Homer Thornberry

Homer Thornberry

CONGRESSMAN, JUDGE, AND ADVOCATE FOR EQUAL RIGHTS

HOMER ROSS TOMLIN

FOREWORD BY THE HONORABLE J.J. "JAKE" PICKLE

FORT WORTH, TEXAS

Library of Congress Cataloging-in-Publication Data

Names: Tomlin, Homer Ross, author.
Title: Homer Thornberry : Congressman, judge, and advocate for equal rights /
    Homer Ross Tomlin ; foreword by Jake Pickle.
Description: Fort Worth, Texas : TCU Press, [2016] | Includes bibliographical
    references and index.
Identifiers: LCCN 2016012858 (print) | LCCN 2016015176 (ebook) | ISBN
    9780875656373 (alk. paper) | ISBN 9780875656465
Subjects: LCSH: Thornberry, Homer, 1909-1995. | Legislators--United
    States--Biography. | United States. Congress. House--Biography. |
    Judges--United States--Biography. | Texas--Politics and
    government--1865-1950. | Texas--Politics and government--1951-
Classification: LCC E840.8.T495 T66 2016 (print) | LCC E840.8.T495 (ebook) |
    DDC 347.73/14092 [B] --dc23
LC record available at https://lccn.loc.gov/2016012858

TCU Press
TCU Box 298300
Fort Worth, Texas 76129
817.257.7822
www.prs.tcu.edu

To order books: 1.800.826.8911

Cover and Text Design by Preston Thomas

In memory of my mother Kate, whose grand idea this whole thing was.

CONTENTS

FOREWORD
Remembrances of Homer Thornberry

WHEN I THINK OF HOMER THORNBERRY, I HAVE A WARM feeling, and a big grin comes on my face. Of course, I think about his eminent service as our US congressman and as a US federal judge. But, most of all, he was a close, warm, personal friend. We liked to be around him. We respected him. We loved him simply because he was a genuine human being.

First, I want to appraise him as a person and then relate these characteristics through a few stories.

Homer Thornberry was an honorable, thoughtful, progressive man. He looked at every issue with this question: Was it the right thing for the average citizen? He was steadfast in his conviction. I do not believe there was an ounce of bigotry, prejudice, or unfairness in his system. By nature he was liberal and progressive, and a lot of that had to do with his upbringing. He grew up in relative poverty, the son of deaf and speechless parents. He was taught to be kind to his parents and to be helpful to them and to others less fortunate than himself. This became a fundamental strength of his character. I believe that the strength of his public service was this sense of integrity and character. He was a liberal-minded person, a liberal Democrat in a progressive Congress, and a staunch defender of human rights as a congressman and as a federal judge.

Thornberry's individual integrity prevented him from doing anything dishonorable. A lot of this character came from his lot in life. As a poor boy, he had to work harder than the average person just to catch up and survive. All of his life he was committed to hard work and honorable service. His legislative support could not be taken for granted. An example of his independence was his vote not to repeal the Taft-Hartley labor law, even though he was close to his labor union friends, and they were supporters and admirers.

I liked Homer Thornberry's sense of humor. He always maintained humor as an ace of support in any type of crisis. His loud, ear-splitting laugh rolled across his audiences and committees. He could slap his hip or knee and say with firm conviction: "Well, I'll say this . . . !" Then he would proceed to make his point and enjoy a good laugh. He was so fair and open in his reasoning that you could not be angry with him. People liked and trusted Homer Thornberry.

Lyndon Johnson took a liking to Homer and helped in his campaign for the US Congress, succeeding Johnson. After Homer's election, LBJ helped Thornberry become acquainted in Washington. He took Homer under his wing because he had such a personal affection and respect for his new congressman. Because of the close relationship that Johnson had with Speaker of the House Sam Rayburn, Thornberry also became a close friend of the Speaker. I often felt Speaker Rayburn considered Thornberry as his "son." That is why he was later assigned to the House Rules Committee. He was considered to be Rayburn's "man" on that committee. Many members of Congress had such confidence in Thornberry that they would vote aye on certain bills just because they had such high respect for Homer individually.

I remember with fondness many events that gave us an insight into this friendly and judicious man. When Homer returned to Austin every fall to "work the district," a few of his close friends—and I was one of them—liked to play a card game called Pitch. Homer loved the game because it was amiable. He could erase the problems of his congressional responsibilities and enjoy himself in the company of friends. One time, our group had reserved the Bastrop State Park facilities for the weekend so we could play golf and Pitch. Homer called from Washington to express regrets that he might not be able to attend because of a congressional conflict. Well, late that Friday night, a knock came at the door around midnight, and there stood Thornberry with little gifts for all of us. He had caught a late flight into Austin, where he rented a car and drove to Bastrop just to be with his friends. You can imagine the joy and laughter that took place when we greeted Homer.

I can recall Congressman Thornberry delivering a toast in the front yard of the LBJ Ranch following a pleasant dinner. The group began to give their toasts, and it came around to Thornberry's turn. He said, "Well, I'll say this . . . I never had a brother, but if I *had* a brother I would want him to be just like Lyndon Johnson." This toast was followed by applause from the group, and one by one each person made a toast. When the circle was completed and came back to Thornberry, he said, "Well, I never had a brother, but if I *had* a brother . . ." whereupon Eloise Thornberry, Homer's wife, who was sitting on the balcony of the front porch alongside Lady Bird, said in a loud voice: "Now, Homer, you've already said that once. Come to bed!" You can imagine the good-natured laughter the entire group gave to Homer and Eloise.

When I was elected to succeed Thornberry in Congress, I asked Homer for his advice about how to handle the duties of the office. He said thoughtfully, "Well, I'll say this . . . God help you with Charlie Green [then publisher of the *Austin American*] and Sarah McClendon [a tenacious reporter]!" Both were difficult to bypass.

When LBJ was elected president in 1964, our group of friends was gathered that evening to listen to the national news. LBJ was in an ebullient mood and said to Thornberry and our group, "Homer, what do you think about a fellow like Pickle? Here I carry every state in the Union, the biggest landslide in US history,* and yet Pickle carries Washington County by a bigger margin than I did. Do you think Pickle is better known than I am?" Thornberry replied, "Well, I'll say this . . . I just think Pickle was more favorably known." That brought out a huge laugh—but not from LBJ. Thornberry settled back in his chair and remained quiet . . . but he still had a big grin on his face.

Homer gave me some good advice. He said, "Before you make some of your quick, flip remarks, Pickle, count to ten first. That will save you a lot of explanations later on. Just slowly count one to ten, and then you won't say it." He also reminded me that this congressional job was "tough," and later, I learned that he was right again. There was glory, recognition, and honor to it, but most of the job was long hours, hard work, and a willingness to work for the people you represent twenty-four hours a day. I think I learned a lot about service from Homer Thornberry.

I think Homer Thornberry was one of the most honorable men I have ever known. He was honest, and his commitment to the public complete. I was proud to call him a friend.

THE HONORABLE J. J. "JAKE" PICKLE

---

*Either Johnson was exaggerating, or Pickle's recollection is incorrect.

ACKNOWLEDGMENTS

I SHOULD HAVE BEEN FLATTERED WHEN MY MOTHER SUGGESTED I write a biography of her father. Instead I questioned her sanity. This was a job for a historian, a scholar, a professional writer—I was none of these. Regardless, she had identified a void in the vast number of publications about Texas's quasi-mythical history and the men and women who shaped it. Indeed, the absence of a comprehensive written account of Judge and Congressman Homer Thornberry's life and contributions qualified as a damn shame. This realization eventually prompted me to reconsider her suggestion, and it became the topic of my undergraduate thesis.

My ensuing monomania was partially fueled by scores of enablers over the next fifteen years, and they shall not remain nameless. My thesis advisers, Distinguished Teaching Professor Carol MacKay and then *Texas Monthly* Editor-in-Chief Evan Smith, graciously guided my awkward first steps into this project. Dr. MacKay deserves special thanks for her support and interest, which lasted well beyond my graduation. Family members and former associates of my grandfather provided indispensable firsthand and previously undocumented accounts of events that occurred before I was born. One of them, the Honorable Jake Pickle, deserves additional credit for contributing the fine foreword to these pages. I sincerely thank the librarians, archivists, and research assistants who helped me unearth thousands of artifacts (usually in paper form), specifically Allen Fisher, Margaret Harman, Tina Houston, Brian McNerney, E. Phil Scott, Linda Seelke, and Bob Tissing at the LBJ Presidential Library in Austin, Texas; Marian Drey and Michael Smith at the US Court of Appeals Library in Shreveport, Louisiana; Kimberly Burpo at the Sam Rayburn Museum in Bonham, Texas; Mike Miller at the Austin History Center in Austin, Texas; and Franna Camenisch at the Texas School for the Deaf Heritage Center in Austin, Texas. Recognition also goes to the unsung staff members at the many public libraries who tidied up the mounds of microfiche and other reference materials left in my wake. No less helpful were the many lifelines that Google and the Library of Congress tossed my way right when hope of finding specific source material was all but lost. Consultations with Dr. Don Carleton, executive director of the Dolph Briscoe Center for American History, and Dr. Light Cummins, State Historian of Texas, proved pertinent in reframing my manuscript in a more scholarly light. I should probably thank my freshman English professor, Dr. Joseph Malof, for teaching me how to write just when I thought I knew it all. Twenty years later, I find myself indebted to another esteemed academic: Dr. Anthony Champagne, who shared his encyclopedic knowledge and ushered me through the final phase of the draft process. Thanks also to Dr. Jim Riddlesperger for likewise reviewing my work and recommending it for publication. I am also beyond grateful to TCU Press for giving me a second chance with a special thanks to Daniel Williams, Kathy Walton, Molly Spain, Rebecca Allen, and Melinda Esco. Finally, I sincerely thank friends and relatives for their counsel, support, patience, and love.

Introduction

THE PREDOMINANT VIGNETTE I CONJURE OF MY MOTHER'S father surfaces from early childhood. Seated in a black lacquered rocking chair adorned with his alma mater's burnt-orange crest, he quietly plays game upon game of solitaire, his lone hobby during his semiretirement. A floor lamp at his right provides the den's only light source. The adjacent bookshelf displays, among other items, a few framed photographs of his two grandchildren as well as tomes about Lyndon B. Johnson and Sam Rayburn. The latter pair is also memorialized in the forms of a miniature bust and commemorative gold coin, respectively. Other than murmurs from the evening news and the hum of a ceiling fan, the snapping of each card as he plays it is the sole audible evidence of human occupancy.

For many of my early years, I perceived my grandfather strictly as an elder by blood with little awareness of his public distinction. My mother's bedtime stories about him notwithstanding, my familiarity with the man was largely limited to his solitaire games, his booming laughter, extensive collection of striped neckties, and quaint habit of tucking his dinner napkin into his shirt collar. Perhaps my earliest memory of him is a conversation we had one evening in his bedroom. My grandmother had already dozed off with the aid of a black eye mask, inspiring him to jest that she was the Lone Ranger. I was six at the time and considered this hilarious. Until that point, I believed the elderly were incapable of humor.

My epiphany about his legacy finally happened in the sixth grade. I was assigned by my social studies teacher Mr. Reynolds a book report on President Johnson. Sifting through several Johnson biographies in my school library, I spotted a listing for Thornberry, Homer, which showed not one but *two* page numbers adjacent to it. After returning home, I excitedly phoned him to report my finding. According to one passage, I explained, he was in the middle of shaving when Johnson called to solicit his advice on whether to accept Senator Kennedy's offer to become his running mate. My grandfather, less enthusiastic than I expected him to be, interrupted my verbatim recitation, swiftly summarized the rest of the story, and then hung up somewhat abruptly. He must have read this book before.

Similar earth-shattering revelations would continue to surface. Grandpa, it turns out, was a lifelong public servant who held several, mostly elected, some high-level, posts in various government bodies. In addition to having a personal friend in President Johnson, he facilitated momentous civil rights reforms as both a congressman and a federal judge. He was also the inspiration for my first name. (When my father, Richard Alan Tomlin, called to inform him of this decision shortly after I was delivered, the judge got too choked up to speak and hung up.)

Just as my grandfather's historical significance felt so surreal at first, so did the fact that his and others' efforts were necessary in a country where all its citizens are supposedly created equal. It seems unconscionable that segregation, acts of violence, and other forms of racial discrimination were societal norms not so long ago. Yet concerted, unyielding efforts by the three federal branches (and brazen activists) were required simply to enforce the nearly two-century-old Constitution's most fundamental protections.

Alas, the landmark civil rights victories of the 1960s have not gone unpunished. As Johnson accurately predicted, his championship of the Civil Rights Act of 1964 spelled the dissolution of his party's hegemony in the South. Desegregation, which my grandfather helped implement by force in dozens of defiant school systems, officially remains the law of the land, but racial divisions still haunt the country's beleaguered educational system. Fifty years after Johnson's signature dried, black children attend poorer schools in extreme disproportion to whites and receive a lower quality of education on the whole.

Likewise, the recent revival of suppressing voting rights has circumvented long-standing protections for vulnerable citizens in several southern states. The US Supreme Court struck down the poll tax in 1966, just after my grandfather helped abolish it in Texas. But lately, political forces have fought to block renewal of the Voting Rights Act of 1965, a Johnson initiative that provides legal safeguards against disenfranchising ethnic and racial minorities. Vital portions of the law were struck down by the US

Thornberry and the author, circa 1980. *Thornberry family collection.*

Supreme Court in 2013. In several southern states, the same forces have spearheaded voting restrictions such as requiring state-issued identification at the polls—ostensibly to prevent voter fraud (which is practically non-existent, as studies have shown), yet clearly intended to deter the poor, minorities, and students—all historically reliable constituent bases for the Democratic Party—from voting. As of this writing, fifteen states, including Texas and the District of Columbia, have passed such restrictive voter ID laws. As US Attorney General Eric Holder bemoaned in 2012, "We call these poll taxes."[1]

The majority of participants in a 2005 *U.S. News & World Report* survey responded that governmental leadership had deteriorated over the twenty years prior, and 73 percent felt that those in power were out of touch with the average citizen. Most survey takers valued honesty and integrity over several other leadership traits presented. In other words, the country had spoken, and it wanted more Homer Thornberrys.[2]

While these pages serve foremost as a chronicle of my grandfather's life-long service to the public, they are also a testament to the rare combination of qualities that enabled his many achievements. My hope is that the reader takes heed of his example, for there is much work to be done in this country.

CHAPTER I

Dedication

A N UNREMARKABLE MASS OF CONCRETE AND STEEL IN DOWN-
town Austin was transformed into a temple of justice on January 9,
1993. Newly enveloped in black marble and rust-colored granite, the four-
story structure cast a refreshingly Texan vibe, just a few blocks from the
state capitol. From then on, it would be known as the Homer Thornberry
Judicial Building.[1]

The site had previously accommodated a postal office, whose conception in 1966 incidentally resulted from federal legislation authored by its
new namesake. Two decades later, congressional funding would repurpose
it in his honor. With a new facade and interior, the 138,000-square-foot
building would house five judges of the Court of Appeals for the Fifth Circuit and two United States Bankruptcy Court judges. The building's rein-
carnation was the brainchild of US Representative Jake Pickle, who took
over Thornberry's congressional seat in 1964. Pickle's sentiments about
the project were so strong they overcame resistance from colleagues who
preferred a posthumous dedication. The $9.1 million remodeling did not
come cheap, but it was hardly a prodigal homage. The judicial center's
courtrooms and chambers would help accommodate a burgeoning number of bankruptcy cases, which also entailed creating a second bankruptcy
judgeship. Why wait?[2]

Held on Thornberry's eighty-fourth birthday on a sunny Saturday
morning, the dedication ceremony took roughly the same form as a church
service. Seated before the speakers—who included Pickle, Thornberry,
several fellow federal judges, and two Methodist reverends—was a congregation of roughly two hundred attendees divided into three sections
within the packed, sunlit lobby. Attendees included family, friends, federal

and state judges across the South, and other regional dignitaries. Addressing the audience from the dais, Pickle extolled Thornberry with religious aplomb. "In an earlier and more enlightened time, he might have been called Saint Homer," he proclaimed. "[He] is a man of deep compassion and understanding, and so far, his opinions seem to spring from the good book of Solomon." Chief Justice Henry Politz, a fellow Fifth Circuit member, added, "He's the quintessential judge. He's fair. He's firm. He has applied his knowledge of the law. He's a principled man, resolute in his principles."[3]

Thornberry, wearing a navy-blue suit and trademark striped tie, characteristically fused equal parts humility and humor in his brief remarks. "I just don't know what I've done to deserve this," he claimed, though conceding, "Every time I come to town, I'll try to find a reason to come down this street and look at my name."[4]

Clearly a groundswell of support had shown that Thornberry's accomplishments indeed warranted enshrinement. The diversity and longevity of his roles in government alone made him a rarity in Texas and American history. How he fulfilled these roles was guided by his fundamental beliefs that equal rights and opportunities should be ensured and that individual responsibility should be expected. He applied these convictions as he worked toward repairing his native region's torn social fabric, which meant reconstructing the monolithic establishment to which he belonged. But first he had to emerge from a briar patch of poverty and prejudice.

CHAPTER 2

Brought into Silence (1909-1918)

T HE TEXAS HILL COUNTRY ONCE EPITOMIZED THE AMERICAN frontier, as much a test of survival as a land of opportunity. Its climate was oppressively hot and dry, yet the rocky landscape, covering much of the state's center, included an abundance of pastures, trees, rivers, and lakes. The region drew a diverse population over time, including Comanches; colonial settlers; transplanted white southerners and their slaves; and Mexican, German, Swedish, and Czech immigrants. Although overwhelmingly Christian, the immigrants' particular denominations were numerous: Methodists, Presbyterians, Cumberland Presbyterians, Episcopalians, Baptists, and Roman Catholics. Austin, which straddled the region's eastern rim, was first populated by settlers along the Colorado River's southernmost extremity in the 1830s and became the capital of the Republic of Texas in 1839. With breezy winds and plenty of sun, Austin was described by early-twentieth-century novelist Amelia Barr as a place "so lovely, and the people so friendly, that any good thing seems possible."[1]

The diversity and independent spirit of these early Texans were well established by the time Texas became a republic in 1836. Its entry into the union nine years later did little to dampen residents' preference for local control over centralized government. The Texas Constitution, written largely by conservative farmers in 1876, reflected a distrust of authority, for it consisted mostly of piecemeal statutory language rather than an overarching set of governing principles. The legendary battles of the Alamo and San Jacinto, which heralded the state's separation from Mexico, formed the basis for Texans' prevailing sense of entitlement, bolstered by the large oil and gas deposits that buoyed state commerce over the course of the twentieth century. Texans considered themselves neither entirely southern nor western but rather a proprietary commonwealth whose peoples would periodically cry out for secession (both pre- and post-Civil War). Texas's status as the union's largest contiguous state further stoked residents' sense of supremacy. It was no coincidence that its statehouse would be larger in gross square feet than any other and be one of two to exceed the United States Capitol in height.[2]

Political alliances and racial barriers cropped up along liberal-conservative lines in the early 1900s, with a new-rich class evolving out of the exploitation of the state's natural resources. Texas and its economy had been predominantly rural and agricultural, but the seminal oil boom at Spindletop in 1901 accelerated its commercial and industrial development. Texas hosted smaller black populations than the other southern states and was therefore less consumed by racial discrimination. Further, cities in rim states like Texas were ripe for industrial expansion, and labor union leaders were compelled to cross racial lines in order to strengthen workers' alliances. Nevertheless, the populism that reigned in the late 1800s gave way to a resurgence of conservatism, which aimed to disenfranchise blacks just as it would disempower organized labor. A state poll tax was passed by the Texas legislature in 1901 and approved by voters in 1902, imposing a regressive economic barrier on the underclass's ability to vote.[3]

Class divisions likewise emerged in Austin as the University of Texas and state government began to shape the city's commercial development. Banks, merchant stores, bars, and saloons gradually sprang up along Congress Avenue, downtown Austin's main artery, to serve a population approaching twenty-five thousand. The state's rapid industrialization at the turn of the century failed to chaperone corresponding quality-of-life improvements or adequate political representation for the lower classes, particularly blacks. Jim Crow laws, unofficial social policies that segregated the races, governed Austin's social fabric as they did throughout the South. Blacks were gradually being herded away from white neighborhoods and into East Austin, which contained but a single, neglected high school. Trolleys reserved sections for whites while blacks sat or stood in the back, even if seats in the front were empty. Segregated water fountains and restrooms were also the norm. Hispanics received more favorable, if uneven, treatment. They were permitted access to whites-only schools and public places, but underlying white bigotry soon rose in proportion to the city's swelling

Mexican migrant population. By the 1930s, they too would be swept out of Austin's heartland.[4]

South Austin was home to many of the city's most deprived citizens. The area was located on the other side of the Colorado River from the rest of the city. A two-lane, cantilevered bridge, whose wood planks covered a stone foundation fortified by iron beams, provided the only convenient passage into town. Most homes in South Austin lacked running water, heating, screens, or door locks. Families used outhouses in their backyards, and a fortunate few enjoyed outside water hydrants for bathing. Unlike much of the rest of Austin, the region was racially mixed, with whites living alongside blacks and Hispanics. Racial tensions in the area were minimal, although blacks and whites attended separate churches. The whites' local Baptist church included some Ku Klux Klan members who were not necessarily accepted by the rest of the congregation. One particularly dramatic Sunday service featured a pro-Klan sermon followed by a slow march down the aisle of white-hooded men bearing a monetary donation to the church. An offended congregation member blocked the procession and voiced his disapproval of their presence. He proceeded to unhood one of the Klansmen, revealed to be an Austin police officer.[5]

South Austin, crisscrossed by just a few major streets, was predominantly residential. Exceptions included St. Edward's College and the Texas Deaf and Dumb Asylum, later renamed the Deaf and Dumb Institute and later still the Texas School for the Deaf. Neighborhood boys called its younger pupils "dummies" and picked rock fights with them. The deaf school, which was the only primary or secondary school for deaf children in Texas, served as the cultural and vocational locus for the city's hearing-impaired. The school, born out of state legislation in 1856, admitted and housed deaf students ages six to twenty-one from across the state. Its first class was made up of only a handful of students. Situated on seventeen acres of farmland, the campus consisted of a few log cabins and a converted smokehouse that housed the school's lone classroom. The school's first thirteen years were a constant struggle, much like life in the rest of the state following the Civil War. During one two-year stretch, the school had no money to pay its teachers, who subsisted by farming on the school's premises and making their own clothing from wool sheared from sheep kept on the grounds. Matriculation and state funding increased slowly and afforded construction in 1876 of a two-story brick building (for a kitchen and dormitory) and a

Texas School for the Deaf campus (with state capitol visible on the horizon),
Austin, Texas, 1908. *Courtesy Texas School for the Deaf Heritage Center.*

stone barn (for the mechanical department). By the 1880s, total matriculation had reached fifty, and the school's expanding vocational department
offered professional tracks in bookkeeping, printing press operation, cosmetology, shoe repair, and other trades.[6]

William Moore Thornberry taught at the deaf school during this time,
and Mary Lillian Jones was a student thirteen years his junior. William and
Mary were of Scotch-Irish and (most likely) Welsh-Irish descents, respectively, and their fathers served on opposing sides in the Civil War. (Mary's
father was a Union soldier, and William's father was a Confederate Army
chaplain.) They had both lost their ability to hear and speak as infants because of illness. Whereas William was shy and reserved, Mary, according to
neighbor Emmett Shelton, was "one of the sweetest women that I believe I
ever knew" and "would make herself known to you without speaking." The
couple married in 1899 after Mary, then age twenty-six, had graduated.
She joined him on the faculty in 1906 and taught elementary grades. They
moved to Johanna Street, at the epicenter of the deaf community. Adjacent
to them lived an African American widow who was raising two sons. On

William Thornberry (standing, far right) and other Texas School for the Deaf faculty members, Austin, Texas, 1890. *Courtesy Texas School for the Deaf Heritage Center.*

the other side lived the family of Simon Gillis, a city councilman who ran a lumberyard. A part-time carpenter, William had built their new house from scratch. Several years would pass before he could afford to install glass windowpanes. "They were just about as poor as Job's turkey," recalled Shelton. "There just wasn't anything that they had at all." The Thornberrys' destitution was not unique among deaf persons, who arguably constituted the city's most disadvantaged subpopulation. "In those days when you were deaf and you couldn't talk, you were completely isolated from the world," Shelton said. "You had an awful hard time making a living. You were a whole lot worse off than the colored people were." The struggling couple relied heavily on friends and neighbors for goods and services, hitching rides into town, for example, on the Gillises' horse and buggy.[7]

Brought into this cradle of adversity and charity was the only child of William and Mary, William Homer Thornberry. Born on January 9, 1909, shortly before the family moved to Johanna, Homer would be shaped not only by his industrious parents but also by the South Austin community. Indeed, the child's middle (and preferred) name had been taken from a

particularly helpful former neighbor. The Thornberrys' dependence on others, however, could only extend so far. Since neither could hear, William and
Mary, who had recently stopped teaching, took turns keeping watch over
young Homer through each night in the event he cried out for attention.[8]

Social science would later substantiate the merits of the Thornberrys'
nocturnal vigilance. Several studies have shown that hearing children of
deaf-mute parents risk developmental impairments because of a lack of
reciprocal communication through speech, which can impair the child's
relationships as an adult. Regular parental neglect like unresponsiveness
to a baby's wails often triggers intense rage and ultimately exhaustion
in the child. The repeated failure of the outside world—in this case the
primary caretakers—to provide comfort can cause long-term emotional
scars that incite impulsiveness, egocentricity, insecurity, and alienation
later in life. On the flip side, children of deaf-mute parents also tend to
develop heightened responsibility and self-reliance as a result of detect-
ing nonverbal cues more readily, leading to improved sensitivity to their
surroundings.[9]

While Homer's parents' attentiveness helped mitigate the chances of
long-term distress, the boy was nonetheless challenged when engaging
with the hearing world. Until the age of three, he was unaware of any
form of communication beyond sign language, as his parents fraternized
almost exclusively with fellow deaf-mutes. His acquisition of oral communication and social skills would require outside assistance. "My mother
would farm me out to the neighbors," recalled Thornberry. "They would
give me the opportunity to talk . . . point objects out, call their names,
and ask me what they were." At one point, a cousin of his was recruited to
live briefly with the family and teach young Thornberry how to develop
his vocal cords.[10]

The written word presented another obstacle as he struggled to bridge
the worlds of oral and written communication:

> I saw the word "town," and I could not recognize it, and I took it to [my
> father] and asked him what it was . . . He'd think about it and he'd [sign]
> "Town." . . . That didn't help me because I had not associated it with anything.
> . . . Then he drew pictures of buildings . . . all over the page, but that still
> didn't help me. But the next day when I went to school, I asked one of my
> fellow pupils what that meant, and he said, "Town." I recognized that.

Mary Thornberry at age 22, Austin, Texas, 1894. *Courtesy Texas School for the Deaf Heritage Center.*

William and Mary were naturally incapable of monitoring their son's vocabulary when he finally mastered speech, including a full range of profanities. Thornberry was oblivious to their taboo nature at first, but not for long. When alerted to their son's bad habit, William and Mary held a stern discussion with Homer that quickly set him straight.[11]

Thornberry at age six, Austin, Texas, 1915. *Thornberry family collection.*

Thornberry's childhood recreation consisted mostly of tagging along with rowdy neighborhood boys. They got their kicks paddling beehives and hornets' nests, smashing a neighbor's pigeon eggs, and fishing for crayfish at a nearby creek. Nursing their bee stings with soda water, the children would regroup on the Thornberrys' back steps to snack on bread-and-butter sandwiches sprinkled with brown sugar. Playtimes, however, soon became scarce.[12]

Although the year 1918 saw the conclusion of World War I, a far deadlier battle continued to be waged at home. While 2,700 US soldiers died overseas during the last week of October, a mysterious illness claimed the lives of 21,000 American civilians over the same stretch. The culprit was a viral epidemic dubbed the Spanish flu which swept across several countries and lingered for months at a time. It dealt swift death to its victims, usually within two to four days of the first symptoms. Affliction led to fevers, nosebleeds, bluish-purplish skin tones, and fluid buildup in the lungs, causing inflammation, hemorrhaging, and cell death. Ironically, the most susceptible candidates were fifteen to forty years of age, normally the healthiest subset of any population. Individuals wore masks in public to avoid infection. Reminiscent of the medieval Black Death, the Spanish influenza is regarded as the deadliest outbreak of disease in human history. It ultimately killed 675,000 domestically, taking more American lives than all twentieth-century American wars combined. Halfway across the globe, twelve to twenty million natives of India succumbed to the epidemic in a single month. Whereas World War I caused ten million casualties in just over four years, the Spanish flu killed an estimated fifty million worldwide in a ten-month period. It was said that one person in every household was infected, and the Thornberry household was no exception. William contracted the flu at its zenith and died within a few days at the age of fifty-eight. Thornberry was nine years old at the time.[13]

Friends and relatives implored Mary to relocate to Goliad, Texas, near her parents' farm. Mary declined on the grounds that her son was unlikely to receive a quality education there. She and her son would take their chances in Austin's rapidly modernizing landscape.[14]

Mary's dedication to her son's education derived from personal experience. Like most children who lose their hearing in infancy, Mary was prone to fits of rage at the slightest provocation. She once swatted her father with a broom simply for frowning at her. In a separate incident, she threw a pail of milk in her grandmother's face after being shown she was milking a cow incorrectly. Mary's intense frustration was shared by disabled humanitarian Helen Keller. Keller became exceptionally unruly at age two when an illness robbed her of the abilities to hear, speak, and see. After her parents consulted numerous health and science experts, including Alexander Graham Bell, Keller began working in isolation with a young graduate of the Perkins Institution and Massachusetts Asylum for the Blind. Keller's tantrums persisted up until a dramatic physical struggle in which her mentor forcefully placed the child's hand under an open waterspout and using the manual alphabet, spelled the word "water" in the girl's palm. It was only then that Keller drew a connection between objects and language, a revelation that permanently attenuated her temper and prompted a lifelong curiosity about the world. Keller proceeded to attend Radcliffe College and became a prominent advocate for the rights of women and the physically impaired.[15]

Like Keller, Mary came to control her rage only after being dispatched into the care of professional educators. Her parents were reluctant to send her away to the Texas School for the Deaf, but their decision paid immediate dividends. Mary's experience at the school facilitated her connections to other people and impressed upon her the importance of education. "She was at the threshold of knowledge and communication," her son later wrote. "This was the real beginning of her life."[16]

The school's curriculum was designed to help deaf children become productive, independent members of a hearing society. Most students were taught how to speak, lip-read, and use sign language. Children with no prior oral education practiced voice-building exercises in order to train their tongues to pronounce vowels and consonants. "Rhythm training" involved placing the student's hands on a playing piano to impart an appreciation of music. The school's offerings also included vocational courses on barbering, auto mechanics, cosmetology, bookkeeping, shoe repair, and woodwork. Physical education encompassed archery, volleyball, bowling, baseball, badminton, soccer, baseball, and ping pong.[17]

The self-reliance Mary acquired through her formal education became especially critical after her husband's passing. Still in mourning, Mary visited her local bank with her young son and pleaded for leniency on a note past due. The outcome was worse than she feared. "I can still see the look of dismay on her face as I translated that the note was not the only one, that there was another one outstanding as well," her son recalled. Determined to achieve solvency on her own, she resumed her teaching position at the school for the deaf. She was forced to borrow money when the school closed each summer, but she managed to pay off her debts over time.[18]

In spite of her tremendous personal tragedy and financial hardships, Mary maintained a positive outlook and rarely complained. She socialized both within the deaf community and in the public sphere, communicating with sales clerks by tablet and pencil. In so doing, she taught her son the importance of building social networks. "All of my life she emphasized to me our need for friends; she, herself, acquired hundreds of them during her lifetime—both among the hearing as well as among the deaf," Thornberry recalled. "She was always loyal to them, and they, to her." Her popularity was greatly aided by her mastery of fried chicken, chicken and dumplings, peach cobbler, biscuits, and lemon pie. In addition to heightened cholesterol levels, collateral effects of Mary's cuisine included flour scattered across the kitchen floor because of her use of sign language while prepping food. She maintained a garden in her backyard, where she would also wash clothes in a black pot of boiling water. She insisted that her son regularly attend services at the neighborhood Methodist church and take lessons from the Bible. "My mother never allowed deafness, the inability to talk, poverty, adversity, or temporary setbacks to stop her in a determination to live a useful life and to provide for her son," Thornberry later wrote. "From the time I was little, I always had the feeling that she carried within her an intense desire that I develop in great depth the senses she was denied."[19]

In addition to stressing the importance of education, religion, and self-discipline, Mary also encouraged her son's interest in public policy. She supported programs for the underprivileged and President Franklin Roosevelt's New Deal programs. Thornberry also accompanied his mother to the local polling location in 1920, the first time women could legally vote. The experience left a lasting impression.[20]

CHAPTER 3

Emergence (1919-1936)

THORNBERRY EFFECTIVELY ENTERED ADULTHOOD WHEN HIS father died. To supplement his mother's minuscule salary, the boy worked after school for the duration of his primary and secondary education, which spanned Fulmore Elementary School, John T. Allan Junior High School, and Austin High School. Prior to completing high school, he worked on a dairy truck before dawn and sold newspapers in the evenings. Newspaper boys chose which of the daily editions to sell, paid thirty-five cents out of pocket per dozen, and sold them for five cents apiece. A good day yielded a quarter in profit. (Thornberry made his "first big financial mistake" by initially selling the less popular midday editions, only to discover that the afternoon versions were in greater demand.) After-school jobs also included positions as an assistant freight clerk at a rail depot, door-to-door bill collector for a plumbing firm, and legislative page at the state capitol. Between his and Mary's accumulated earnings, they could finally afford wallpaper to replace the newspaper that had lined their home's interior.[1]

Thornberry's diligence eventually earned him acceptance into the University of Texas at Austin, which tamed some of his aimlessness. "I wandered into the university without any real purpose, with no real goal," he said. "My mother wanted me to go to the university very badly, so I thought I'd go a year or two to please her and then find myself a job." He soon discovered that the school provided "an opportunity to find myself, to learn how to get along with people, to make enduring friendships." Joining the Acacia Fraternity, where he lived for part of his college years, afforded his primary social outlet.[2]

Thornberry's Texas legislative page portrait, age fourteen, Austin, Texas, 1923. *Thornberry family collection.*

UT was conceived by the same legislative act in 1839 that designated Austin as the state capital (although the school did not become operational until 1883). A growing student body would necessitate more housing on campus in the 1910s. Oil royalties from UT-owned land endowed by the legislature helped the school finance additional expansion during the Great Depression. By the time Thornberry enrolled in the late 1920s, UT had achieved the equivalent standing of established state institutions in Michigan, Virginia, and Missouri. Students on campus passed the time dancing at the student union, playing horseshoes, and blaring the swing music of Paul Whiteman and Glenn Miller through the open windows of their dormitories and boarding houses. Students paid a monthly average of $10.39 for room and $23.84 for board. In his 1965 Distinguished Alumnus acceptance speech, Thornberry reflected fondly on these formative years:

> It is no exaggeration to say that I landed on the "Forty Acres" [UT's approximate size and nickname] a rather bewildered young man. . . . And yet, through all of this long and confusing experience, I caught a glimpse— perhaps a fleeting one—either from friends among the student body, from the classroom, or from the spirit of the institution itself—of a challenge to try to be of service to my community, my state, and the nation.[3]

Public affairs and economics piqued Thornberry's interest, and like his mother, he found inspiration in President Roosevelt's efforts to rescue the country from its economic quagmire. Thornberry felt strongly that the New Deal was a proof-positive illustration of government's rightful role during hard times:

> I spent most of my spare hours . . . in the Old Library looking up references assigned in class. I'd get immersed in some periodical, start reading about public affairs, about economics, about the stock market crash of 1929, and the steps Franklin Roosevelt took to set things straight in 1932. These things made a deep impression on me.

Thornberry likewise viewed the Democratic Party as the political vehicle most capable of correcting socioeconomic inequities. Other like-minded future Democratic leaders also found their political calling at UT at this time: elected student body presidents during the 1930s included future Governors Allan Shivers and John Connally and future Congressman Jake Pickle.[4]

Albeit enlightened by his undergraduate experience, Thornberry frequently felt so overwhelmed by the burdens of schoolwork and employment that he considered withdrawing from the university. But his mother's steadfast insistence that he finish his degree swiftly reversed these inclinations. Thornberry remembered, "Every time I wanted to quit, and there were those times, my mother insisted that I continue." He was thus motivated to endure several unsatisfying side jobs, including grueling summertime construction work in a Baytown, Texas, oil field where he lugged buckets of concrete up ladders all day long.[5]

For all the obstacles Thornberry overcame to enter and complete college, the color of his skin gave him a distinct and unfair advantage as a resident of a former Confederate state. Like many schools in this era, UT lacked any semblance of social diversity. Mexican Americans were slowly being admitted in the 1920s, but otherwise no nonwhites constituted any portion of the student body or faculty. The university's first black undergraduate was admitted in 1938, but blacks were denied entry into the school's graduate programs. (This practice would cease following the 1950 Supreme Court case *Sweatt v. Painter*, which came about when a black applicant was rejected by UT's law school because of his race.) Blacks had emigrated from Texas en masse in the 1920s largely because of pervasive discrimination, dropping their proportion of the state's population to 14 percent by decade's end.[6]

A reprieve from Thornberry's construction job arrived in the form of a telegraph that would permanently reroute his professional trajectory. Family friend and Travis County Commissioner John E. Shelton Jr. had recommended the struggling college student for an administrative position under Travis County Deputy Sheriff Coley White. White had been fined for hoarding public funds rather than disseminating them to other state offices. In lieu of suing White once his term expired, Shelton opted to place a trustworthy source there who could observe White. Shelton referred Thornberry to County Clerk Fred Malone for the position, although the young man was hesitant. "I had some funny ideas about sheriffs when I first came to work in Sheriff [White's] office," said Thornberry. "I had an idea they packed six shooters and spent most of their time flashing badges. I guess it was an idea picked up from movie thrillers." He accepted the position on the condition that he work part-time so he could focus on his studies.[7]

Thornberry's new line of work wound up being mostly procedural but still gratifying. The sheriff's office primarily collected fees on behalf of the county whenever papers were served or an arrest was made. He was enthralled by the daily activities at the county courthouse, where he got to witness the legal system in action. Because the county sheriff's position was subject to popular vote every two years, office employees were obligated to drum up voter support for the incumbent. These grassroots activities marked the first time that politics "got in my blood," Thornberry later said.[8]

Thornberry as Travis County Sheriff, age twenty-one, Austin, Texas, 1930.
Thornberry family collection.

In 1930, on his twenty-first birthday, Thornberry became the youngest deputy sheriff commissioned in Travis County history. The *Austin Evening Statesman* wrote that Thornberry's combination of youth and intelligence defied the "burly, two-fisted, fighting, scowling" stereotype commonly attributed to law enforcement agents. Thornberry continued to work in the sheriff's office for roughly three more years. During his tenure he cultivated relationships with the community that would one day propel his own run for public office. He later recalled:

> Those five years helped me in the future. [They] taught me that hard work in life was necessary and also gave me an opportunity to meet lots of people. I was there in the courthouse, and people would come in. I'd meet them, and when I ran for office, that was not a handicap.[9]

After earning his undergraduate degree in business administration in 1932, he immediately applied to UT's School of Law. Despite generally disliking his law school experience, he managed to graduate in the top 15 percent of his class four years later. He did so while keeping his post as deputy sheriff before switching midway to a less time-consuming position as an assistant school superintendent for the Austin public school system. Thornberry credited his mother for regularly refueling his perseverance. "When I was discouraged, and knew I was too tired to keep going through all that school," Thornberry later commented, "it was my mother's determination, spelled out in the language of her hands, that made me go on."[10]

Thornberry's own determination and lust for politics prompted his decision to vie for a seat in the Texas legislature at age twenty-seven, despite both his relative inexperience and the fact that he had not quite finished law school. "I was greatly concerned . . . that I [would not make] my grades," he later recalled. "I could see myself running for office and saying, 'Well, I'm sorry. I failed [my classes].'" Thornberry initially dithered over his decision until a pivotal road trip to Chicago with family friend Hubert Jones. Jones not only urged Thornberry to run for office but also offered to lend him one hundred dollars to pay the candidate entry fee. It was an offer Thornberry did not refuse.[11]

CHAPTER 4

The Immortals (1936-1940)

T HORNBERRY'S CAMPAIGN FOR THE TEXAS HOUSE OF Representatives depended largely on the support of friends and neighbors, especially of those in the deaf community. His platform centered on improving child labor laws, raising state salaries on a par with the cost of living, increasing appropriations for public education, and opposing a general sales tax. In addition, he supported taxation on natural resources, efficient and economical reforms in the state government, conservation of natural resources, and strict regulation of liquor traffic. "I believe that the citizens of the state expect a member of the legislature to remain free from the influence of special interests, to stand for what is right regardless of political pressure, and to give due consideration to the rights of all the people," Thornberry told the *Austin American*.[1]

Thornberry's chief opponent for the Eighty-Second District, Place Five seat was its incumbent, insurance salesman Jack Padgett, who was among the state's top vote-getters in the previous election. Padgett's popularity had gone to his head in the interim, and his vanity quickly alienated his supporters. He was also ostracized within the state government after pressuring employees in the governor's and state comptroller's offices to buy his company's insurance products. Thornberry, who had yet to complete his law degree and couldn't afford to buy his own car, hitched rides to Democratic precinct meetings, where he got to know voters face-to-face.[2]

Owing both to his own diligence and to Padgett's hubris, Thornberry won the 1936 Democratic primary election into the Forty-Fifth Texas Legislature. He collected more votes (8,586) than did both Padgett (4,849) and fellow candidate Lee Satterwhite (2,440) combined. He would run unopposed in the general election.[3]

In his first term, Thornberry received committee assignments to Appropriations; Judiciary; Public Lands and Buildings; and Privileges, Suffrage, and Elections. An early conundrum stemmed from a bill that would postpone implementing the new state bar exam required of aspiring attorneys. Thornberry had already entered legal practice and was therefore exempt from the exam, and if passed, the bill would likewise absolve many of his former classmates who were about to graduate. He nevertheless helped vote it down, so that new graduates would indeed be required to take the bar. "I decided that in view of all of the experience that we had been having in Texas with all the fly-by-night schools granting law licenses that it had to be stopped," he later explained. "That did not make me very popular among my classmates . . . but I'm convinced that was the thing I had to do."[4]

Assisting Austin's deaf population was a top priority during his first term. In 1937, he secured appropriations for a placement officer at the Texas School for the Deaf, where his mother still taught (she would retire three years later). The funding afforded $1,700 in annual salary and $800 in travel expenses. Although the total amount was less than Thornberry had hoped, the school was most appreciative. "We believe such a placement officer will be of inestimable value in assisting the young school graduates in being placed in ideal positions after leaving school," read a piece in the school's monthly newsletter. Its author also commended Thornberry for "rapidly endearing himself to the deaf of this state through his wholehearted interest in their welfare." Thornberry addressed attendees at the Texas Association for the Deaf Convention in Dallas around this time, one of many instances in which he would appear before deaf assemblies over his career.[5]

Another of Thornberry's objectives as a state representative was to facilitate Austin's rebound from economic devastation:

> The Depression made a deep impression on me because I could see that an ordinary person—when the economy dropped—that person was the first to lose his job. There was a good deal of dissatisfaction in those times, too . . . And having been fortunate enough to be elected, I was brought immediately to the forefront of what people were feeling.

Optimism for a statewide recovery took the form of zealous Democratic Governor James Allred, who had earned Thornberry's support. Inaugurated in 1935, the youthful Allred entered office at a time when hope was in short supply. Allred was the only Texas governor of the era who fully committed to the New Deal and would ultimately be considered among the most liberal governors in the state's history. His initiatives included a state pension program for poor Texans, concurrent with Congress's passage of the Social Security Act. Allred also proposed a tax hike on natural resources and chain stores as well as a statewide sales tax to provide economic assistance to the poor. Although neither proposal gained traction, token taxes were eventually levied on chain stores and pipelines. The Texas Liquor Control Act was also passed during Allred's term in November 1935, which established a regulatory board and imposed taxes and fees on liquor sales. The measure raised close to $5 million annually, roughly three-fourths of which was earmarked for pensions for the elderly with the remainder going to public schools. Allred was reelected in 1936, which was no small feat ("It was easy to become unpopular during the Depression," affirmed Thornberry). His governorship nevertheless upset the state's fulminating New Deal detractors.[6]

Thornberry's own (uncontested) reelection in 1938 coincided with the beginnings of a paradigm shift in the state's political landscape. The aftermath of Roosevelt's appointment of Allred to a federal district judgeship created a vacuum that would be filled for decades by conservative governors who catered more to the business community than to the average taxpayer. The most divisive among them was Anti-New Deal Democrat Lee "Pappy" O'Daniel, who succeeded Allred and served from 1939 to 1941. He upset a number of constituents by trimming state pension checks and reneging on campaign promises to block any new sales taxes and to abolish the state's decades-old poll tax. He also waged endless legal, political, and legislative battles against workers' unions, which preferred taxation of natural resources, pipelines, and utilities to O'Daniel's proposed sales tax. Funds for the Texas Department of Public Safety were slashed to the extent that Texas Rangers had to borrow ammunition from highway patrolmen. Austinites were further appalled by his decision to veto appropriations for state hospitals serving orphans and the mentally ill.[7]

Thornberry was among several dozen state legislators greatly aggrieved by O'Daniel's performance. Most of their irritation swelled from the governor's push for a 2 percent retail sales tax, which would have disproportionately burdened low-wage earners and small businesses. His plan would also establish a cap on certain severance taxes, a proviso designed to aid the

oil and gas industry. Thornberry and fifty-five other legislators were nicknamed the "Immortal 56" for their collective stance against these measures. They united to prevent O'Daniel from permanently amending the
state constitution to effect his regressive tax proposal, which belied repre-
sentational government in the Immortals' eyes. "I decided that that would
not be fair to people in the future and also not a good way to legislate,"
Thornberry later said. "We should not place legislation of that sort in the
Constitution but . . . pass a law that we could amend or change later on."
O'Daniel, sensing a critical mass of opposition, next tried attaching his
sales tax plan to Senate Joint Resolution 12, a constitutional amendment
levying a tax on gas and electricity use, telephone service, oil and natural
gas drilling, sulfur production, and admission to amusement parks. The
fifty-sixers, who included future governor Price Daniel, were united in
their obstruction. The sales tax proposal "contained a lot of horrible provisions in addition to voting a sales tax," Daniel later said. "One of the worst
things . . . was the fact that it had a ceiling written in it assuring the natural
gas-oil industry that no additional taxes would be levied for social security
purposes in this state."[8]

After his sales tax measure died in the house, a vengeful O'Daniel
vowed to purge the legislature of the "disgraceful bunch of fifty-sixers."
He took to denouncing each one by name on his Sunday morning radio
show and in his car, using a loudspeaker as he drove along Congress Avenue. Thirty-three of the fifty-sixers ran for reelection in 1940, but only a
handful survived. (Thornberry did not seek reelection after two terms.)
O'Daniel's own reign ended in the following year, when he successfully ran
for the US Senate. His popularity would gradually erode there, however,
and he resigned in 1949.[9]

O'Daniel's gubernatorial star power was evidence of the unique appeal of what historian V. O. Key called the "old-style, patronage-minded top
leadership" that endured in Texas. Key cited O'Daniel and fellow former
Governor Ma Ferguson (who discernibly served as proxy for her impeached
husband) as quintessential politicians who subsisted solely by showmanship
and hollow overtures to voters. Key observed that O'Daniel "talked the
language of the lesser people but on the whole he acted and voted about
as a *Chicago Tribune* Republican." Texas's panoply of political curiosities was
evidently commonplace across the region. Wrote Key: "From afar, outland-
ers regard southern politics as a comic opera staged on a grand scale for the
amusement of the nation."[10]

The far-right Texas Regulars, a conservative Democratic faction formed in 1944 and championed by O'Daniel, called for the restoration of so-called "states' rights" to enforce white supremacy and dismantle the New Deal's "communistic" legacy programs. O'Daniel's immediate gubernatorial successors, fellow segregationists and Texas Regulars Coke Stevenson and Beauford H. Jester, likewise aligned with civil rights antagonists as well as the oil industry. Although racism was not as overt in Texas as it was in other southern states (mainly because of its relatively low black population), the percolating intra-party divisions over civil rights augured a tornado on the horizon.[11]

As state legislators earned a mere three hundred dollars for four months of each regular, biennial session, Thornberry sought concurrent employment with the Austin law firm Powell, Wirtz, Rauhut, and Gideon during his two terms. The firm was known for serving clients in the oil business, notably the burgeoning construction company Brown and Root. At the firm, Thornberry focused on civil law at the county, state, and federal court levels. His primary responsibilities involved civil litigation, condemnation cases, divorce actions, workers' compensation, and appeals of rulings by the Railroad Commission of Texas, which regulated the oil and gas industry. In his first litigation case, a divorce dispute in which he represented an untruthful client, Thornberry "learned as most lawyers must, not to accept a prospective client's appraisal of his or her case at face value." Partner Alvin Wirtz, a former state senator and future lobbyist for Brown and Root, enjoyed mentoring his firm's younger lawyers including Thornberry, whom he encouraged to stay in public service for the long term.[12]

Although the firm paid him a paltry seventy-five dollars per month—less than what he made in the sheriff's office during college—Thornberry felt fortunate to be employed at all. "People who were in my class did not have high-paying jobs," Thornberry reflected. "Most people had to work pretty hard to exist if they were going to educate their children." Thornberry's social circle was equally strapped. Thornberry and Herman Jones, a fellow state legislator and future state district judge, shared a mutual friend in Budweiser lobbyist Martin Winfrey, who was married to Smithville native Marian Harris. Their circle included Price Daniel and fellow legislator Alf Roark, a former teacher from Cleveland, Texas, who was elected to the state House in 1932. The coterie frequented the Austin Motel for thirty-five-cent shrimp cocktails. When it was his turn to pay, the miserly but charming Daniel closely monitored each person's take and particularly liked ribbing Thornberry when he purportedly took more than his fair share. The group relied on Thornberry for transportation, since he was the only car owner among them, yet he never solicited contributions toward his gas expenses.[13]

At the national level, the Roosevelt-led Democrats enjoyed a rare opportunity in American history to govern the country unilaterally. Roosevelt "was on the crest of a political wave, and only two or three times in our history has the other political party been so weak," Vice President John Nance Garner later commented. "How he would have fared under normal political alignments can only be conjectured." Garner, who hailed from Uvalde, ranked among several Texans in the upper echelons of national party leadership. Garner protégé and Bonham native Sam Rayburn, having joined the House in 1913, had just begun his storied stint as Speaker in 1940. US Senator Tom Connally of Marlin was instrumental in shaping the Democratic agenda as well. Jesse Jones, a business and community leader from Houston and friend of Garner, was appointed by Roosevelt in 1933 to chair the Reconstruction Finance Corporation (RFC) before his elevation to US Secretary of Commerce in 1940.[14]

Texas's prowess on the big stage aside, fallout from the Depression continued to limit opportunities for job seekers as the national unemployment rate peaked at 25 percent in 1932. Austin lagged behind most urban areas in terms of living conditions and prosperity. According to a 1934 federal survey of housing conditions in sixty-four cities, over 20 percent of all Austin homes were deemed "either in dangerous disrepair or even unfit for habitation," compared to the national average of 18.1 percent. Only 80 percent of Austin homes had running water compared to 95 percent nationwide. Within a three-block radius of Congress Avenue, a family of eight to ten members could be found living in a single room measuring twenty feet by thirty feet. A single water hydrant provided the only potable water for more than one hundred locals, who also shared an outdoor toilet. Over five thousand heads of households were unemployed in the worst of these times, and those who had jobs could barely make ends meet.[15]

At this time, an ambitious twenty-something Lyndon Baines Johnson was eager to remedy the destitution pervading his home state. He had jumpstarted his career through the New Deal's National Youth Administration (NYA), which was designed to find employment and student aid for college graduates and prospective students. Johnson had convinced key legislators to appoint him director of the NYA's Texas regional office in July of 1935. After eighteen months on the job, Johnson had helped nearly thirty thousand people between the ages of sixteen and twenty-five find work or go to school. He was obsessed with his job, working seven days a week and up to eighteen hours a day. An acquaintance remembered, "You'd ask him about the weather, and he'd start talking about the projects."[16]

Like Thornberry, Johnson grew up in hardship. He and his four siblings were raised by their parents in a three-room house in Stonewall, Texas. His father, Samuel Ealy Johnson Jr., was a Populist Democratic state representative from Gillespie County. The family lived in the isolated "jackrabbit country" that was southwest Texas, where the education system was widely substandard. Partly in pursuit of better schooling, the family of seven moved to rural Johnson City (population 323), a hamlet with no electricity, no indoor toilets, and little running water. As a teenager Johnson worked as a page in the legislature at the same time as Thornberry, although the two were not acquainted. ("Lyndon . . . was six feet tall and twelve years old," recalled Wright Patman, a Democratic state representative in the 1920s and later a congressman. "But little Homer Thornberry . . . was half as tall as Lyndon and the same age.") Johnson worked his way through school just as Thornberry did, ultimately earning an education degree from the Southwest Texas State Teachers College.[17]

Johnson parlayed his NYA experience into a victorious run for the US House of Representatives in a 1937 special election. Representing the Tenth Congressional District, which served Travis County and surrounding areas, Johnson steered more federal largesse to Texas businesses and low-income residents. Austin was a prime beneficiary of his efforts, netting construction funds for Bergstrom Air Force Base, a fish hatchery, and a magnesium plant. He saw to rural issues as well, persuading the Rural Electrification Administration to deliver electric power to underserved residents in the Hill Country. With the help of Mayor Tom Miller, Johnson convinced the Austin City Council to establish the Housing Authority of the City of Austin (HACA) to provide shelter for homeless persons. After the 1937 Wagner-Steagall Housing Act provided $500 million in loans for low-cost housing projects across the country, Johnson petitioned the United States Housing Authority for a $450,000 loan, followed by an additional $700,000 over two years that helped the HACA produce 186 affordable units for low-income families previously living in squalor.[18]

In addition to catering to a wide range of his constituents, Johnson was also driven by an insatiable hunger for power. The successful launch of his own radio station cemented his identification with the business community, and he could comfortably rely on a steady stream of corporate funding to ensure his political career's longevity. In exchange for decades of lucrative government contracts, Brown and Root steadily bankrolled the Johnson machine. Thanks to Johnson's mastery of the legislative process, the company would be awarded a contract to build the Mansfield Dam just northwest of Austin, completed in 1942. While favoritism clearly factored into the award, the project was hardly frivolous, as the region had sustained tens of billions of dollars in flood damage since the dawn of the century.[19]

Thornberry first made Johnson's acquaintance during the latter's initial run for Congress in 1937. Thornberry had just started his first term in the Texas House, and he occasionally paid visits to Johnson's campaign headquarters. Despite similar backgrounds and philosophies, they were polar opposites in nearly every other respect. At six feet and four inches, Johnson towered over the slim and slight Thornberry. Johnson's domineering stature and outsized personality doubtless helped him get what he wanted, whether via cajolery, intimidation, or rage. Thornberry, on the other hand, preferred building rapport through reserved deference and humor. And while both men were career driven, Johnson's appetite for power was substantially larger. Yet for all their differences in appearance and style, they shared a compassion for society's disadvantaged that shaped their formative years as elected officials. "When I thought about the kind of congressman I wanted to be," Johnson reflected. "I . . . promised myself that I'd always be the people's congressman, representing all the people, not just the ones with money and power." Likewise, Thornberry's experience as a legislator caused him "to have a good deal of sympathy or interest in people who are not as fortunate as others."[20]

POLITICS AND RACE IN THE SOUTH: A BRIEF RETROSPECT

The post-Civil War New South's long-awaited socioeconomic reboot began in earnest with the New Deal, whose wake would also unforeseeably upset the region's political dynamics. Although Democratic President Franklin Roosevelt's stimulus programs eventually polarized members of his own party, they were roundly welcomed by southern leaders at their inception. The

Great Depression had crushed the South's already weak agrarian-centered economy and exposed inadequacies in many cities' public services. The region had suffered from decades of agricultural overproduction while share-croppers and tenant farmers, composed mostly of freed slaves, remained bereft of property rights. Southern conservatives in Congress voted for most New Deal programs, and their few liberal counterparts felt emboldened to advance other progressive social reforms such as strengthening labor rights and repealing state poll taxes. But the New Deal ultimately fell short of fully reviving the national economy, and its aftermath threatened Democratic dominion over the South, partly because of dustups over civil rights issues.[21]

Despite their prevailing resistance to Roosevelt's overall aspirations, southern conservatives welcomed the modernization of infrastructure afforded by his programs, which had the side benefit of attracting outside industry. Although the South's economy continued to languish, its private sector benefited from federal contracts that generated additional tax revenue for cities and improved municipal functions. Roosevelt tolerated the region's pervasive racial discrimination and deplorable labor conditions so as not to disrupt autonomy at the state and local government levels. Notwithstanding such acquiescence, Roosevelt included blacks in a number of key positions within his administration, welcomed being photographed with black leaders, and was the first president in almost sixty years to publicly condemn lynching. He also helped create the Good Neighbor Commission in Texas to improve race relations. The New Deal's civil rights initiatives were chiefly responsible for luring black support away from the Republican Party, which had hitherto enjoyed most blacks' allegiance since President Abraham Lincoln's abolition of slavery. Other New Deal programs benefiting southern blacks included federal housing projects, the Civilian Conservation Corps, and funding for new black schools and hospitals. Discrimination was nevertheless prevalent in New Deal agencies.[22]

The cultural and political landscape where Thornberry and Johnson built their careers had long baffled outsiders. The South was almost entirely Democratic, yet its political system remained highly decentralized and disordered. "The South really has no parties," political scientist V. O. Key wrote at mid-century. "Its factions differ radically in their organization and operation from political parties." This lack of regional solidarity despite one-party hegemony was attributed to corrosive race relations, rampant poverty, and general voter apathy toward politics. Because of white-dominated Democratic primaries and suppressed social mobility, Populism failed to gain traction in the 1890s, leading to the South's near-monopoly by conservative Redeemers (a Bourbon Democrat wing).[23]

Thornberry's home state of Texas, Key observed, was among a core of southern states characterized by "a far more chaotic fractional politics" that enabled continued suppression of many citizens' civil rights. Since Reconstruction, the South's white establishment—with the aid of the Ku Klux Klan—had succeeded in subduing black and labor agitation by institutionalizing Jim Crow and antiunionism. In 1902, Texas joined ten other southern states (Georgia would become the eleventh six years later) in imposing a poll tax to thwart Populist electoral support and discourage racial and ethnic minorities and the poor from voting. Furthermore, the Texas legislature passed a law in 1923 that restricted participation in primary elections to whites only. Blacks had been more adversely affected than whites by the economic crisis of the 1930s, yet they enjoyed few short-term gains through New Deal programs. As in the rest of the region, whites in Texas received preferential treatment under the Federal Emergency Relief Administration and Civil Works Administration, while public service facilities and economic opportunities remained separate and unequal. Key concluded that the southern establishment's only common denominator was the suppression of the region's black population. The Democratic Party's solidarity thus hinged on largely eschewing economic issues in favor of race, making blacks' depressed social status the primary conduit for southern unity. The white upper class would continue to rely on a disorganized political structure to protect interests and thwart sustained disobedience by the lower classes. Backlash to the New Deal had thus strengthened southern conservatives' alliance with industry reactionaries, giving rise to a resurgent and reconstituted Republican Party in time.[24]

Although the New Deal did little to curtail white oppression, it engendered opportunities and inspiration for disadvantaged groups. Funding was made available for federal housing projects, schools, and hospitals for racial and ethnic minorities. Blacks began winning seats in state legislatures in the South. Civil rights organizations, both revived and newly conceived, featured more blacks in leadership roles. The University of Texas at Austin's Young Democrats student group launched the Texas Committee to Abolish the Poll Tax. The state's poll tax would remain a fixture for several more decades, but Texas's whites-only primary was soon vanquished in the 1944 Supreme Court case *Smith v. Allwright*. Arguing for the plaintiff was NAACP attorney Thurgood Marshall, whom future President Lyndon Johnson would elevate to become the first black US Supreme Court Justice.[25]

CHAPTER 5

Fractures (1940-1948)

A FTER FOUR YEARS AS A STATE LEGISLATOR AND PRIVATE ATTORNEY, Thornberry made his next career move when he ran for Travis County district attorney. In a campaign speech, he interpreted the district attorney's role as the "people's lawyer," one who "must not be afraid of the truth." He faced a grossly congested criminal docket, which had grown by three hundred cases over the past three years, and lamented its burden on taxpayers as costs piled up from frequent trial postponements. Thornberry also decried what he found to be an unsettling trend in the county court system, in which murder cases were resulting in steadily reduced or suspended sentences. "The time has come to return to the day when the offense of murder was prosecuted without fear or favor," he declared. Thornberry would defeat incumbent Edwin Moorhead on Election Day in 1940 by a thirty-nine-vote margin.[1]

Moorhead contested the election outcome and filed suit for an injunction against the inclusion of certain ballot boxes. He was convinced that Thornberry was somehow responsible for miscounting ballots. Moorhead petitioned for a recount, claiming that he should have received "at least seventy-five more votes" and that the ballots were "intentionally and illegally" recorded in his opponent's favor. Moorhead's vengefulness backfired. Local Judge George Best told a local newspaper that "Moorhead is slapping at some of his best friends and has cast reflections not only on my honesty and integrity but on the honesty and integrity of every worker at our polls." Fellow Judges Buckner Fitzgerald, T. F. Caldwell, Sam Hill, and L. B. Burnette agreed. Judge Hill stated that he himself had "never countenanced any irregularities," while Judge Caldwell accused Moorhead of "taking a step too far." Moorhead's injunction predictably fizzled before the Court of Civil Appeals.[2]

Taking office on January 1, 1941, Thornberry was responsible for representing the state of Texas in hundreds of civil and criminal cases each year. Contending with a heavy backlog and a small staff, Thornberry reprised his familiar workhorse role. "I was personally actively engaged in the trial of every major case," Thornberry recounted later. "This necessarily required my constant presence in courts." On his first day, a whopping 973 criminal cases were pending on the docket; one year later, only 259 remained, even though an additional 308 cases were filed in 1941. In 1942, 119 cases were filed with 274 cases spilling into the next year—a slightly larger carryover compared to the previous year but a significant net reduction from when Thornberry first took office.[3]

Thornberry's new job ended prematurely after Pearl Harbor was bombed by Japanese war planes. With the United States's subsequent entrance into World War II, Thornberry enlisted in the Naval Reserve in spite of the navy's reservations about his recent arm fracture. He was assigned as a lieutenant commander to the Naval Air Station in Corpus Christi, Texas, from 1942 to 1946. His patriotic zeal ebbed when his assignments tended toward the humdrum. "I was involved in a good many things that involved problems of people who were against the war and also foreign people who were considered dangerous," Thornberry later said. "And most of the time it was just doing a lot of checking, and while I enjoyed it, I felt like it was a laborious job." He occasionally boarded foreign ships and interviewed their commanders about enemy activity. But Thornberry's legal expertise provided the most value to the navy. On one occasion a black steward accused of striking an officer asked him to represent him before a court martial. Thornberry took the case because otherwise the man had "little opportunity to get the right sort of defense." Thornberry was ultimately removed from the defense team against his will by a superior officer. Thornberry demanded to remain on the case ("That old stubborn nature came out in me," he recalled later) but was rebuffed. He developed a surly reputation that was further aggravated by another stormy court martial, but as he conceded in private, he was "one of these tough guys outside and a 'sissy' inside." For all his discontent in Corpus Christi, he scored a personal triumph in landing his future wife Eloise Engle, who was serving as a civilian assistant to a naval officer.[4]

Following an honorable discharge, Thornberry resumed private practice in Austin, starting up a firm with friend and former fellow state legislator

Herman Jones. The only affordable office space they could find was a par-
titioned corner of a converted garage operated by a savings and loan institution. "We didn't really get off the ground running," recalled Thornberry.
"We handled the loan business for the savings and loan association, and we
had some practice; but it was slow going." (Thornberry shrank his bottom line even further by paying his clients' dollar parking fines out of his
own pocket rather than indulging their requests to "fix" them.) He and
Jones worked on civil cases before county, state, and federal courts on
wide-ranging legal matters that included title examinations, preparation
of liens, mortgages, conveyances, and real estate transactions. They also
advised savings and loans associations, counseled the Austin public housing
authority, and represented clients in labor disputes and workman's compensation litigation. Thornberry joined the Travis County Bar Association,
the State Bar of Texas, and the American Bar Association. For the time being, Thornberry resisted friends' urgings that he return to elected office.[5]

The political climate in Austin had reached a boiling point during
Thornberry's sojourn from the public sector. Racial and class tensions di-
rected at the white and wealthy establishment swelled in the late 1940s.
Liberal angst also lingered over the 1944 firing of progressive UT Austin
President Homer Rainey, the victim of a politically motivated ouster by
UT's conservative Board of Regents. Thornberry had been supportive of
UT's direction under Rainey for engendering "a more progressive atmo-
sphere in Austin" at a time when conservative forces were dominating state
leadership and business. Meanwhile the regents, all appointed by Governors O'Daniel and Stevenson, had demonized Rainey for pushing to admit
blacks and purportedly enabling communism and a "nest of homosexuals"
at the school. In addition to the Rainey incident, the regents' termination
of four untenured economics professors, who were outspoken supporters
of organized labor, earned censure by the American Association of University Professors. Students organized a mock funeral march for the symbolic
demise of academic freedom.[6]

The Rainey incident was illustrative of the prevailing anti-government
sentiment across Texas. As historian Randolph Campbell wrote, "The average voter's ingrained distrust of the national government, dislike of taxes,
and lack of concern about civil rights would not change easily." The Democratic Party's ideological dynamics continued to shift rightward as the
ultraconservative Texas Regulars faction gathered more support. Liberal

Thornberry in naval garb with Mary Thornberry (standing, right) alongside
unidentified friends, Austin, Texas, circa 1943. *Thornberry family collection.*

forces suffered another setback three years later when Rainey, hoping to
capitalize on the backlash to his firing, was soundly defeated in the gubernatorial runoff election by former Railroad Commissioner Beauford Jester,
who had publicly chastised his opponent for being a "nigger lover."[7]

Austin's City Council leaned nearly as far right as the state's leadership at this time, much to the ire of oft-dissenting liberal council member
Simon Gillis, one of the Thornberry family's neighbors who helped teach
Homer to talk. Gillis opposed minimum income-level requirements of
certain public housing programs, which had excluded the city's poorest
from participating. Following Gillis's resignation from his at-large seat in
early 1946, South Austinites feared their interests would lose representation. Friends and neighbors pushed Thornberry to run for Gillis's spot, but

Thornberry stands outside his law firm, cofounded by Herman Jones, Austin, Texas, 1947. *Thornberry family collection.*

preoccupation with his struggling law practice and personal matters deterred his pursuit of yet another low-paying government job. Surprisingly, he also lacked the full endorsement of the departing incumbent, despite their long-standing relationship. "Mr. Gillis had known me as a boy, seen me grow up," said Thornberry. "He really didn't think I had the capacity to do it. . . . I was still a boy to him!" A small legion of South Austinites disagreed and generated seventeen petitions with seven hundred signatures across town. Thornberry finally relented. "I am responding to the desires of the people who have nominated me, and I'll do the best job that I can," he told the *Austin Evening Statesman*. The city council had the power to appoint Gillis's successor unilaterally, but after consulting with Mayor Tom Miller, it opted to hold a special election instead.[8]

The city's most pressing issue was an $18,173,000 municipal bond—at the time the largest amount ever proposed in Austin. The bond's measures primarily dealt with infrastructure upgrades, the new construction of Brackenridge Hospital and a low-water dam, and improvements to the municipal airport. The most controversial project was an interregional highway that would replace East Avenue and relieve downtown congestion. Some questioned the need for a superhighway while others were concerned it would bolster the physical boundary that segregated the city's white majority in central Austin from most of its black population on the east side. "It looked like we were creating a more intense barrier," said Thornberry, who nevertheless agreed with the highway department that "it was apparent we couldn't run [all] the traffic through Austin on Congress Avenue." Actual public vehemence was minimal, partly because Austin's black community focused more on survival than public protestation. All measures—including the superhighway, which eventually became part of Interstate 35—would pass by wide margins, perhaps attributable, in part, to the state's poll tax and other voting obstructions that kept blacks and the poor away from the polls.[9]

Although May's bond vote preceded the June election for Gillis's council seat, both Thornberry and his opponent, local merchant S.B. Price, campaigned on the major bond issues. Price had voted for every measure, for he believed Austin needed to prepare for future growth and follow the example of the City of Houston, whose upcoming $133 million bond issuance would finance major infrastructural improvement. In line with his customary cautiousness about public spending and concern about legal issues, Thornberry had supported some but not all of the ballot measures. Specifically, he preferred conserving the city's financial resources and limited labor and materials for what he considered to be the city's most pressing needs, which included schools, roads, and sewers. He opposed funding construction of the low-water dam because, as he said, "I did not see the need for such a project now, that it was inflationary, and that it would take material needed for veterans' housing." Taking an attorney's perspective, Thornberry also warned against proceeding without legal authorization from the state supreme court. He coasted through the special election on June 3 by a 1,383 to 225 vote. Thornberry conscientiously declined to issue a public statement until election officials verified the plainly decisive results.[10]

Immediately after being sworn in to the council, Thornberry introduced a resolution commending Gillis for his thirteen-year service, despite not receiving his ex-neighbor's endorsement. "I cannot take the place of Mr. Gillis," Thornberry stated, "but I can emulate his acts in working for the best interest of all of Austin." Judge Ben Powell, who had given Thornberry his first job as an attorney, vouched for the new council member as "a man of energy who is not afraid of work and a man of convictions who is not afraid to express them." Thornberry next joined the rest of the council and Mayor Miller in bartering rights-of-way with East Avenue property owners to clear land for the new superhighway.[11]

City council meetings tended to be mundane affairs. In conjunction with the mayor, its members primarily handled city management and budgeting, zoning, and permitting issues; ordinance adjustments; and private citizen requests for public service improvements. The discussions with East Avenue property owners dragged on for several years. The city manager was authorized to handle the negotiations, but the council entertained property owner protests over the city's valuations of their properties.[12]

More memorable council meetings involved disagreements over beer and liquor licensing. Whereas most license seekers were approved without debate, those operating near schools and churches drew scrutiny from the council as well as local residents. Thornberry butted heads with Mayor Miller over a spot-zoning case in which a black business owner requested permission to sell alcohol in an otherwise dry locale. Since spot-zoning was generally frowned upon by the zoning board, Miller recommended that the entire block be rezoned in order to permit alcohol sales there.

Thornberry took issue because of the business's close proximity to both an elementary school and a Baptist church. A pastor of the church, already perturbed about a nearby drug store that sold alcohol, argued that additional vendors would "make worse the very objectionable moral condition already existing there." Miller claimed Thornberry's opposition to the permit was subjective and alleged that Thornberry was a prohibitionist, which he was not. Miller also contended that denying a black applicant's request was discriminatory since several white liquor storeowners nearby had received permits. Thornberry shot back, "I am not giving consideration to this on a moral issue, but I have to look to my own conscience, and I want to vote so I can look my mother in the face when I see that a bad situation already exists and that granting this zoning change would make the situation worse." (Mary, a devout churchgoer and teetotaler, surely supported her son's feelings on the matter.) After a few procedural deferments, the rezoning application was approved by vote of the council. Thornberry was the lone dissenter.[13]

Thornberry's protectiveness extended to illegal gambling. During the council's meeting on January 30, 1947, Thornberry lamented, "It is well known that wherever professional gamblers are allowed to ply their vicious and immoral trade, crime in general becomes prevalent." Thornberry thus proposed a resolution that laws against gambling be more strictly enforced for the sake of his fellow citizens and their children, whom he claimed "come here to obtain their education, free from the influence and presence of the professional gamblers and their organized crimes." The motion carried.[14]

On occasion the council dealt with discriminatory restrictive covenants, which were provisions in deeds or leases to real property that imposed limits on that land's use by the owner. Over the first half of the twentieth century, these covenants, in conjunction with lax zoning laws and racist federal housing policies, allowed land developers to impose deed restrictions that permitted only whites to move into certain areas of town. Covenants restricting Jews were commonplace. In the spring of 1947, the City of Austin received an application for annexation to it by two communities that forbade Jews from living there. According to Morris Polsky, the Thornberry family's Jewish dermatologist, Thornberry railed against the measure during a council meeting:

I'm just back from a tough war where we fought a vicious enemy whose
whole program was to erect barriers, including death, to certain minorities.
I didn't fight that war to come home and allow that same evil in my hometown. I denounce these restrictions, and I demand they be removed!

The communities held firm, but Thornberry prevailed in denying their
applications.[15]

Austin's black community generally kept to its side of town, but its
members occasionally filed complaints with the council over inadequate
city services. Examples included insufficient street lighting, trash collection, fire and police protection, sewer lines, street paving, and parks and
playgrounds. The mayor and council were generally receptive to these
complaints but usually referred them to the city manager and chief of
police to be resolved. (A sign of the times was the city council minutes'
identification of blacks as "colored." It was otherwise assumed that the person of note was white and needed no such descriptor.) Only once during
Thornberry's tenure did the council hear accusations of overt racism. At
the council's August 21, 1947, meeting, representatives of the National
Association for the Advancement of Colored People (NAACP) complained
of discrimination and poor emergency service at the new Brackenridge
Hospital, which kept separate facilities for the two races. This matter too
was referred to the city manager's office.[16]

Thornberry's colleagues had elected him mayor pro tempore in May
1947, which entailed substituting for Miller at meetings in his absence.
Thornberry remained on the council for another thirteen months.

LOVE AND WAR

For all of Thornberry's achievements by age thirty-five, he had yet to discover love. But in the midst of a world at war, that all changed.

Eloise Engle was an attractive, magnetic twenty-five-year-old who
hailed from San Antonio. Like most heads of households during the Depression, her parents, George and Kate Engle, struggled mightily to support their family, which also included Eloise's younger brothers George
and Wallace. Following foreclosure on their home in Houston, they moved
to San Antonio, where George found sporadic work at a friend's gas station, and Kate entertained at children's parties. Near the end of 1939 they

relocated to Austin and rented out rooms in their house to college students. Eloise attended San Antonio Junior College before completing her undergraduate degree at UT Austin in 1942.[17]

At a restaurant during one of their first dates, Thornberry became distracted by another alluring female sitting nearby. Once both parties had finished dinner, Engle deviously instructed Thornberry out loud to hold hands with a little girl standing near the exit, giving the false impression that he was a family man and therefore off the market. The ruse appeared to work. "I needed somebody who in spite of my looks, age, contrariness, shortcomings, poverty, lack of future, could be loyal to me, put up with me and still think I was the best man," Thornberry later wrote to a friend. "And that is what I got."[18]

Their relationship hit a bump when Engle returned to Austin while Thornberry stayed behind to complete his military service. Their distance and the time apart pushed them to the brink of a breakup, but Thornberry refused to let that happen. In a letter to Engle in September 1944, he effused:

> It seems to me that both of us need to find out something right about now—and that is how this business of living and getting along is when we don't have any contact with each other. Of course, one of the answers to this thought is that we can still be friends. But I just ain't interested in this old business of 'Can't we still be friends.' There is something more involved here than that. I know this to be true and I think that you know it to be true.
>
>   . . . . I feel that we are . . . trying to find something somewhere else— when here it is. Like Sir Launfal when he traveled the world over to find the Holy Grail and there it was just at the point from which he started.[19]

His petition did the trick, and within months of its receipt, the couple announced their intention to marry. The announcement came as a surprise to Mary, who had yet to meet her soon-to-be daughter-in-law. On February 24, 1945, not long after Thornberry's wartime obligations ended, Engle and he exchanged wedding vows at the University Presbyterian Church in Austin. Lyndon Johnson was invited but could not attend (he mailed a congratulatory letter in lieu). Over the next five and a half years, the couple would welcome three children—Molly, David, and Kate. Washington newspapers would later label Eloise a "campus beauty" and "the perfect type of congressional wife" and describe the children as having the kind of "good looks you see in magazines."[20]

Eloise and Homer Thornberry at their wedding, Austin, Texas, 1945. *Thornberry family collection.*

Speculation sprouted in 1948 over Thornberry's interest in filling Johnson's vacant Tenth District seat in the US House of Representatives when the latter decided to run for the Senate. By this point Thornberry was well acquainted with Johnson, who occasionally met with Austin City Council members on return trips from Washington. Thornberry's connection to Johnson and familiarity with the district gave him a competitive advantage in the race. "I was not a handpicked successor," Thornberry later said. "On the other hand, I think it's fair to say that he [Johnson] thought I would run . . . [and] that he had told people that I would be the next congressman." Thornberry was nevertheless hesitant to succeed Johnson for a number of reasons. For one, it would likely require transplanting his wife, mother, and children to the nation's capital and also incur a sizable debt. Thornberry initially deferred the opportunity to liberal attorney Ralph Yarborough, who declined the offer (he preferred to continue his law practice) yet pledged to endorse Thornberry if the need arose. The Thornberrys ultimately decided that the opportunity to serve the public "on a broader and more important scale" was too great to pass up.[21]

CHAPTER 6

Nation, State (1948-1953)

S INCE THE TEXAS REPUBLICAN PARTY FIELDED NO CANDIDATES in 1948's nine congressional races—including the Tenth District—the only hurdle facing Thornberry was the Democratic primary. Six candidates (four from Travis County including Thornberry) had set their sights on Lyndon Johnson's vacated seat. Austin attorney Creekmore Fath, considered Thornberry's closest competition, could count on most of the region's liberal contingent while Thornberry would inherit Johnson's business support. Thornberry's experience in public office, coupled with Johnson's backing, gave him a clear advantage, but his courtship of black voters would agitate conservatives in the region.[1]

Racial tensions were relatively moderate in Texas, where blacks were relatively few compared to other southern states. They accounted for 14.4 percent of Texas's population in the 1940s, compared to 49.2 percent in the racial hotbed of Mississippi. Nevertheless, rural areas in Texas, including parts of the Tenth District, harbored "an intense feeling about blacks," according to Thornberry. Further, as of March 1948, only 14 percent of the state's residents supported President Truman's civil rights program, including its anti-lynching law. Still, Austin's church-led black communities were gaining prominence in the 1940s, and their votes had become coveted.[2]

Thornberry recognized the importance of black constituent support, but he also had to weigh white backlash. "Votes of blacks—it was tough then, and you had to know how to handle it," Thornberry recalled. "You wanted them to vote for you, but you weren't sure." An opponent circulated photographs of Thornberry shaking hands with blacks in rural areas in hopes of race-baiting white voters.[3]

Racial stirrings notwithstanding, Thornberry handily won the primary and became the uncontested Democratic nominee for the Tenth District seat, assuring his entry into the Eighty-First US Congress in November. His new constituency comprised ten counties: Bastrop, Blanco, Burleson, Burnet, Caldwell, Hays, Lee, Travis, Washington, and Williamson.[4]

Unlike Thornberry, Truman was opposed in the general election, where he faced heavily favored New York Governor Thomas E. Dewey. Truman's hard-fought campaign included a cross-country tour in a commercial rail caboose dubbed the "Harry Truman Special." Johnson, having won his primary election for the US Senate, accompanied Truman to several of his Texas stops.

Austin was one of Truman's destinations, and Thornberry convinced his wife Eloise, who was expecting their second child, to attend the rally downtown. Upon the train's arrival, Johnson spotted Thornberry in the crowd and summoned him aboard. He promptly introduced Thornberry both to President Truman and to House Speaker Sam Rayburn. Following Rayburn's brief address to the crowd, Truman regaled attendees with "one of those 'Give 'em hell' speeches," recalled Thornberry.[5]

Once the rally ended, Thornberry began to bid his farewells before the Truman Special proceeded north. Johnson intervened. "Well, wait a minute," he said. "We're going to go up to Georgetown—it's in your district. You ought to stay on here and show up there." Thornberry happily accepted without consulting Eloise. "I had forgotten that she couldn't drive, so I said, 'One of these ladies will take you,'" recalled Thornberry. "I just was too excited. I couldn't be worrying about my pregnant wife."[6]

En route, the conductor requested to see each passenger's ticket. Alas, Thornberry had no money on him. "Thornberry, don't you even have one dollar?" Johnson barked. "Well, hell, I'll loan you a dollar." Thornberry later remembered, "That was my first experience in seeing a president of the United States, and I was broke at the time." Going forward, he pledged he would always "remember to have at least a dollar in my pocket."[7]

Thornberry's respect for President Truman owed as much to their shared values as to the president's policy agenda. Like Thornberry, Truman had grown up poor, served in the military at a time of war, and devoted most of his professional life to public service. Truman had pushed an aggressive civil rights agenda following his unabashed State of the Union address on January 7, 1948, when he told the American people, "Our first goal

President Harry Truman addressing Georgetown, Texas, residents from the
"Harry Truman Special," with Senator Lyndon B. Johnson and Thornberry, 1948.
LBJ Library Photo by Frank Muto.

is to secure fully the essential human rights of our citizens." Although Truman
would win reelection later that year, his outspoken liberal aspirations—
notably his stance on civil rights—alienated southern conservatives in
his own party. Anti-New Dealers stewed over his affirmation of President
Roosevelt's social programs that supported national health insurance, public housing, minimum wage increases, public education, conservation of
natural resources, and aid to farmers. Indeed, Truman failed repeatedly to
win over the Democrats' southern bloc. The New Deal's unraveling began
in earnest at the watershed 1948 Democratic National Convention in Phil-
adelphia, where senatorial candidate Hubert Humphrey's rousing pro-civil
rights speech exacerbated intra-party divisiveness.[8]

Homesickness soon beset Thornberry upon moving to Washington.
He initially shared a hotel room with fellow House freshman and Texan
Lloyd Bentsen before temporarily moving in with Lyndon Johnson's family. "Washington [is] such a funny place," Thornberry wrote his wife, who
stayed behind with their children. "Everybody [is] in a hell of a hurry to go
somewhere, but when I think of our hurried trips what good does it do?
. . . I get sort of an amusement out of it as I watch from the sideline." At first

the Thornberrys tried to maintain permanent residence in Austin, lest his tenure in Congress be brief, but the experiment was short-lived. "I surely get tired of this place quick," Thornberry wrote. "This business of being a bachelor belongs to another age. I always had the sneaking notion that because I was a bachelor so long that it wouldn't hurt me to go through a temporary period of being alone for a short period when it was necessary, but I am wrong."[9]

Eloise struggled to cope with the arrangement as well. Among other reasons, she was unsettled by the heightened public exposure of being a congressional spouse. Her husband reinforced the necessity of active public relations: It "reminds folks that we are representing them and that I am up here working. In addition you do such a wonderful job in meeting people—give a good impression, etc. . . . it's part of the job." Financial purse-pinching contributed to their distress as well. Thornberry had accrued a sizable debt from his election campaign, and not all travel costs were reimbursable. Brown and Root, a client of Thornberry's former law firm and the chief benefactor of Johnson's political ascension, graciously funded the Thornberry family's visits to and from Washington following the election. (Thornberry resisted the firm's periodic entreaties to reciprocate on certain House votes.) Homer and Eloise ultimately decided that the whole clan, including Homer's seventy-six-year-old mother Mary, should permanently move to Washington. (The trip marked Mary's first time on an airplane.) Their new home was around the corner from the Johnsons.[10]

Johnson had made certain that Thornberry inherited his former office space. He also schooled his successor on his new constituency. "He knew the district, and he would tell me about some parts of it and tell me about how to work with other people," Thornberry said. "And throughout the time that I was in Congress, he was very helpful to me in many, many ways." Johnson also ordered his staff aides to help the Thornberrys become acclimated to their new surroundings, which included chaperoning the newcomers' house hunting. Notwithstanding Johnson's hospitality and the reunion of his own family, Thornberry remained apprehensive. "I had entered into a job that was not an easy one," he later said. "I was succeeding a man who had been very successful. He was a very popular congressman with this district." Thornberry's anxiety was mitigated somewhat by his initiation into the fraternal Texas delegation. He was heartened to discover that his congressional brethren were "twenty-three of the most able, just, and sincere men to be found anywhere."[11]

The most widely respected member in the House, if not in all of Congress, was Speaker Sam Rayburn. "It seemed to me that he was a very aloof man, very formal," recalled Thornberry. "I didn't recognize him as having the warmth and wonderful personality that he had." The reserved sixty-seven-year-old Rayburn was a bald, stocky fellow known for making poor first impressions and keeping others at a distance. Yet Thornberry managed to win over the Democratic stalwart, and they forged a close, enduring relationship at once personal and professional. "No other experience would cause me to be more indebted to Senator Johnson than that I came to know the Speaker Rayburn," said Thornberry.[12]

Thornberry was assigned by Rayburn to the House Committee on the Post Office and Civil Service in his inaugural session. Few vacancies existed elsewhere, given the many fellow Texans who sat on various committees. Said Thornberry:

> [The Committee on the Post Office and Civil Service] was not supposed to be one of the highest-ranking committees, but from it I learned a good deal. I learned how to work on a committee. I learned how to study legislation. I learned how to listen to people who testify. It was a good experience for me.

During his two years on the committee, he introduced and supported legislation to increase retirement benefits and unemployment compensation for civil servants. He was particularly protective of postal workers and sought to raise their overtime pay, salary base, and retirement benefits. He was more ambivalent about entitlement programs for the elderly. While he understood the need for a more affordable healthcare system, he was also sensitive to the medical community's concerns about their profit margins. (Legislative traction would not reach critical mass until the creation of Medicare in 1965 after Thornberry's departure from Congress.) Overall, compassion for the average retiree factored most heavily into Thornberry's voting patterns. He subscribed to the spirit of the Townsend plan, a revolving pension fund proposed by an eponymous physician that had influenced social security's conception in 1935 and that would advance its augmentation in the decades to come. During his tenure in the House, Thornberry regularly supported amendments to the Social Security Act that increased elderly and survivor insurance benefits, both timeless mainstays in House floor debates and legislation.[13]

Thornberry joined the vast majority of his colleagues in their wholehearted support for military funding, particularly during wartime. Legislation in this vein periodically provided financial aid for veterans pursuing higher education, a subject dear to Thornberry. More commonly, it concerned procurement and military base construction, motivated largely by concerns about communist imperialism during the Korean War. Thornberry sided with Truman and most congressional members in hastily ramping up US intervention abroad, yet he felt equally strongly about maintaining fiscal responsibility. In a letter to the Austin business community during the early stages of the war effort, Thornberry wrote:

> I fear that we are confronted with two serious enemies—communism and inflation. . . . If we are to gain any lesson at all from our experience in the last war, it is that we cannot have effective control against inflation if we are to impose controls only on part of our economy. I do not believe in making an exception of any special group. I have voted for imposition of controls on prices, wages, and credit—clear across the board. . . . Our first duty during these days is to cut nonessential spending to the bone, so that we can send bullets, guns, tanks, and airplanes to our men in Korea.

An editorial appearing in the *Austin Statesman* months later applauded Thornberry's steady backing of the military:

> The sense of national peril is acute here in Texas. Some have come to share it only recently. It is reassuring that the representative of central Texas in Congress has had the vision and the foresight and the realistic purpose to go down the line for total mobilization from the beginning.[14]

After enjoying another uncontested general election in 1950, Thornberry joined the Committee on Interstate and Foreign Commerce, which Rayburn prized and previously chaired, where he acquired a deep sympathy for the struggling farming industry. The cattle and cotton trades prevalent in his district were among the hardest hit of all domestic agricultural producers in the early 1950s. By December 1952, farm prices across the country declined by an average of 12 percent from the previous year and were at their lowest in two years. Farm employment levels meanwhile plunged to seasonal nadirs not seen since 1925. Making matters worse, federal appropriations to support farming had been reduced; farm equipment prices had remained high since the start of the war; and bank loans were more difficult to obtain. From the House floor on June 8, 1953, Thornberry recited a despondent formal letter sent to him by members of the Lee County Cattlemen's Association and Lee County Farm Bureau. An excerpt reads:

> Many of our local cattle raisers are standing a huge loss, while some have failed to meet their notes as they come due. . . . We believe it imperative that we either support cattle along with price-supported commodities or take the support price from all agricultural products. No money can possibly be made feeding cattle at this time.

Furthermore, the percentage of farmers with phone service had dropped from 32 percent in 1920 to 17 percent in 1945. "And for the farm family just as for the city family, telephone service provides a link with neighbors and the outside world that can do much to increase the enjoyment and contentment of family living," Thornberry said in a floor debate on H.R. 2960 to fund rural electrification. "This is not a fight between free enterprise and socialism, but it is indeed a fight to preserve free enterprise against monopoly and socialism." The bill was ultimately passed and signed into law, but the tide would turn with the passage of the Agricultural Act of 1954. This new law, which was opposed by Thornberry and other members representing districts with heavy agriculture, replaced existing fixed price support with flexible price support, which was generally lower and adjusted according to the supply of commodities. The majority of the members in Congress who supported the act believed that fixed price supports would no longer be necessary with the conclusion of the Korean War one year prior. An undeterred Thornberry fought for an increase in farm price supports the following year for producers of basic commodities like peanuts, of which Texas was the country's largest producer. As Thornberry pointed out in a floor debate, peanut farming was not only a critical part of his home state's economy, it also aided the war effort (peanut oil was used in the manufacture of munitions). Alas, congressional support for fixed prices had fizzled irretrievably by that point.[15]

Perhaps the most contentious issue Congress tackled during Thornberry's early years was the revisited anti-union Labor-Management Relations Act of 1947, better known as the Taft-Hartley Act. The right to organize had been previously guaranteed under the National Labor Relations Act, passed in 1935 under Roosevelt. But the ensuing Republican-controlled Congress succeeded in overriding Truman's veto of Taft-Hartley, which

Thornberry in 1954. *Thornberry family collection.*

imposed strict limitations on labor union activities. Conservatives' resentment toward the New Deal's legacy and Truman's Fair Deal was palpable at this point. Truman supporters in Congress, whose chambers had both returned to Democratic control in the 1948 election, launched a counteroffensive and made abolishing Taft-Hartley a key part of the party's platform. During a House floor debate on H.R. 2032 to repeal Taft-Hartley, Washington Democrat Hugh Mitchell argued, "The spirit of the Taft-Hartley Act is a malevolent one—to create dissension and dissatisfaction within the ranks of labor, to turn each worker against his brother, and all against their chosen leaders." Alas, most southern Democrats, including Thornberry and Johnson, refrained from siding with H.R. 2032 supporters, who included Truman and Rayburn. On May 4, 1949, Thornberry joined the slim majority of 212 against 209 House members on a motion to recommit H.R. 2032 to the Committee on Education and Labor, thereby preventing a floor vote and effectively killing it. Eight other Texans joined Thornberry and Johnson; eleven dissented.[16]

Thornberry's opposition to repealing Taft-Hartley notwithstanding, he was not fundamentally opposed to unions. A conflicted Thornberry later explained at a Rotary Club meeting in San Marcos, Texas, that management and labor relations were "one of the most complicated and challenging problems facing us today" and that he would never "take sides with either labor or management against the other." (He acknowledged in hindsight, "If it weren't for organized labor, a lot of the great social reforms would never have happened in this country.") Nevertheless, his stance on Taft-Hartley and his subsequent opposition to raising the minimum wage would cost him the support of labor forces—however weak they were in Austin—for most of his fifteen years in Congress. "I was independent, and I didn't always do just exactly what . . . labor wanted me to do," explained Thornberry.[17]

Johnson likewise laid claim to being "against anyone who thought he was bigger than the people and the government, whether big labor bosses or big business." Yet Johnson had taken a clearly pro-management stance when he voted for Taft-Hartley while he was still in the House, which not surprisingly drew the ire of the American Federation of Labor. ("I have voted for many bills that benefited the working man," Johnson said in his own defense.) His identification with the business class was partly attributed to his ownership of a highly profitable radio station which, in his view, might be threatened by the union movement. In the end, Taft-Hartley, which survived numerous repeal efforts over time, set in motion the long, slow erosion of American labor rights. Texas and twenty-one others would eventually become right-to-work states, providing yet another indicator of the New Deal's unraveling.[18]

Another contentious issue raised during Thornberry's first years in Congress pertained to states' jurisdictions over offshore natural resources, particularly lucrative subterranean petroleum deposits. Since the

1901 discovery of the Spindletop oilfield in southeast Texas, the ensuing oil boom buttressed the state's economic development over the course of the century. Elected officials from coastal states, including Texas, regularly rebuffed the federal government's claim to leasing rights and fees from offshore oil wells. Truman had supported a recent Supreme Court decision that denied these states' offshore mineral entitlements, and he opposed legislation by their representatives to reclaim them. Thornberry joined the Texas delegation against Truman and the Supreme Court ruling, contending that the revenue was needed to sustain his state's public school system, which Thornberry considered sacred. (The $150 million Texas public school fund was largely supported by revenue from oil leases in the Gulf of Mexico.) Thornberry and others also pointed to the conditions of Texas's annexation to the union in 1845, in which the state was guaranteed sole entitlement to its offshore territories. From the House floor, Thornberry laid out a vigorous defense of H.R. 4484, which would have erased the Supreme Court's decision. "The loss of three million acres of submerged Gulf lands . . . is a catastrophic blow to the foundation of our state school system," Thornberry stated, adding that the bill would "restore their [tidelands'] 100-year heritage to the school children of Texas." The bill was passed by the House on July 21, 1951, but later died in the Senate. Even if it had cleared both chambers, Truman likely would have vetoed it. (Dwight Eisenhower's ensuing presidency would reverse the White House's stance on tidelands issues. In early 1953, Thornberry introduced H.R. 1941, which would return to coastal states their tidelands rights within three leagues of their coastlines. The bill was rolled into H.R. 4198, which passed the House 285-108 on April 1 and was signed into law as the Submerged Lands Act of 1953 the following month.)[19]

Of course, far more divisive than tidelands and labor legislation was the matter of civil rights reform, which carved deep divisions between the White House and the South. In 1948 Truman had issued Executive Order 9981 to end discrimination in the military and guarantee fair employment in the civil service, a move coldly received by most southern members of Congress. Through another controversial executive order, Truman created the President's Committee on Civil Rights to propose measures that would strengthen civil rights protections in the United States. He also called for anti-lynching legislation, the creation of the Fair Employment Practices Commission (FEPC), and a constitutional ban on the poll tax (still in effect in seven former Confederate states, including Texas). Truman had thus pushed the strongest civil rights program of any president theretofore. As a result, he seriously jeopardized his chances for reelection.[20]

As Truman, a midwesterner, came to learn, racism was infused into southern culture and would not be uprooted solely by the stroke of a pen. After all, the South's resistance to large-scale social reform precipitated the devastating Civil War, and while slavery was abolished in its aftermath, segregation and other forms of institutionalized discrimination persisted through Reconstruction and the New Deal. Although black organizations were on the rise as of the late 1930s, access to public facilities and socioeconomic parity remained separate and unequal. Southern politics had long revolved around the subjugation of black rights, particularly in places like Mississippi, where whites were greatly outnumbered. Polls showed that only 23 percent of white southerners supported federal anti-lynching laws, compared to 51 percent of non-southerners. Consequently, Truman's efforts to curb racial violence succeeded only in intensifying southern political resistance. By the end of the 1940s, the southern Democratic bloc could no longer rely on the national party to represent its interests, and it began to align with conservative Republicans to obstruct the president's agenda.[21]

Following the 1948 elections, middle-of-the-road Texans like Johnson, Thornberry, and Rayburn felt pressure to join southern conservatives in opposing Truman on several key domestic issues, including civil rights, during his last term in the White House. Johnson's position on civil rights had ostensibly reversed once he began serving in the national spotlight. Prior to joining Congress, he was a staunch advocate of equal rights; as Texas NYA head he had, for example, ignored race as a factor in his hiring decisions. And unlike many southern leaders, his election campaigns avoided race-baiting white voters on hot topics like segregation. But upon joining the House and then the Senate, the pragmatic Johnson curried favor with white constituents for the sake of his own political survival. Johnson even criticized Truman publicly on his civil rights initiatives despite their alliance on most other issues. Indeed, Johnson, who would eventually become the country's most powerful champion of equal rights, regularly voted against civil rights reforms for the first three-quarters of his twenty-four years in Congress.[22]

Thornberry also consistently voted down civil rights legislation, but, as with Johnson, this did not necessarily equate to bigotry. To be sure, Thornberry had voted against a constitutional ban on the poll tax in federal

and state elections (H.R. 3199) and against the Fair Employment Practices Act (H.R. 4453), which would have reauthorized the Fair Employment Practices Committee to investigate complaints of discrimination. But
his behavior in public and private painted a different picture. Thornberry
openly courted blacks during the 1948 primary in the face of rural white
backlash, for instance. (Much later, during a family dinner in which his
mother-in-law made a passing reference to "some nigger," Thornberry
gently requested that she substitute "negro" instead.)[23]

Rayburn, too, opposed civil rights measures, but unlike Thornberry, he
answered to a stridently segregationist district. In response to a letter in
early 1948 from a constituent white couple, Rayburn firmly assured them
of his loyalty on the issue:

> I have voted in this Congress against federal repeal of the poll tax law. I am
> against the so-called federal anti-lynching law. I have been opposed to the
> Fair Employment Practices Commission and still am and shall vote against it
> and against any bill that has any tendency towards crippling our segregation
> laws or any other part of the program that has to do with, in what I consider,
> interference of our local rights.

Texas representatives routinely abstained from floor debates on civil rights
bills, but Georgia Democrat Henderson Lanham essentially spoke on their
behalf when he argued that renewing the FEPC "violates the Constitution
of the United States and as a corollary, invades the province of the states
and the personal freedom of individual employers." All twenty Texas House
members joined the majority of their southern colleagues in voting against
H.R. 4453, which nonetheless passed the House before succumbing to a
southern filibuster in the Senate.[24]

Questions about Congress's constitutional limitations were also presented under southern members' claims that they were powerless to banish
the poll tax in federal and state elections. The US Attorney General's office
countered that they had it backwards: Congress indeed had the power to
lift the tax, and the tax itself was unconstitutional. To the first point, the
attorney general showed that Congress is positively endowed with

> the authority to enact anti-poll-tax measures to effectuate its guarantee of
> a republican form of government to every state, to eliminate state interfer-
> ence with the manner of holding national elections and to eliminate the tax
> imposed upon the exercise of the national function of suffrage.

Regarding the poll tax's legitimacy, the attorney general issued the following statement in July 1949:

> The poll tax is an arbitrary, unreal, meaningless requirement intended and operating as a means of disenfranchising approximately 10,000,000 American citizens, of which 7,000,000 are white and 3,000,000 are Negro, in seven of our southern states. . . . On some citizens the tax imposes a burdensome inconvenience; others are altogether deprived of their vote because of their financial inability to meet the arbitrarily established condition precedent to voting.[25]

At first blush, Thornberry's position on the poll tax seemed curiously contradictory, which was out of character for the straight-shooting Texan. On one hand, he had compared the poll tax to "a shackle—a bridle pulling back on this guaranteed right of all citizens of Texas and America to vote." He further denounced the poll tax's thinly veiled design to disenfranchise the lower classes, for which he held a kindred sympathy. In an address to Austin's Committee for Poll Tax Amendment in 1949, Thornberry bemoaned the drop in statewide voter turnout from 71 percent in 1900 to 39 percent in 1904, which he ascribed to the introduction of the state's poll tax on state elections in 1902. In a separate speech, he credited Johnson for opposing the poll tax in Texas, quoting him, "'I do not believe in the poll tax as a prerequisite for voting. I have advocated and do advocate the repeal of the constitutional provision of Texas which makes the payment of a poll tax necessary before a person can vote.'" On the other hand, Thornberry voted against lifting the tax in 1949 and went so far as to publicly endorse the same position held by the late Texas Governor Beauford H. Jester, an unabashed racist.[26]

How to reconcile Thornberry's contempt for the poll tax with his refusal to help repeal it? Although he never defended his position on the tax from the House floor, his previous comments during the tidelands debates might explain his reluctance to push early civil rights reforms on the whole. During a speech before the House on July 27, 1951, he made the case that the federal government had "limited powers formed to do for the states what they could not do for themselves in the fields of national defense, the conduct of foreign relations, and the control of commerce and navigation." (By the same rationale, Thornberry's personal crusade to guarantee farm price supports was, in his opinion, supported by such "control of commerce" obligations of the federal government.) Whereas other southern Democrats invoked the states' rights defense primarily to preserve institutionalized racism, Thornberry did so out of constitutional fealty, much the same way that fellow Texas Democrat Thomas Pickett denounced the movement to repeal the tax as one that "invades the fiscal affairs of the seven states in which they have a poll tax. . . . It would then prohibit a public official from doing what he may be required to do under the constitution and laws of his own state." Their constitutional defense aside, the likes of Thornberry and Pickett felt pressure from both peers and constituents not to upset the established order. As a result, Thornberry joined the majority of his fellow Texas House members 18-2 against H.R. 3199's proposed ban of the poll tax, which nonetheless passed the House before foundering in a Senate committee. For the time being, the poll tax would continue to stand.[27]

It would take an escalation of racial violence as well as intensive soul-searching before Thornberry and a select few of his southern colleagues flipped their positions and helped reinvent the national Democratic Party as the party for civil rights. In the meantime, the nation-versus-states debate would resurface over the poll tax and other forms of institutionalized discrimination, particularly racial segregation in schools and public spaces.

THE "BOARD OF EDUCATION"

Thornberry's close friendship with Sam Rayburn was hard earned. "I stood in awe of him," said Thornberry. "It was hard for me . . . to approach him for a long time." Terribly shy as a child, Rayburn kept his personal life tightly guarded and never discussed the details of his brief and only marriage. After overcoming his initial intimidation, Thornberry became one of Rayburn's few confidantes.[28]

Rayburn's influence in the House was unprecedented. He first entered the Sixty-Third US Congress in 1913 before becoming majority leader (1937 to 1940), Speaker (1940 to 1946, 1949 to 1952, 1955 to 1961), and minority leader (1947 to 1948, 1953 to 1954). Congress convened in June 1961 to commemorate Rayburn's tenure as Speaker—an impressive sixteen years and 273 days, or twice that of the next longest-serving occupant. At his zenith, Rayburn was considered the second most powerful man in the country after the president. Somewhat paradoxically, he was a pro-New Deal native of an ultra-conservative southern town (Bonham, Texas) as well as a strong supporter of both unions and the oil and gas industry. Like Thornberry, he opposed federal intervention in civil rights and tidelands rights.[29]

The Speaker hovered over the most powerful House committees, particularly the Committee on Ways and Means and the Committee on Committees. Although Rayburn could not vote or otherwise exercise direct influence on these bodies, he held vicarious veto power through personal relationships with their members. Ways and Means members were ostensibly elected by the Democratic members of the House, but rarely did they receive enough votes without his blessing. Thornberry passed muster: after just one term in the House, he was placed on the powerful Committee on Interstate and Foreign Commerce, which Rayburn had once chaired.[30]

The Speaker's standoffish nature notwithstanding, his dense moral fiber and stout work ethic earned the loyalty of his allies and the respect of his enemies. A divorcee with no children, Rayburn expended his "parental love" on the House, often going into his office on Saturdays and spending each Sunday preparing for the forthcoming week. He liked to impress upon freshmen members the virtues of compromise: "If you want to get along—go along." Rayburn's ideals echoed those of his party's founder, Thomas Jefferson, who had said, "The whole art of government consists in the art of being honest." As such, many of the Speaker's maxims, or "Rayburnisms," spoke to the merits of honesty and integrity. One among them, originally coined by Mark Twain, particularly resonated with Thornberry: "I always told the truth, so I wouldn't have to remember what I said the last time." Thornberry idolized Rayburn for being "entirely honest. He always . . . said right off how he stood. . . . And he never tried to put on any kind of attitude that he was better than anyone else." Like Thornberry, he resisted being pigeonholed, preferring that his record be assessed in a vacuum, not through an ideological prism. Their moral compasses were perfectly calibrated with one another.[31]

The Speaker occupied a second office, known simply as "The Room," which provided refuge in the downstairs of the Capitol beneath his formal office. There he hosted private, usually informal discussions with the closest of his compatriots, a group nicknamed the "Board of Education." Board regulars were an exclusive and tight-knit group. According to Thornberry:

> [Rayburn] was very careful in the people he invited by, very careful that no one who represented any special interest had entrée. . . . It was a confidential, off-the-record meeting, and he didn't intend for anybody to come who would go and report what had been said. Because we discussed everything in that room that you could think of.

In addition to Thornberry, Board members included fellow Texans Lyndon Johnson, Lloyd Bentsen, Wright Patman, and Jack Brooks, who could all depend on the Speaker's support and influence. Another benefit was the free-flowing bourbon that Rayburn served whether on the rocks or with water.[32]

Thornberry's special relationship with Rayburn extended beyond the Capitol and the board. "Mr. Sam" was a frequent diner at the Thornberrys, where they enjoyed southern staples like buttermilk, buttered corn on the cob, and chilled raw onions. Thornberry was also among the rare insiders invited to attend fishing trips with the Speaker. Indeed, Rayburn approximated a paternal figure to Thornberry, a void unfilled ever since his father's death when he was nine. When he eventually left Congress in 1963, after fifteen eventful years in the US House of Representatives, Thornberry reflected, "The real highlight of my Washington service was the close association with Mr. Rayburn."[33]

CHAPTER 7

Civil Warfare (1955-1957)

T HORNBERRY'S STATURE IN THE HOUSE ROSE CONSIDERABLY
after his placement on the House's powerful Committee on Rules
following the 1954 elections. He had been content serving on the Committee on Interstate and Foreign Commerce, but House Speaker Sam Rayburn
had other plans for him. Rayburn considered the Rules Committee "closer
to the leadership of the House than any other." Thornberry later explained
that the Speaker "was always concerned about having somebody from Texas
on the committee that he was close to, that he could work with."[1]

The Committee on Rules was one of the House's most powerful standing committees in addition to being among its most longstanding. Formally
implemented on April 2, 1789, it had two primary obligations. One was
setting the special rules—terms and conditions of floor debates on particular issues. Its other main responsibility was original jurisdiction, which
pertained to changes in the standing rules of the House or measures con-
taining special rules. In other words, it had virtually unlimited power to
rewrite portions, and even the entirety, of any given piece of legislation,
schedule bills for floor consideration at its choosing, and kill bills deemed
unworthy by the committee's majority. The 1954 elections returned House
control to the Democrats after a two-year hiatus, and they would retain its
majority for decades to follow.[2]

The Rules Committee also produced its own brand of headaches. Its
members had to deal with disgruntled colleagues when the committee stalled
their bills. Thornberry bore the added burden of Rayburn's expectations:

> Mr. Rayburn would communicate with me since I was the Texas member
> whether or not he felt that [a bill] would be able to come to the floor of the
> House. Sometimes he'd say, "Now don't just let that bill come out in a hurry.

Let's wait and see." If he did not want a bill to come to the floor of the house, well then he would tell me. And it was a committee that was a tough one. Men had been on it a good while, and you could understand that they felt strongly about their position and what they could do.

In addition, a conservative alliance between Republicans and southern Democrats dominated the Rules Committee and prevented many progressive measures from reaching the House floor, earning it the reputation as a "graveyard for much 'liberal legislation.'"[3]

Thornberry joined all but one of his fellow twenty-one Texas House members in voting against raising the national minimum wage rate in 1955. And like the vast majority of House members, Thornberry voted to expand social security benefits for disabled veterans and their family members. Thornberry also supported amendments to the Agricultural Act of 1949 to preserve agricultural price supports and boost employment of Mexican immigrants by needy domestic farmers. (Thornberry would later accompany President Eisenhower and Senator Johnson on a diplomatic visit to Mexico City in 1959 to discuss several issues, including the two countries' mutual interest in renewing a US-Mexico treaty preventing the exploitation of illegal immigrant workers.)[4]

Racial apprehensions in the South had reached a tipping point following the Supreme Court's landmark 1954 ruling in *Brown v. Board of Education of Topeka*, which rendered segregation of public schools, a southern institution since Reconstruction, to be unconstitutional. While *Brown* was a major victory for the civil rights crusade, the ruling's immediate impact was actually quite marginal, partly because the high court declined to impose strict guidelines or deadlines for achieving full desegregation. The ruling also invigorated state legislatures in the South to pass hundreds of pro-segregation measures over the next decade. Texas Governor Allan Shivers's strident opposition to desegregating public schools and frequent criticism of the Truman administration won over many state residents. Following the *Brown* ruling, Shivers declared, "All my instincts, my political philosophy, my experience, and my common sense revolt against this Supreme Court decision." A spring 1954 poll showed 45 percent of Texans were opposed to integration compared to 35 percent for it.[5]

Like civil rights issues, the New Deal's legacy was a lightning rod in Texas and other southern states. Animosity toward federal programs had billowed following rapid postwar population growth in Texas and a "wholesale manufacture of new members of the upper economic orders," observed political scientist V.O. Key. Key wrote in 1949 that the state's bounty of natural resources fostered a sense of entitlement among nouveau oil barons, who regarded government as little more than a nuisance:

> In forty years a new-rich class has risen from the exploitation of natural resources in a gold-rush atmosphere. By their wits (and, sometimes by the chance deposit in eons past of an oil pool under the family ranch) men have built large fortunes from scratch. Imbued with faith in individual self-reliance and unschooled in social responsibilities of wealth, many of these men have been more sensitive than a Pennsylvania manufacturer to the policies of the Roosevelt and Truman administration.

To a growing contingent of southern Democratic segregationists, or Dixiecrats, the national party's leadership seemed less attentive to their concerns and more attuned to urban interests, organized labor, and civil rights reform. Visible cracks in the party's foundation had formed during the 1948 Democratic Convention, which was punctuated by Hubert Humphrey's emphatic pro-civil rights speech. Truman enjoyed moderate southern approval in the ensuing general election, but it had steadily eroded by the end of his final term. Five-star general Dwight Eisenhower became the first Republican presidential candidate since 1928 to win at least one southern state: he took three, including Texas by a narrow margin. (The only non-Democratic southern victories in the interim occurred in 1948 when Dixiecrat Senator Strom Thurmond, running on the third-party States' Rights ticket, siphoned off four southern states from Truman in the general election. Texas was not among them.) With Eisenhower's surprising support in the South (albeit meager overall), it was clear that top Democratic leadership was losing control of the party. The Democrats' identity crisis was spotlighted when Texas Governor Shivers endorsed Eisenhower over his own party's presidential candidate, Illinois Governor Adlai Stevenson, in 1952. (Shivers was rumored to have considered defecting from his party to become Eisenhower's running mate that year, but land and insurance scandals involving several of his appointees at state agencies convinced Republican power brokers to look elsewhere.)[6]

Evidence of Texas's definitive rightward shift can also be traced to Shivers's victories in the 1952 and 1954 gubernatorial primaries over populist Ralph Yarborough. Shivers once supported the New Deal when he entered the Texas legislature in the 1930s, but he had changed into a champion of conservatives and big business by the time he became lieutenant governor in 1947. Rayburn and Johnson entrusted state affairs to Shivers when he inherited the governorship following the death of Beauford Jester in 1949. They erred in assuming that all blue states would take direction from the national party. They particularly miscalculated in their home state, where Shivers's eager defense of states' rights had taken root. He branded New Deal legislative acts as constructs of communism and pushed to have any affiliation with the Communist Party be a criminal act punishable by death (he was unsuccessful). Shortly after taking office, Shivers swiftly went to work removing liberals from the State Democratic Executive Committee and replacing them with like-minded, right-wing "Shivercrats." His supporters likewise began infiltrating the Texas delegation at the national convention.[7]

Irreconcilable differences over the New Deal and civil rights led to the Texas Democratic Party's acrimonious subdivision into moderate loyalists and ultraconservative Texas Regulars. The loyalist camp, which included Johnson, Rayburn, Thornberry, and others, believed that party solidarity trumped individual and regional differences over the party's direction, a precept roundly rejected by the Shivers-led Regulars. Shivers's reneging on his promise to endorse Stevenson and his backing of Eisenhower instead were particularly distressing to Rayburn. Said Thornberry:

> Mr. Rayburn . . . just did not understand people being independent. . . . Governor Shivers didn't think of himself as a national party man. . . . While I had Mr. Rayburn's viewpoint, I can understand other people's viewpoint of saying, "Just because I vote Democratic in Texas because of tradition, background, and everything, [there is] no reason I have to follow what some national convention does."

Exacerbating matters were Johnson's ultimately vain efforts to regain Shivers's support, efforts that only served to alienate liberals in the party.[8]

The tussle between loyalists and Regulars for the reins of the state party was on full display at the 1956 Texas convention. A national news magazine declared "It's War Among Texas Democrats" after Johnson clashed with Shivers for chairmanship of the Texas delegation to the national convention. Johnson won by a three-to-one margin at statewide precinct conventions, but Shivers, dubbed the "Pied Piper of Texas" by cobiographers Sam Kinch and Stuart Long, continued to denounce both Johnson and Rayburn. Disunity in Texas foreshadowed Stevenson's weak reception at the ballot box during his second run for the presidency in 1956. Despite concerns about his health following a heart attack suffered one year earlier, Eisenhower won reelection by a landslide electoral margin (457 to 73). He again captured Texas.[9]

Nearly half of the US Congress formally declared their segregationist sentiments with their issuance of the Southern Manifesto in 1956. The document represented a collective pledge to defy *Brown* and reject the Supreme Court's order to integrate school systems. All one hundred signatories—nineteen senators and eighty-two representatives—were from former Confederate states. They included five Texas representatives and the entire delegations from Alabama, Arkansas, Georgia, Louisiana, Mississippi, South Carolina, and Virginia. Johnson, Rayburn, and Thornberry were among the eighteen Texans who did not add their names. But, distancing themselves from the segregation issue did little to aid the civil rights movement.

In fairness, civil rights legislation was a profoundly difficult and complex area for middle-of-the-road elected officials from the South. Johnson's decision not to sign the manifesto was motivated largely by his long-term presidential ambitions; he figured a national audience would need to see improvement in his civil rights voting record. But Johnson had dodged civil rights bills only partly for political survival:

> At the time I simply did not believe that the legislation as written was
> the right way to handle the problem. Much of it seemed designed more
> to humiliate the South than to help the black man. Beyond this, I did not
> think there was much I could do as a lone Congressman from Texas. I
> represented a conservative constituency. One heroic stand and I'd be back
> home, defeated, unable to do any good for anyone, much less the blacks
> and underprivileged.

Although not a manifesto signatory either, Rayburn was held somewhat captive by his heavily conservative district, which compelled his regular defense of segregation and silence on Ku Klux Klan activities at home. In a letter to a constituent, he wrote:

I have been too long voting on those [civil rights] matters to change. Every opportunity I have had, I have voted against federal repeal of the poll tax law, and have vote[d] three times, in the 67th, 75th, and 76th congresses, against the so-called anti-lynching law. Of course I am going to do everything I can for my state to protect our segregation laws.[10]

Like most southerners, Thornberry's position on civil rights was influenced by his upbringing at a time when discrimination was the norm. In a 1984 interview, Thornberry recalled:

When I was growing up, of course we were part of the South and we treated the blacks pretty badly, put them off in poor schools. . . . We made them ride in the back of the streetcar, back of the busses. I grew up thinking that's what they were supposed to do. . . . I thought [segregation] was the way it ought to be. It was how I was reared. My mother thought that blacks were an inferior race.

It was thus out of bewilderment rather than scorn when, on a crowded Washington bus one afternoon, Thornberry asked Johnson why he surrendered his seat to a black woman. Johnson responded, "I'd hope that if my mother got on the bus, someone would get up and give her his seat." The inertia of cultural heritage coupled with a herd mentality enabled nascent equal-rights proponents like Thornberry to rationalize their participation in a race-based caste system. Tom Miller, Austin's popular mayor from 1933 through 1948, supported equal rights and services for racial and ethnic minorities, but he loathed the idea of their bathing with whites in Barton Springs or using the same libraries. Racism was so casual and ingrained that many whites were unaware that certain demeaning words and gestures could be construed as racist.[11]

The Rayburn-Johnson-Thornberry triad had become more reform-minded by the fall of 1956, a development that jelled in a dramatic backyard gathering at Thornberry's home. He was hosting Rayburn one afternoon while recuperating from a recent operation when Johnson burst in on the scene:

I heard Senator Johnson come in the house and ask my wife, "Now where are they?" She said, "They're out in the back yard." And he came out, sort of greeted us, but he didn't take much time. He said, "Now Mr. Speaker, we've got this bill. . . . We haven't let them [blacks] vote, and it's just not right, and it's time to turn them loose." And Mr. Rayburn said, "Well, I think you're right." And I knew right then that the time had come when we would be having legislation of that sort and that both houses would be engaged in passing it.

Eking out the first modern civil rights bill would require intrepid effort and bipartisan support. A total of 110 civil rights bills were filed in 1955, yet none made it to the president's desk. While Rayburn had come around on the issue, Thornberry required more convincing. He nonetheless respected Johnson's valor. "I thought it was a great plus [that] a man who a lot of people thought had all of the prejudices of our section [the South] could do something like that," said Thornberry later about Johnson's follow-through.[12]

Guidance on civil rights would not come from the White House, at least not yet. Eisenhower was ambivalent about the issue and mostly skirted it during his two terms. He resented lawmakers who attempted to attach anti-segregation amendments onto legislation, and he declined to publicly endorse the *Brown* ruling. At an informal White House dinner held when *Brown* was being adjudicated, Eisenhower gave a toast to John W. Davis, counsel for segregationist states. Afterwards, he reportedly urged fellow dinner guest Chief Justice Earl Warren to side with the segregationists. Following Warren's ruling to the contrary, Eisenhower reportedly expressed regret for having placed Warren on the court. Eisenhower believed that legislating morality and people's beliefs was not the government's responsibility (although civil rights proponents pointed out that they merely sought enforcement of the Constitution's guarantee of equal rights). Consequently, Eisenhower refrained from introducing any civil rights legislation during his first three and a half years in office. Nonetheless, he ordered an end to segregation on military bases and dispatched federal troops, albeit reluctantly, to maintain order at an Arkansas high school on September 4, 1957, when nine black students, famously remembered as the "Little Rock Nine," broke the color barrier.[13]

Escalating racial tensions ultimately prompted both the executive and legislative branches to address states' roles in handling civil rights issues on their own. H.R. 6127, a bill drafted by Eisenhower and introduced into the House, proposed reforms that were equal parts modest and ambitious. Parts I and II called for the creation of both a civil rights division in the

Left to right: Senator Johnson, Lady Bird Johnson, and Speaker Sam Rayburn deplaning as Thornberry and others greet them, Washington, DC, 1956. *LBJ Library Photo by World Wide Photos.*

Justice Department and a Commission on Civil Rights to investigate voting discrimination. The far more impactful and controversial Parts III and IV endowed the attorney general with unprecedented authority to initiate desegregation lawsuits and issue injunctions against civil rights violations.

After being voted out of the House Judiciary Committee, H.R. 6127 came before Thornberry and his fellow Rules Committee members. As characterized by the *New York Times*, the Rules Committee "held the keys to action on civil rights and to the adjournment date." The House was more receptive than the Senate to civil rights legislation, but Rules played the ultimate gatekeeper to the House floor. Committee Chair Howard W. Smith of Virginia chafed at Rayburn's persistent efforts to influence the clearance of particular bills, including H.R. 6127. Smith was one of four southerners on the committee alongside Thornberry, William Colmer of Mississippi, and James Trimble of Arkansas. The other eight, all northerners, voted to clear H.R. 6127, overcoming the four southerners' nays. Smith could have forestalled the outcome out of spite but chose not to.[14]

No Texan participated in the many floor debates over H.R. 6127, which were typically reserved for the staunchest advocates and opponents. Michigan Democrat Thaddeus Machrowicz defended the bill from the floor: "This is indeed a moderate civil rights bill. It contains a mere minimum of what is most certainly required from us as representatives of a democratic people in this great democracy of ours." Uncompromising Democrat W. Arthur Winstead of Mississippi countered with the familiar states' rights tune: "What this so-called civil rights bill has the audacity to say to our states is that we in the South do not know what justice is and must have it forced upon us by the federal government from Washington." Thornberry, as well as the other Texas House members (except Rayburn, who as Speaker could not vote), voted nay on the first version of H.R. 6127, but it still passed 286-126.[15]

Largely as a result of Johnson's tenacity, the Senate passed a modified version of H.R. 6127, overcoming South Carolina Democrat Strom Thurmond's twenty-four-hour filibuster, the longest one ever carried out by a lone senator without a break. The Senate's new version of the bill required another pass through the House, starting over at the committee level, before it could reach Eisenhower's desk. Smith was less receptive this time around, refusing to call a Rules meeting on it. On August 19, Rayburn moved to force the committee to convene by invoking a House rule that empowered the majority of a committee's members to call a meeting if the chair had not set a date within a ten-day timeframe. Coaxed by Rayburn, Thornberry and Trimble switched to join the northerners this time, voting to set a meeting by a ten-to-two margin. Upon convening, the committee voted along the same margin to send it to the floor. On the following day, the House passed the Senate version, save for two amendments, by the count of 279-97. This time Thornberry voted aye for passage, cementing his complete reversal on H.R. 6127 and civil rights legislation in general. He was joined by eleven other Texas House members versus five opposed and four abstaining. Described as "the most vexing issue of this session" by the *New York Times*, H.R. 6127, better known as the Civil Rights Act of 1957, was signed into law by Eisenhower on September 9. Its passage would not have been possible without Johnson's horse-trading in the Senate and Rayburn's strong-arming in the House, backed at the end by Thornberry and other Rules members. (Texas Democratic Election Executive Committee member Jake Pickle later wrote that Thornberry "played a key part in getting enough southerners to support the bill," but did not elaborate.)[16]

While the Civil Rights Act of 1957 did provide a useful stepping-stone for future legislation, civil rights proponents were largely disappointed with its final form. Southern conservatives had weakened it by gutting Parts III and IV. Had those sections survived, the Justice Department would have been empowered to desegregate the many schools that had chosen not to comply with *Brown*. Civil rights figurehead Jackie Robinson, who had broken Major League Baseball's color barrier ten years prior, issued a wired statement that he was "opposed to [the] civil rights bill in its present form. Have been in touch with a number of my friends. We disagree that half a loaf is better than none. Have waited this long for bill with meaning—can wait a little longer." The US Commission on Civil Rights birthed by the bill was ultimately incapable of aggressively curbing discrimination. Thurgood Marshall, chief counsel for the NAACP, called the new law "just barely progress." *Brown* and the 1957 Civil Rights Act had now provided civil rights advocates with symbolic victories, but a leveled social order remained a wishful fantasy.[17]

YES MAN?

Thornberry's job security over his fifteen years in Congress was rarely in question, but if he felt any complacency it did not diminish his attentiveness to his constituents. He spent the entirety of October 1955 (a nonelection year) traversing his district from six in the morning until midnight, canvassing one hundred communities by the end of the month. "There's nothing better for an officeholder than renewing his acquaintance with the people," Thornberry told the *Austin American*. "It makes you keep your feet on the ground. A fundamental of good public service is to remember

Thornberry hosting Speaker Rayburn in his backyard, Washington, DC, 1957.
Thornberry family collection.

who you're working for." A characteristic rural destination was Caldwell City (population one thousand), where he was treated by locals to home-cooked fried chicken and green grape pie. "Chicken fries," which were usually organized by civic leaders, were also popular in places like Bastrop, where one dollar fetched a plate of poultry cooked in a giant iron kettle. After Caldwell City, a spaghetti dinner prepared by churchwomen awaited him in Luling. "Some officeholders 1,600 miles from home develop a kind of mental barrier, get to feeling they've lost contact with the people," Thornberry said. "When that happens, they make things worse by growing hesitant to go back home."[18]

While his popularity endured, Thornberry naturally could not please all the people all the time. His midstream reversal on the 1957 Civil Rights Act not only agitated white conservatives but also fueled criticism that he was a sycophant of Democratic leadership. These sentiments were voiced in waves of unflattering letters mailed to his Washington and district offices, many of them originating from extreme right-wing groups. Critics

Thornberry visiting constituents in Oakalla, Texas, 1951. *Thornberry family collection.*

fixated on what they perceived to be his submissiveness to Rayburn and Johnson and later, to the Kennedy administration. But he regularly went along with his Texas colleagues (and most southern Democrats) on issues like agriculture price supports, coastal states' tidelands rights, limits on organized labor rights, retention of the poll tax, and opposition to other civil rights reforms. Rarely did he introduce legislation that made it to the House floor, for he prematurely withdrew many bills in deference to authors of similar versions. Thornberry's modesty and slight physique lent additional credence to a perception that he was soft. He was also indebted to Johnson for facilitating his entry into Congress and to Rayburn for his brisk elevation once inside. Indeed, Johnson used to call Thornberry "my congressman." Johnson's eccentric younger brother Sam dismissed Thornberry as "Lyndon's neighbor, errand boy, and I think that he'd even be honored to be called that," adding, "Homer used to laugh at Lyndon's jokes before he ever got the point."[19]

While overly deferential in his critics' minds, Thornberry's untroubled, altruistic nature earned the respect of many colleagues and observers. At a large public dinner held in Georgetown in 1958 to fete Thornberry, Johnson hailed the honoree as "agreeable when he's disagreeing" and as one who "knows how to sacrifice and compromise without forgoing principles." Thornberry was also generally averse to the spotlight, preferring to deliberate on bills in private. A *Williamson County Sun* editor wrote, "Not a publicity-seeking politician, Congressman Homer Thornberry is, nonetheless, a very effective and respected one." A *Dallas Morning News* columnist asserted, "Liberals frequently charge an unholy alliance exists between the southern conservatives on the committee and the Republicans. Thornberry has aligned with neither the conservative nor liberal bloc, but weighs each piece of legislation on its merits as it comes along."[20]

Whereas Johnson sometimes resorted to coercion to achieve his ends, Thornberry preferred rapport building. As the product of deaf-mute parents, he had a special appreciation for the art of communication and recognized its importance in forging alliances. Charm was important. Contemporary community organizer Saul Alinsky wrote that "humor is essential, for through humor much is accepted that would have been rejected if presented seriously." A testament to Thornberry's affability was his uncommon ability to stay in good standing with Texas's two larger-than-life senators: Johnson and arch-liberal Democrat Ralph Yarborough, whose animosity toward one another polarized their respective allies and cleaved their party's support base. "I hope I was able to keep the friendship of them both [Johnson and Yarborough] without in any way being disloyal to either one of them," Thornberry said. "I'm sure [Yarborough] knew me well enough to know that I wouldn't in any way be disloyal to that friendship [with Johnson]."[21]

Thornberry's disagreements with Rayburn were few but heated at times. A prime example followed a House debate on whether to repeal the controversial, union-stripping Taft-Hartley Act in 1949, Thornberry's freshman year. President Truman and Rayburn pushed hard for the repeal while their fellow party members in the Democratic-controlled Congress were divided. Rayburn needed support for Truman, whose earlier veto of Taft-Hartley was overridden by a two-thirds vote of Congress and thereby enacted into law. Nevertheless, Thornberry, who opposed federal involvement in labor-management relations, voted against the repeal. Rayburn was "hot and furious" over his protégé's decision, remembered Jake Pickle. "If you were close to [Rayburn]," Thornberry later explained, "it would worry you a good deal about not doing what he wanted you to do. He had a right to expect somebody who was close to him and who was supposed to be a part of his leadership to go with him."[22]

Rayburn also became unhinged over Thornberry's support for the Labor-Management Reporting and Disclosure Act of 1959, or the Landrum-Griffin Act, which imposed heavy restrictions on unionization. Thornberry voted for the act because "it was trying to eliminate some of the corruption, but labor just felt it was a big test." (Unions had recently earned a bad rap over corruption and racketeering charges. Senate investigations had exposed illegal organized labor practices within the Jimmy Hoffa-led International Brotherhood of Teamsters.) Conversely, Rayburn considered Landrum-Griffin too punitive toward unions, a stance attributed to his personal conviction that legislation should not target particular organizations (like the Teamsters) or individuals (like Hoffa). Further, a prominent party figure like Rayburn was expected to appease big labor as it constituted the national party's largest constituency.[23]

Acrimony over Landrum-Griffin beleaguered the House to an extent not seen since a fight over public-utility-holding companies in the 1930s. Incensed voters demanded a crackdown on labor corruption; meanwhile union lobbyists threatened to use all resources in their power to oust uncooperative Democrats in future election cycles. Against Rayburn's wishes, Thornberry voted for Landrum-Griffin and its subsequent substitute bill, joining roughly four-fifths of Texas House members (as well as both Johnson and the populist Yarborough in the Senate). Rayburn was so offended by the Texas delegation's overwhelming defiance—especially from the likes of Thornberry and fellow protégé Frank Ikard of Witchita Falls—that he suspected Johnson had gone behind his back to kill the bill. After a tongue-lashing from Rayburn for breaking rank on a vote, Thornberry was in tears when he returned home that evening. Weeks elapsed before the Speaker's fury subsided. Said Thornberry later in Rayburn's defense:

> He carried loyalty almost to an extreme. . . . He could be pretty rough when
> he thought that you weren't doing right by him. On the other hand, if you
> had told him that 'I can't do this—it could hurt me politically back home,'
> he would understand. I don't think he jumped on many people. I think it was
> sort of like, 'whom the Lord loveth, he chastiseth.'[24]

Thornberry's clashes with Johnson were likewise seldom (indeed partly because they never occupied the same chamber) but could also get ugly. Much later, as Thornberry was preparing to leave Congress for the judiciary in 1963, Johnson grew irate over Thornberry's desire to return to Texas rather than join the nearby Washington, DC, Circuit Court of Appeals. The Thornberrys took a trip to the Johnson ranch afterwards, and Johnson shunned the whole family during their entire visit.[25]

Johnson's much-documented irascibleness came naturally and indiscriminately. Outside of playing pressure politics, Johnson tested some male visitors to his ranch by hunting game on the premises or swimming nude in his pool. Johnson biographer Doris Kearns Goodwin concluded that his father's own humiliating tests of manhood affected Lyndon so profoundly as a boy that he spent his adulthood in constant pursuit of the upper hand over friends and enemies alike. As Thornberry said, "If he is your friend, then he is *really* your friend." The occasional difference of opinion notwithstanding, Johnson and Thornberry deeply respected one another, and the two men were able to preserve both their professional and personal relationships. Thornberry later reflected:

> He [Johnson] would leave me very free. As a matter of fact, I do not remember his ever, ever just coming directly to me and saying that I should vote this way or that. . . . I would seek his advice quite often. I didn't always vote as he advised. I think he had a sense of my feelings. I imagine he had a sense about how I would ordinarily vote on issues, but so far as him trying to tell me how to vote, he never did do that, ever. I know a lot of people thought perhaps he did, but he did not. In fact, he was very, very careful not to find himself in the position of telling me how to vote.[26]

Upon review, Thornberry was not so much a "yes man" as he was a loyal lieutenant under Democratic leadership while in Congress. As one Rayburnism went, "You cannot lead people by trying to drive them unless you know how to follow too." Hubert Humphrey's early congressional years illustrate the consequences of venturing too far outside the party establishment: his pro-civil rights speech at the 1948 Democratic Convention not only roused the powerful southern bloc, it also undercut his influence in the chamber. The Senate was a particularly conservative body in which southern members who disagreed about other issues were in lockstep against civil rights reforms. (For this reason, liberal southern senators like Arkansas Democrats J. William Fulbright and John Sparkman remained part of Senate Majority Leader Richard Russell's anti-civil rights coalition. Both Fulbright and Sparkman voted against the Civil Rights Act of 1957 and were among the signatories of the Southern Manifesto.) After defying his party's conservative base, Humphrey became ostracized in the Senate during his early years, stunting his political capital. The House and the Senate were hostile environments for those freshmen members who too often spoke out, particularly on civil rights. In this respect, an agreeable Thornberry fit right in.[27]

Ralph Yarborough suffered a fate similar to that of Humphrey. He had little appetite for compromise, and his defiance of Johnson in particular contributed to his permanent isolation from the party's core. Johnson had befriended Yarborough when the latter headed the Lower Colorado River Authority, and the two had consistently voted together in the Senate. But Yarborough never forgave Johnson for endorsing the ultraconservative Allan Shivers over him in the 1954 gubernatorial race (and against Rayburn's wishes for a more liberal candidate, no less). Johnson did so partly because he feared that Shivers might eventually challenge him for his Senate seat, and partly in an ultimately futile attempt to restore party unity. Cementing Yarborough's marginalization were his repeated rejections of Johnson's conciliatory efforts. According to future Johnson White House aide Jack Valenti, Yarborough bore the chief responsibility for his becoming a "passionate but isolated figure in Texas politics."[28]

Unlike Yarborough, Thornberry adopted a "go along, get along" mentality that paid handsome professional dividends. His loyalty to Rayburn facilitated an eleven-year membership on the most powerful House committee and later, his appointment to the federal judiciary. As future Johnson cabinet member John Gardner penned in *On Leadership*, "Proximity to power is a source of power."[29]

Of course, politicians' going along with the status quo at this time prevented the civil rights movement from gaining much momentum, and any middle ground on civil rights was quickly becoming untenable. Because Congress had done little to tamp down racial discrimination, the public could not easily differentiate between the two major parties on the issue. Eisenhower had originally introduced the Civil Rights Act of 1957 and later signed the final version into law; meanwhile, Democratic leaders were credited with pushing it through both chambers of Congress, however inert the act became in the process. Growing public unrest finally forced Texas loyalists like Thornberry and the few other moderate-to-liberal Democrats in the South to buck the system in bold, decisive fashion.[30]

Thornberry with wife Eloise and children (standing, left to right) Kate, David, and Molly, Washington, DC, 1963. *Thornberry family collection.*

Thornberry's turnaround on the 1957 civil rights bill was partly motivated by a personal revelation during a visit to his district. While canvassing various establishments around Austin, Thornberry entered a barbershop where he shook hands and chatted with its employees and patrons. Afterward, one of the barbers informed an associate of the congressman, "He doesn't know how to electioneer. He came in and shook hands with every one of us and didn't shake hands with the [shoe] shine boy [who was black], and he got control over more votes than any of us." It was then that Thornberry realized that his culturally ingrained belief that blacks were second-class citizens had not only contributed to his overall neglect of Austin's black community but had also clouded his thinking about government's role in removing racial barriers. He considered this lesson a "tremendous transformation" that irreversibly altered his view on engineering civil rights reforms.[31]

By suddenly deciding to become proactive supporters of civil rights reform, Thornberry, Rayburn, and Johnson were risking both their own political fortunes and their party's long-term viability. But their shared values about equal rights and loyalty to each other remained firmly intact.

CHAPTER 8

At Society's Margins (1958-1961)

S OUTHERN PREJUDICE AGAINST BLACKS WAS CENTURIES IN THE making. Regional white supremacism originated in the colonial slave trade, and it became ingrained during the cotton industry explosion of the early 1800s. Reforms of substantially greater magnitude than the toothless 1957 Civil Rights Act were necessary to remake a society that had fought to the death to preserve racial suppression one hundred years before.

The Confederacy arose when seven slave states, including Texas, declared their secession over the 1860 presidential election of Republican Abraham Lincoln. Four more states would eventually join them. Lincoln delivered on his anti-slavery platform by declaring the freedom of over three million slaves through his Emancipation Proclamation on January 1, 1863. A cascade of transformational events followed over the next several decades: the Civil War, slave liberation, Reconstruction, the New Deal, and transformation of the southern economy. Although the South underwent dramatic political and economic restructuring, pervasive racial discrimination within its culture and legal system persisted. Black marginalization took the forms of Jim Crow laws, segregation in public schools and spaces, disenfranchisement, employment discrimination, and other forms of intimidation and cruelty.

Following the South's devastation during the Civil War, the federal government initiated a series of interventionist programs to rebuild the region. Reconstruction provided federal funds to modernize the southern economy and infrastructure. It also installed federal troops in nine former Confederate states (including Texas) and military governors in some cases.

Between 1865 and 1870, Congress ratified the Thirteenth, Fourteenth, and Fifteenth Amendments, which collectively abolished slavery, bestowed citizenship upon blacks (overturning the 1857 Supreme Court case *Dred Scott v. Sandford*), and guaranteed due process and voting rights.

But for all its postbellum heavy-handedness, federal leadership eventually adopted a conciliatory approach to racial injustice. Reconstruction and federal intrusion effectively came to a close with the grand Compromise of 1877, in which the installed governors and troops abandoned the region in exchange for the South's recognition of Republican Rutherford B. Hayes as the victor in the disputed 1877 presidential election. Later, the Supreme Court case *Plessy v. Ferguson* (1896) determined that segregation of the races was legal, so long as it was "separate but equal," which resulted in separate institutions that were anything but equal. Marginalization snowballed with the Supreme Court's ruling in *Williams v. Mississippi* (1898), which legitimized state poll taxes and literacy tests, thereby disenfranchising racial and ethnic minorities and the poor. The first three presidents of the twentieth century—Republicans William McKinley, Theodore Roosevelt, and William Howard Taft—refrained from intervening on racial matters in hopes of repairing relations with the region.[1]

Later federal efforts in the South failed to minimize systemic mistreatment of blacks. Every southern state exploited "separate but equal" by establishing inferior schools, courtrooms, residential districts, and libraries for blacks; denying them access to white-owned hotels and restaurants and even to sidewalks; and banning intermingling between the races. Jim Crow laws remained harshest in states like Mississippi where larger proportions of black populations resided. Areas where blacks comprised the majority prompted the most anxiety and activity among resident whites to reinforce their dominion. Rim states in the South like Texas, Florida, and Arkansas, where blacks were proportionately fewer, were less preoccupied with enforcing white supremacy. Industrial expansion in the first part of the century was rapid in these states, and working class and union leaders crossed racial lines to strengthen their coalitions. However, every gain for blacks led to intense pushback from whites. Blacks saw their median income increase between 1940 and 1960, but racial apprehensions had simultaneously given rise to the Dixiecrat movement, promulgating race-related angst and violence.[2]

Albeit moderate compared to other southern states, racial tensions in Texas were such that blacks felt mostly unwelcome living there. The early twentieth century's oil boom begot a resurgence of conservatism, which drew strength from suppressing the lower classes' ability to vote. The legislature introduced the state's first poll tax in 1902, which kept many blacks out of general elections. In 1923, the state passed a law that restricted participation in primary elections to whites only. The Supreme Court ended this practice in *Smith v. Allwright* (1944), but Democratic Party officials found other ways to discourage black participation in primary elections, such as taxation and intimidation at polling locations. With whites agitated over the growing numbers of blacks and Hispanics, Texas's urban areas witnessed the reemergence of the Ku Klux Klan, the largest white supremacist order, which held significant sociopolitical sway. In 1918, the KKK organized a march down Austin's Congress Avenue. Four decades later, Ralph Yarborough lost to segregationist Price Daniel in the race for governor. Yarborough's defeat made it apparent that Texans remained unwilling to accept desegregation in any form.[3]

Thornberry's hometown of Austin may not have fostered the same levels of racial animosity or violence as hotbeds like Little Rock or Montgomery, but Jim Crow reigned nonetheless. Blacks were not allowed to mingle with whites, share public spaces, or patronize the same stores and businesses. Since the 1910s, blacks had been herded into the eastern part of town, which contained just one high school to educate black children. In 1928, the Austin City Council approved a city plan that practically segregated the city and permitted more forceful and underhanded means to push blacks into East Austin. (At about this time, in response to debates and peaceful rallies, the council also built a recreational center and library especially for blacks.) Many black tenants were at the mercy of negligent landlords and were flatly refused housing loans from banks. Used textbooks were inherited from white schools across town. Businesses along Congress Avenue permitted only whites to use their restrooms, forcing blacks to use gutters or alleyways instead. Brackenridge Hospital kept separate public facilities for the two races. Black patients were relegated to the basement there and received treatment much inferior to that afforded whites.[4]

At the close of the 1940s, Austin leaders were becoming gradually more sensitive to the mistreatment of blacks, who represented 13 percent of the city's population. The city council now included populists; unions had become a powerful force; and the Austin Housing Authority was more aggressive in constructing low-cost housing. Nevertheless, blacks largely continued to reside, attend school, and do business in separate parts of town from whites.[5]

In many ways, the student and faculty bodies at the University of Texas, the city's cultural hub as well as Thornberry's alma mater, were emblematic of the civil rights debates between progressives and conservatives. Students and professors had protested the board of regents' firing of president Homer Rainey in 1946 over his efforts to admit black students. Their demonstrations grew larger after the UT School of Law turned down a black applicant named Heman Sweatt on the grounds that the Texas Constitution prohibited integrated education. Sweatt was ultimately awarded enrollment by the Supreme Court in *Sweatt v. Painter* (1950), which paved the way for the more consequential 1954 ruling in *Brown v. Board of Education* that outlawed segregation altogether. Campus demonstrations over the *Sweatt* case likewise energized Austin's black community. "The University has had a very profound effect on Austin," Thornberry later reflected. "Economically, of course. And . . . in many ways it keeps Austin from being . . . anti-human rights." Two years after *Brown*, UT became the first college in the South to become fully integrated (although most blacks continued to pursue higher education elsewhere).[6]

Its checkered past on race notwithstanding, Austin was an anomaly compared to the racial flashpoints that spanned the South, where elected officials and school heads openly defied *Brown*. One month after the Supreme Court's decision, politicians from all eleven former confederate states convened in Virginia and unanimously pledged to disobey the ruling spelled out in the Southern Manifesto. Three years later, Arkansas Governor Orval Faubus ordered his state's National Guard to join segregationists' physical blockade to prevent nine black students from attending Little Rock Central High School. Eisenhower dispatched federal troops to ensure the safety of the "Little Rock Nine," fearing a violent outbreak might metastasize. Many states, including Texas, opted to close public schools rather than integrate them. As a result, most black students were confined to substandard, often squalid schools while most public facilities remained segregated or off-limits.[7]

White defiance also took the form of court challenges, Ku Klux Klan marches, and new voting impediments, including literacy tests. At its worst, southern racism manifested as public terrorism, including lynchings of minorities and sniper fire targeting integrated buses. Just 23 percent of white southerners approved of federal intervention to stem such extreme violence, compared to 51 percent of non-southerners.[8]

Civil rights groups responded with their own forms of civil disobedience and typically followed Martin Luther King Jr.'s example of passive resistance. In February of 1960, four black college students in Greensboro, North Carolina, gained national attention upon refusing to leave the Woolworth's lunch counter until they were served. The incident inspired similar sit-ins in cities across the South, largely the doings of student activists. Demonstrations soon spread to beaches, parks, swimming pools, libraries, and other public places across the country.

But for all the momentum it had generated, the civil rights movement had few tangible results to show for its audacious efforts by the close of 1959. *Brown* represented a significant step forward, but most southern classrooms remained segregated five years after the fact. The ruling also incited backlash from legislatures in all eleven former Confederate states, taking the form of 450 pro-segregation measures over the ensuing decade. As for the two-year-old Civil Rights Act of 1957, only four civil rights cases were brought to the Department of Justice under the law's auspices, and just sixty sworn complaints about voting obstructions would be submitted by late March of 1960. The Civil Rights Commission that received these complaints comprised a small group of unenthusiastic conservatives, and its authority was limited to issuing recommendations. All told, after a century of hard-fought efforts by both the establishment and outside forces to create a post-racial paradigm in the South, blacks remained stranded at society's margins.[9]

Thornberry and other sympathetic members of Congress set about building upon the 1957 Civil Rights Act. Several civil rights bills had been introduced in 1960 by Johnson, Hubert Humphrey, and a coalition of liberal Democrats and Republicans in both the House and Senate. H.R. 8601, the only one among them to gain much traction, called for federal inspections of voting polls, penalties against parties obstructing the right to vote, and the extension of the underused Civil Rights Commission. Georgia House

Democrat Prince Preston, a staunch segregationist and Southern Manifesto signatory, argued that the commission's poor track record failed to justify its continuation, much less warrant one of H.R. 8601's provisions to increase its annual budget from $778,000 to $900,000. "Now, is this not amazing, that this one million dollar agency which has been fiddling around with a mere handful of complaints on voting rights that the proponents of this legislation would have you believe is a must, represents a great demand on the part of the American people?" Preston posed to the House floor on March 24, 1960. "No, there has been no groundswell for this legislation. I am not getting any mail for it or against it." Defenders of the commission pointed to its hearings on civil rights violations and to its 1959 report on voting rights abuses, which showed that only a quarter of the black population in the country had registered to vote, as sufficient reasons for renewed funding. Connecticut Democrat Robert Giaimo argued that the commission should be viewed not as an end but as a means: "The Civil Rights Commission . . . has done its job of developing the facts and presenting to the Congress the information it needs to legislate. The burden of such responsibility for enacting adequate laws now rests upon the Congress."[10]

Thornberry was among four of twenty-one voting Texas House members to support an early version of H.R. 8601, which passed 311-109 on March 24, 1960. Passage in the Senate required astute political maneuvering by Johnson, who helped overcome a filibuster lasting 125 hours and 31 minutes, the longest continuous Senate session in history. After fifty-three days of debate, the bill had been thoroughly watered down by southern conservatives, who limited its purview to voting rights; it would pass 71-18 on April 8. The Senate's amended version required another cycle through the House. Thornberry was the lone southerner on the Rules Committee to vote for clearance of this new version, which passed out of committee 8-4 on April 19. On the House floor vote two days later, he was one of just six Texas House members to vote for this version, which passed 288-95 despite massive southern resistance. As his last term was coming to a close, Eisenhower signed the bill on May 6, and it became known as the Civil Rights Act of 1960.[11]

The final product did not please all of its advocates, but the act did provide modest improvements over its 1957 predecessor and marked a second legislative victory in three years' time. The 1960 version established federal referees of local registration polls, imposed penalties against anyone obstructing registration, extended the life of the Civil Rights Commission, and closed certain loopholes in the 1957 version. In practice, however, the 1957 and 1960 Civil Rights Acts raised black voter turnout by a mere 3 percent. Despite recent victories in the courts and in Congress, fewer than one in four voting-age blacks registered and voted in the 1960 election. Nevertheless, in addition to boosting its adherents' morale, the law laid another stepping stone toward the more impactful 1964 Civil Rights Act and 1965 Voting Rights Act, which included enforcement and protection of a number of civil entitlements beyond voting.[12]

With his aye votes on both the 1957 and 1960 Civil Rights Acts, Thornberry had formally abandoned his belief that the government should distance itself from legislating civil rights issues. Moreover, 1960 marked Thornberry's definitive break from the conservative coalition. Whereas he had voted for 82 percent of bills supported by the majority of southern Democrats and Republicans in 1959, his support plummeted to 37, 30, and 25 percent over the following three years. Alas, his and others' defiance of the southern conservative order would incur devastating long-term political consequences for their party.[13]

Thornberry was in the middle of shaving on the morning of July 14 when he received a phone call from Johnson, who sought his friend's counsel on whether to accept Senator John Kennedy's offer to be his running mate. The dynamics at play were arresting: Kennedy was an Ivy League-educated, inexperienced junior senator from the North, and Johnson was a bootstrapped, battle-tested veteran from the South. Johnson, having been trounced in the primaries, now had twenty-four hours to decide whether to play second fiddle to a man he did not highly regard. The offer carried the potential to become vice president of the United States, a position John Nance Garner characterized as "not worth a bucket of warm piss." Johnson also risked losing the loyalties and cachet he had acquired as Senate Majority Leader. For these reasons, Thornberry, along with Rayburn, advised against it:

> I knew that there would be a sharp reaction from many of his friends in Texas who did not like Senator Kennedy . . . and [he] would feel that maybe he was letting them down . . . I also didn't think that being vice president was as good a job as he had as majority leader and as senator from Texas.

But immediately after hanging up, Thornberry asked himself, "Who am I to be telling somebody that they shouldn't be willing to be vice president?" He phoned Johnson back and informed him of his change of heart. Rayburn, who initially called the idea "idiotic," came around as well. Supporters believed that Johnson's absence from the Democratic ticket would spell certain victory for Republican candidate Richard Nixon, given southerners' apprehension about a Catholic Yankee occupying the White House. (Johnson's ultimate decision to accept Kennedy's offer would prove decisive in light of their narrow margin of victory. Many historians consider their triumph a rare instance—perhaps the only one—in which a running mate influenced the outcome of a general election.)[14]

Thornberry, who again ran uncontested in the primary and general elections, helped coordinate campaign efforts in Texas for Kennedy and other candidates. "You can't get that many people together that you don't have problems, hurt feelings," Thornberry later said. "But on the whole, it was a remarkable effort." An impromptu assignment forced Thornberry to cancel a fishing trip with Rayburn and instead escort Harry Truman to deliver stump speeches. The former president created a mild stir in San Antonio when, according to Thornberry, he extemporaneously suggested that a growing contingent of Republican-leaning farmers should "go to hell." A discomfited Thornberry and two aides gingerly asked the former president to watch his language, particularly at their next stop in the predominantly Baptist town of Waco. Truman, who also was reprimanded by his wife over the phone, promised to stick to his script.[15]

The Kennedy-Johnson ticket won seven of eleven former Confederate states despite both candidates' recent support for the 1960 Civil Rights Act, but their victory was far from unsullied. In addition to winning the White House, Democrats retained the upper hand in the Senate (64-36) and controlled 60 percent of House seats. But Democratic control of the South continued to slide, with three former Confederate states voting Republican and all eight of Mississippi's unpledged electors writing in segregationist Senator Harry Byrd of Virginia even though he never announced his candidacy. Although Johnson's home state of Texas went Democratic, its margin of victory was a relatively tenuous 46,233 out of more than two million ballots cast. "I was surprised that the election was as close as it was in Texas," Thornberry said. "I just did not realize the deep-seated feelings that still existed on the religious issue [Kennedy's Catholicism] in Texas."

Control of Texas Democratic leadership teetered atop a fragile union between Johnson moderates and Yarborough liberals. Meanwhile, the conservative Shivercrats, who were once again excluded from the Democratic
National Convention, continued to drift away from the party's core, largely
in response to the national party's civil rights crusade.[16]

Kennedy and Johnson received the overwhelming majority of the country's black vote, but plenty of room for improvement remained. Despite
new civil rights laws, favorable court rulings, and outreach efforts by the
NAACP and Southern Christian Leadership Conference, blacks remained
largely underrepresented at the polls.[17]

The House Rules Committee, on which Thornberry had served since
1955, would be critical to advancing Kennedy's progressive New Frontier.
After eight years of working under a Republican White House, Thornberry's
party loyalty could now blossom in full splendor. Thornberry, who told the
Austin American he was "proud to be known as one of [Kennedy's] strongest supporters," voted for 95 and 78 percent of Kennedy-supported bills
in 1961 and 1962, respectively; by comparison, Thornberry's legislative
support for the Eisenhower administration averaged just over 50 percent
during his two terms (see Table 1). He was also the lone southern Democrat to back Kennedy's ultimately vain effort to create the Department
of Housing and Urban Development, whose conception had to wait until 1965 under Johnson's presidency. "There were some southerners on
[Rules] who were just against the Kennedy program . . . and I was trying
to support the program as best I could," said Thornberry. "That's of course
when the turnaround came on civil rights."[18]

Two of the New Frontier's biggest impediments were Rules members
Howard Smith of Virginia and William Colmer of Mississippi, who contributed to an even six to six ideological split on the committee. Hoping
to break up the deadlock, Rayburn devised a plan to increase the committee's membership by three. Doing so would naturally prevent stalemates
enabled by an even number of members. More importantly to his wing
of the party, the addition of at least two allies would provide the White
House a reliable eight-to-seven margin on divisive issues like civil rights.
Said Thornberry:

> Of course the hardest fights were the bills on allowing blacks to vote, blacks
> to have an education. In fact that was the big fight I had to face when I went

Thornberry and President John F. Kennedy at a cocktail party, Washington, DC, circa 1962. *Thornberry family collection.*

on the committee. There just weren't enough [liberal] Democrats on the committee to get it out because two of the Democrats were from the South, and understandably they could not support [civil rights reform]. So the House had to vote to increase the membership in order to get the bills out, but that wasn't easy.

Ohio Republican Clarence J. Brown unfavorably compared the committee's expansion to Franklin Roosevelt's "court packing" scheme that tilted the Supreme Court's ideological balance in his favor. Due largely to Rayburn's efforts, the House was able to pass legislation increasing Rules membership from twelve to fifteen on January 31, 1961, by a razor-thin 217-212 margin. Conservative backlash was intense. A group of young Republican congressmen called out Rayburn as a "traitor to the United States as well as to Texas" for his role.[19]

Despite such efforts to advance the president's agenda, civil rights reform was not a high priority in the New Frontier. Kennedy felt that the

Department of Justice, headed by his brother Robert, should help preserve a middle ground between federal intervention and state sovereignty on the matter. He also feared backlash from black communities lest additional civil rights legislation fall short of expectations. But, as with Eisenhower, racial violence pushed Kennedy into action. In October of 1962, the president dispatched federal marshals to quell riots after James Meredith became the first black student admitted to the University of Mississippi at Oxford. Kennedy's televised address about the incident sent a clear message that for once, the White House was emphatically against segregation. However, Kennedy's subsequent, piecemeal initiatives disappointed civil rights leaders. His efforts included extending the life of the limp Civil Rights Commission and providing technical assistance to the small number of schools willing to desegregate. A 1962 constitutional amendment abolishing the poll tax in federal elections also netted little impact as five states, including Texas, found ways to continue imposing the tax.[20]

Martin Luther King Jr. said that racial discrimination in the South was "so great that the Negro cannot fight it alone." That is, meaningful civil rights reform would require a revitalized and concerted effort on behalf of all three branches of government. Thornberry's contributions would ultimately emanate from two of them.[21]

Midway through Kennedy's abbreviated term as president, Thornberry began itching for a career move. For starters, he was weary of Washington's escalating partisanship, and he claimed to have sensed some appetite for change from his constituency. More importantly, he had long yearned to become a federal judge, and he was ready for that day to arrive. Also, the lifetime tenure associated with a judicial appointment held much more appeal than the two-year election cycle as a US Representative. Indeed, he often reused the same line in relevant missives: "To serve on the federal bench is the dream of most members of my profession." Furthermore, he had tired of certain inconveniences of Washington living, particularly shoveling snow off his driveway in the wintertime. "I had thought maybe I would try to be appointed to one of the judgeships in Washington, but somehow it just didn't appeal to me," Thornberry said. "It still cost a whole lot. It was expensive to live in Washington, and I was a little tired of Washington." He yearned for an appointment in Texas, preferably in his hometown of Austin. Since federal judges were not subject to term limits, foreseeing a desirable vacancy was a challenge.[22]

TABLE 1. Breakdown of Thornberry's Congressional Voting Record, 1949-1962[a]

YEAR	CONGRESS	ADMINIS-TRATION	SUPPORT OF PRESIDENT'S POSITION (%)	PARTY UNITY SUPPORT[b] (%)	BIPARTISAN SUPPORT[c] (%)	CONSERVATIVE COALITION SUPPORT[a] (%)
1949	81st, sess. 1	Truman	N/A	85	79	N/A
1950	81st, sess. 2		N/A	90	64	N/A
1951	82nd, sess. 1		N/A	86	94	N/A
1952	82nd, sess. 2		N/A	74	86	N/A
1953	83rd, sess. 1	Eisenhower	56	88	90	N/A
1954	83rd, sess. 2		58	90	87	N/A
1955	84th, sess. 1		73	87	93	N/A
1956	84th, sess. 2		26	25	37	N/A
1957	85th, sess. 1		53	73	75	N/A
1958	85th, sess. 2		58	84	71	N/A
1959	86th, sess. 1		46	85	97	82
1960	86th, sess. 2		63	82	98	37
1961	87th, sess. 1	Kennedy	95	93	94	30
1962	87th, sess. 2		78	81	82	25

TABLE 1

SOURCES: *Congressional Quarterly Almanac* 5-19 (Washington, DC: Congressional Quarterly Service, 1949-1963)

NOTE: *CQ Almanac* changed its methodology in 1955. Previously, announced positions on bills were included and treated the same as actual votes. All instances of nonvoting became excluded beginning in 1955. *CQ* retroactively amended the 1954 percentages for these votes, reflected here, but none before then. In Thornberry's case, the new formulae produced only marginally different results.

[a] Voting data for 1963, Thornberry's final year in Congress, is unavailable because of his transition to the judiciary one month before completion of his term.

[b] Voted with the Democratic majority against the Republican majority.

[c] Voted with majorities of both parties.

[d] Voted with majorities of both Republicans and Southern Democrats against the majority of Northern Democrats.

Johnson, who seeded Thornberry's judicial aspirations years before, promised to help realize his friend's dream. Recalled Thornberry, "I wasn't sure if I could be appointed, and secondly I didn't know if I was qualified, being up in Congress that long. . . . [Johnson] said, 'Don't you worry about that. You can be appointed if there's ever a Democratic president.'" Ultimately the decision lay with Kennedy, who as president had the sole authority to nominate federal judges, and he would likely have reservations about losing a loyal lieutenant in Thornberry.[23]

However, Kennedy's feelings were of less concern to Thornberry than was Rayburn's reaction. Seeking the Speaker's blessing for his egress could easily strain their relationship. Thornberry prepared himself for the worst before entering the Speaker's office to make his plea. "I hated to do it worse than anything on the earth," he remembered. To Thornberry's astonishment, Rayburn told him, "Homer, of course I'll help you. If I've got a better friend on earth than you, I don't know it." Thornberry was nearly moved to tears.[24]

Through Rayburn's and Johnson's lobbying efforts, Kennedy reluctantly consented to appointing Thornberry to the judiciary. "I think it bothered him a good deal because they had had so much trouble in the House with the composition of the Committee on Rules." But for the time being, Thornberry's departure remained on hold until a desirable vacancy materialized.[25]

Rayburn's health began deteriorating around this time. His customary workhorse pace had slowed of late because of waning energy levels and persistent backaches. "I never did realize he was seriously ill," said Thornberry.

"I can remember in sixty-one talking to him, and he just seemed just as healthy and fine as he could be. He failed in a hurry." Rayburn continued to report for duty anyway, commenting, "I want to die with my boots on and with my gavel in my hand. They are going to have to carry me out of here, God willing. I love this House." Doctors at Baylor University Medical Center in Dallas discovered the spread of cancer throughout Rayburn's body, and he passed away six weeks later on November 16, 1961, at age seventy-nine.[26]

Funeral services were held at First Baptist Church in Rayburn's hometown of Bonham, Texas, and drew over twenty thousand people. Attendees included Kennedy and Johnson, former Presidents Truman and Eisenhower, over one hundred members of Congress, and fifteen thousand friends and constituents from the Fourth District. CBS News journalist Eric Sevareid said that Rayburn "did not merely believe by the evidence, in the strength, goodness—the rightness—of America, he assumed it." Rayburn had no children of his own, and Sevareid commented that he "expended his parental love on the House of Representatives. It was his home. . . . Mister Sam was a little bigger than life; a little bigger than Texas." Thornberry was among the scores of representatives to eulogize the late Speaker from the House floor on January 18, 1962:

> I was afforded the privilege of what I like to believe was a close friendship which occurs only a few times in a man's life. His was more than a fatherly interest in me. . . . Mr. Rayburn walked with kings and notables during his lifetime—and yet never lost the common touch. He talked with crowds and never lost the simple dignity which earned for him the affection, admiration, and devotion of all who ever knew him.[27]

Johnson became Thornberry's chief political benefactor with Rayburn's passing. As with Rayburn, Johnson's relationship to Thornberry was both professional and deeply personal. The Johnson and Thornberry families lived within three blocks of each other in northwest Washington, DC. Their proximity permitted frequent joint dinners with children's after-school visits, slumber parties, and Easter egg hunts. The Thornberry children referred to Mr. and Mrs. Johnson as "Uncle Lyndon and Aunt Bird." They vacationed together on fishing trips, beach getaways, and visits to the exalted LBJ Ranch. The ranch featured three hundred acres of green pastures and rolling hills; hordes of livestock, including bulls, cattle, pigs, goats,

The Ikard, Thornberry, and Johnson families vacationing at a California beach, 1955. *Thornberry family collection.*

and sheep; fishing ponds filled with bass and perch; a swimming pool; a children's entertainment room; and a front porch conducive to storytelling and stargazing. On one particular visit, the two Thornberry daughters (Molly and Kate) and another guest took an unauthorized afternoon golf cart ride that resulted in a minor collision with a cattle guardrail. Fortunately for them, "Aunt Bird" was as magnanimous as she was hospitable. She hardly batted an eye once when a careless individual knocked over a tray of crystal glasses, shattering them to pieces. (Likewise, in 1976 she would generously commission her family's jet to whisk Thornberry, who had undergone several unsuccessful surgeries to remove a gall bladder infection, away to the Mayo Clinic for a lifesaving operation.)[28]

Like his genteel spouse, Johnson left his own brand of impressions on the Thornberry children. He tried to phone Thornberry at home one evening only to discover that the children were alone. Ten-year-old Kate answered and explained that she was under parental orders not to reveal her father's whereabouts. An agitated Johnson pressed with his need to reach Thornberry, but Kate, who soon found herself "sweating bullets," held her ground. The following morning, her father instructed her that going forward, she was to make an exception to his house rule for the vice president of the United States. Years later, high school senior Molly handed the phone to her newly arrived date, explaining that "Uncle Lyndon" on the other end wanted a word with him. It was only after he hung up that the young man was informed he had been speaking not to a family relative but to the leader of the free world.[29]

Johnson's heart attack in 1955 forced Thornberry to cancel his Fourth of July plans with his family and attend to his stricken neighbor. Thornberry spent nearly every evening of Johnson's hospital stay with him, entertaining the senator with their storied dominoes contests. Johnson accused Thornberry of letting him win each time, but accounts varied. "He tells it as if I let him beat me," Thornberry contended. "In spite of my best efforts, he was very skillful. He really wanted to win; he liked to win." Indeed, Thornberry provided a soothing presence for Johnson during their fifteen years together in Washington. According to reporter Liz Carpenter, Johnson was so charmed by his friend's "Santa Claus laugh" that prior to speaking before large groups, he told his aides, "Put Homer out there in the middle of the audience. I don't just want polite smiles or chuckles—I want a real belly laugh."[30]

GALLAUDET

Lost in most civil rights discussions is the enduring plight of deaf persons. The physiological constraints caused by the inability to hear and speak severely restrict access to the public sphere, yielding fewer privileges and opportunities than those available to individuals able to fully communicate. Like non-natives inarticulate in the local tongue, deaf individuals consider themselves minorities in both linguistic and cultural respects (while generally eschewing labels like impaired or disabled). Yet, whereas racial and ethnic minorities' struggles have historically drawn plenty of publicity, marginalization of the deaf has not.[31]

As the child of deaf-mutes, Thornberry made it a priority during his congressional years to shine more light on society's disadvantaged and boost their self-sufficiency. In 1953, he headed opposition to H.R. 5246, which would have drastically cut funding for state vocational programs, primarily for the blind, including a $2.4 million reduction for Texas. The Texas Commission for the Blind, Texas Vocational Association, and Vocational Rehabilitation Association had reached out to Thornberry to fend off these cuts. He delivered. "I believe in the long run more economy will be achieved in giving handicapped people an opportunity not only to earn a livelihood for themselves but to contribute to our economy," he spoke from the floor on May 25. An amended version of the bill that restored the original funding amount was ultimately passed by the House the very next day. It was promptly passed by the Senate and eventually signed into law by President Eisenhower. The following year, Thornberry supported amendments to the Vocational Rehabilitation Act (VRA) to increase federal funding for rehabilitation services, facilities, undergraduate training programs, and research serving the mentally ill. Albeit heartened by the VRA's expansion, Thornberry fretted over the prevailing neglect of the deaf population.[32]

At the time, the country's only four-year college for deaf-mutes was Gallaudet College in Washington, DC. The school's inception in 1864 was made possible by $56 million in federal funds, and its charter was signed by President Abraham Lincoln. Originally called the Columbia Institution for the Instruction of the Deaf and Dumb and Blind, it was renamed the Columbia Institution for the Deaf and Dumb in 1865 and yet again as Gallaudet College in 1954 in honor of nineteenth-century humanitarian Thomas Hopkins Gallaudet. Born in Philadelphia in 1787 to French immigrants, Gallaudet became arguably the greatest champion of deaf-mute persons in history. He originally intended to enter into the ministry before his keen interest in a neighbor's deaf daughter set him on a different path. He soon mastered sign language in his interactions with her and set out to find others like her. He discovered a concentration of deaf persons in Connecticut with no place to obtain a formal education. In addition to their isolation, the deaf were perceived as less competent than the hearing and were even prohibited from voting in the state of New York. After touring deaf-mute schools in Europe, Gallaudet returned to Connecticut to build an educational asylum in 1818 that exclusively served deaf-mutes in the Northeast. As the school's first principal, he spent much of his time locating and recruiting uneducated deaf-mutes in the region. Traditional universities took note of his rising stature and tried to lure him into their own ranks, but their efforts were in vain. He finally retired in 1830 after years of rigorous missionary work, having doubled his school's student body to 140 over the last five years of his tenure.[33]

Gallaudet envisioned the use of sign language by both the deaf and hearing populations, but the subject of integration would gradually polarize the deaf world. Some believed sign language was an essential binding agent to

Thomas Hopkins Gallaudet, circa 1855. *Courtesy Gallaudet University Archives.*

maintain cultural solidarity and independence. Others wanted to abolish sign language altogether, which they considered an undesirable contributor to their separation from the public sphere. Such disunion roughly paralleled the divide among blacks between the isolationist Malcolm X and the assimilationist Martin Luther King Jr.[34]

Unlike the civil rights movement's unfolding in plain view by main-stream society, deaf persons found the gates to the public domain locked from the inside. The deaf enjoyed far fewer educational opportunities than other subpopulations and were neglected as much by elected officials as by the general public. Home-schooling deaf children was prevalent, often presaging a life of quiet solitude. Unemployment rates among deaf persons were high, and opportunities were generally limited to educating their own kind, as both of Thornberry's parents had done. As of the mid-1950s, roughly 40 percent of all Gallaudet graduates taught at deaf high schools. Audism, the term for institutional discrimination of deaf persons, was not limited to education and employment. Author Myron Uhlberg, another son of deaf-mute parents, was sickened by the audistic treatment of his father in public. "I would note with despair and shame, and then anger, the way in which the hearing world would ignore him as if he were nothing more than an inanimate, insensate block of stone, something not quite human," Uhlberg wrote in his 2009 memoir, *Hands of My Father*. "This sheer indifference seemed worse than contempt."[35]

After joining the Columbia Institution's board of directors in 1954, Thornberry introduced several pieces of legislation on its behalf. One was ultimately withdrawn in favor of the identical H.R. 6655, written by California Republican and fellow board member John Phillips, which included appropriations for a ten-year construction program on the school's campus. The estimated $250,000 in proposed funding allowed for a new library-classroom building, power plant, and extra gymnasium space. Another $410,000 was sought for salary increases and other expenses. A chief aim of the bill was to enhance the school's reputation by helping it become a fully accredited learning institution. Without either this designation or adequate salary rates for its faculty, the institute would continue to struggle recruiting quality instructors, according to President Leonard Elstad. The bill also proposed renaming the institute Gallaudet College after its founder. On the House floor, Illinois Republican and institution board member Fred Busbey called the school's housing conditions a "disgrace" and argued, "Gradually, year by year, we can make this into a first-class institution of its kind in the world." Not only were campus buildings dilapidated, but the school was so cramped for space that it had to cap its annual admission at 100 out of 170 recent applicants. Because the institute remained the world's only place of higher education for the deaf, rejected applicants had little recourse. "We ought to be large enough to take care of all of the students who qualify, and right now we cannot do that," Elstad testified before the House Committee on Education and Labor on May 6.[36]

Thornberry's statements on H.R. 6655 at the same committee meeting and later on the House floor touched on both the school's financial predicaments and its disproportionately low support from the government. Thornberry compared its funding to that of two other federally chartered private schools—the American Printing House for the Blind and the historically black Howard University. Whereas Gallaudet had received no federal funds for new construction since 1917 (and prior to that, 1870), Howard had taken $25 million for new building projects in the interim. Addressing the committee, Thornberry argued:

> Other handicapped, the blind, the crippled, can go to any institution in the United States that is already established, either by the state or by private institutions, for their education, because they can hear and talk . . . . There is nowhere an eligibility for a person to receive [similar] assistance for the mere reason that he is deaf. . . . Nowhere in the Social Security program do you recognize them as you do the blind; nor do you set up a program for the physically handicapped as you do for the blind. . . . One of the most shameful things in the history of this country is the way we have had . . . a college to educate the deaf and the way we have neglected them, by this Congress and by the federal government. . . . It is not easy to have a college or an educational institution for a few people who do not have a political voice; and in time, people have just forgotten that they are there.

Thornberry also mentioned his mother's and his own shared belief that education formed the cornerstone of self-empowerment: "History shows that where [deaf people] have been given the opportunity, they go out and make a living for themselves." At the same hearing, Linton M. Collins, attorney-secretary of the institute's board of directors, commended Thornberry and Phillips for championing the deaf community: "During my service on the board, we have never had more cooperative sponsorship than we have had from these two gentlemen. . . . They have been about the only members of Congress who have attended . . . the graduating sessions of the institution to see what we are doing."[37]

With Eisenhower's signature on June 23, 1954, H.R. 6655 allowed the renamed Gallaudet College to triple its student body. A dedication ceremony was given for the new library on February 2, 1957, the school's Founder's Day. Guest speaker Bradshaw Mintener, former assistant secretary in the US Department of Health, Education, and Welfare, which carried out H.R. 6655's terms, stated that the new library and other building projects marked a "new era for Gallaudet." In 1960, Thornberry introduced legislation (which was rolled into another bill that became law) that relieved Gallaudet of its quasi-governmental status, cancelled its deed of trust to the United States, and quieted its title. That is, the school was made financially independent.[38]

For his efforts, Thornberry received an honorary doctorate from Gallaudet in 1954. In 1963, he served as Gallaudet's graduation speaker and delivered the commencement address in sign language, in which he said:

> I am grateful that my years of service in the Congress have permitted me to fulfill the privilege of serving on the board of this finest educational institution of its kind in the nation—and in the world. Grateful as I am for Gallaudet, for the role it fills, for the example and inspiration it offers, I am and we all should be the more grateful for the society and system which supports efforts such as this to open wider the doors of opportunity to all.[39]

Thornberry's crusade for the deaf rubbed off on Johnson. While in the Senate, he had prodded Thornberry, "You ought to be telling me what I can do for Gallaudet College. I want to help them." As president, Johnson would sign into law legislation establishing the National Technical Institute for the Deaf in Rochester, New York, in 1965. NTID would provide deaf students a technical alternative to Gallaudet's liberal arts programs and focus on reducing deaf unemployment rates. In a letter to President Johnson, Hugo Schunhoff, president of the Conference of Executives of American Schools for the Deaf, called the NTID's inception "the most important event in the education of the deaf since the signing of the bill establishing Gallaudet College." Johnson followed that by delivering a surprise commencement address to the institute's 1966 graduating class. "I was like the little boy in the mountains who didn't get an invitation to the dance," Johnson joked. "I just sat down and wrote myself an invitation." The scheduled keynote speaker that day, an equally surprised Democratic House member John Fogarty, described Johnson as one of the "greatest patrons of education and health in our country today." The Alexander Graham Bell Association for the Deaf would recognize Johnson in 1967 for Distinguished Service to the Deaf.[40]

Thornberry's wife Eloise also became involved in deaf charities and even learned sign language from her live-in mother-in-law. Eloise served on an advisory group during NTID's incipiency and also joined Gallaudet's National Advisory Committee in 1966, while serving with her husband on the school's board. President Johnson referred her for several other governmental and nongovernmental committees related to deaf education.[41]

Thornberry's deaf-mute mother Mary reconnected with several old friends from Austin who had since found work at Gallaudet. She became popular in her son's workplace too. Described as a "slight, spunky little lady with sparkling blue eyes" by Liz Carpenter, she endeared herself to the Texas delegation, which threw her an eightieth birthday party in May 1953. Senator Johnson, one of two hundred in attendance, had grown particularly fond of her. "You possess an inner beauty of soul that is transformed into an outward radiance and glow," Johnson wrote her in March of 1957. "Yours is the kind of strength of character and force of personality that makes great mothers of great men."[42]

It was around this time that Mary's health deteriorated. She was forced to spend the last months of her life in a nursing home, until finally passing away at the age of eighty-five. The costs of Mary's assisted-living care were so substantial that the Thornberrys almost had to sell their house. A decade later, Johnson confided in Eloise that the financial strain of Mary's medical care partially inspired him to launch Medicare during his presidency. A condolence letter from a Texas School for the Deaf faculty member read, "Teachers will have to race down the path of progress to surpass some of the old timers here, and your mother was one of them. I have not forgotten how she was given the problem kids whom others did not want and how she taught them not only their lessons but good behavior and good manners as well."[43]

Sometime after his mother's death, Thornberry set to work on a brief narrative about her inspirational life, which he submitted to Reader's Digest in 1962. The piece centered on the lessons she instilled in him, including a work ethic and compassion for the less fortunate. He also mentioned that she never grew comfortable with the insecurity of her son's profession, signing, "I wish Homer could get a good, steady job." Although Thornberry's story submission was rejected for unspecified reasons, one theory held that the magazine's conservative editorial board was unwilling to publish anything by a left-leaning politician. A sympathetic Digest editor responded,

Mary Thornberry, circa 1953. *Thornberry family collection.*

"I seldom find myself in disagreement with their judgment, but I believe they're 100 percent off this time." (The story, "My Most Unforgettable Character," is presented in the afterword.)[44]

Mary's passing invited not only sympathy but legislative action on Johnson's part. To Thornberry, he wrote:

> I vividly remember the enlightened expression that came into her eyes when she realized in the south Austin grocery market that she had met Homer's friend. . . . I recognized what a great woman she was every time I saw her, and it has been indelibly impressed upon me through the years as I saw evidences of your concern for human welfare, your sense of justice and your constant search for the course that would result in the greatest good for the greatest number. . . . I don't know of a greater credit to any man. . . . Just as sure as my name is Lyndon Johnson and I live till next week, we are going to have a monument at Gallaudet to Mary Thornberry.

Johnson pitched the idea to Gallaudet President Leonard Elstad during a dinner given by the Texas delegation. Elstad later recapitulated that conversation:

> He [Johnson] turned to me, we had finished eating. . . . He said, "You ought to name one of your buildings for Mrs. Thornberry." I said, "Well, we've

never done that." He said, "There's got to be a first time sometime." I said, "Well, I'll talk to my board about it." He said, "You do that."[45]

The Mary L. Thornberry Hearing and Speech Center was established at Gallaudet College on October 19, 1959. In addition to modernized diagnostic testing, the $475,000 center offered training courses for graduates interested in teaching as well as research tools for postgraduates. Importantly, it featured soundproof suites that reduced ambient noise during auditory tests that had previously been conducted in a poorly insulated basement. Inside the new facility, modern equipment permitted clinical tests of hearing aids while also allowing "integrationists" to improve their lip-reading skills through the use of video and booths with mirrors. Center director Robert Frisina told the *Washington Post*, "We're not making hearing people out of them. We're trying to get each one to develop the potentialities he has."[46]

The announcement of the new facility included a statement from President Elstad and the Gallaudet Board of Directors praising Homer Thornberry as one who "continuously maintains his interest in the education of the deaf and who is one of those most responsible for the development of a nine million dollar building program for the college." In a written statement, Thornberry responded that he was "deeply grateful for this wonderful tribute to my mother." The building would be officially dedicated a decade later on May 18, 1969, and would display an oil painting of Mary. Thornberry and a few associates seeded a scholarship fund in Mary's name that primarily benefited students from Texas. "This idea for a memorial is typical of his usual generosity when the deaf are involved," Elstad said.[47]

Educational opportunities for the deaf exploded over the twenty-five years following H.R. 6655. A 1985 US General Accounting Office (GAO) report on Gallaudet and NTID showed substantial improvement in their student and faculty capacity, degree offerings, and graduates' employment rates. Gallaudet's enrollment had risen from one hundred to two thousand since H.R. 6655, and the number of students at NTID exceeded 1,300 since opening its doors to seventy-one students in 1968. In addition to providing elementary and secondary education, Gallaudet now included three schools of higher education: the College of Arts and Sciences, School of Communication, and School of Education and Human Services. Programs included an associate's degree in interpreting, a bachelor of arts in twenty-six fields, a bachelor of science in four fields, a master's in seven areas, a specialization in education, and a doctorate in Special Education Administration. The school would also offer career counseling and job placement services. Within eleven months of graduating, over 80 percent of Gallaudet's 1982 to 1983 graduating class was either employed or pursuing continuing education. Of the ninety-four graduates, a mutually inclusive forty-nine were working in education with forty-seven employed in institutions serving the deaf, including seventeen at Gallaudet. At the time of the GAO report, NTID offered certificates and associate's, bachelor's, and master's degrees in thirty-seven technical programs within three schools (business, visual communications, and engineering and science). NTID boasted employment rates comparable to those at Gallaudet at this time. In 1986, one year after the GAO report, Gallaudet became a fully accredited university. Future legislative milestones benefitting the deaf would include the Civil Rights Act of 1964, Rehabilitation Act of 1973, Education for All Handicapped Children Act of 1975, Individuals with Disabilities Education Act of 1990, and Americans with Disabilities Act of 1990. Collectively, these laws would protect against discrimination in the workplace and public spaces; expand access to educational services; and guarantee equal access to important forms of communication through the provision of interpreters, hearing aids, and television captioning.[48]

Gallaudet's impressive results notwithstanding, the school could not fully reconcile its community's competing philosophies: assimilation versus independence vis-à-vis mainstream society. In 1987, one year after the school was granted university status, the board of directors appointed Elisabeth Zinser to become Gallaudet's first-ever hearing president, a decision greeted by campus protests as well as a march on the Capitol. The uproar led to the replacement of Zinser with Irving King Jordan, who was deaf. Alas, controversy resurfaced in the spring of 2006 over Jordan's successor, Jane Fernandes. A purist contingent of students, faculty, and alumni felt Fernandes was "not deaf enough" on account of her upbringing, which involved reading lips and communicating orally rather than using sign language. Protestors objected to her more inclusive vision for the university, which would expand enrollment to those with only mild deafness, including those with cochlear implants. Contributing to the rancor was the school's suddenly declining graduation and employment rates. Amid persistent protests, hunger strikes, and mass arrests, which lasted well into the fall of 2006 and drew national media attention, the school's board finally rescinded Fernandes's appointment.[49]

Three years after the Fernandes fiasco, a dilapidated and disused Mary Thornberry Building was demolished. The university called it "a bittersweet ending to fifty-one years of service to the community." Mary's portrait and other commemorative materials would be displayed in the relocated Hearing and Speech Center's front office.[50]

Despite Gallaudet's more recent difficulties, educational opportunities for the deaf in the post-H.R. 6655 era extended beyond its main campus. Starting in the late 1970s, six Gallaudet University Regional Centers (GURCs) would be launched to provide educational and professional development resources for deaf persons across the country. The centers would also help coordinate the National Academic Bowl for Deaf and Hard of Hearing High School Students, hosted annually at Gallaudet. The Southwest GURC, serving Texas and seven neighboring states, opened in January 2011. Partnering with Austin Community College, the new center would be located just east of the Texas School for the Deaf, where Thornberry's parents first met one century before.[51]

CHAPTER 9

A Good, Steady Job (1962-1963)

T HORNBERRY'S LONGEVITY IN CONGRESS HAD BENEFITED FROM a complete absence of Republican challengers to his seat. The 1962 election season would not only break this cycle, it would also epitomize the snowballing transformation of the region's political landscape. Texas Democrats had enjoyed a false sense of security ever since 1876, the last year the Lone Star State had been governed by a Republican. Democrats' complacency about their hegemony overrode concerns about internal discord over civil rights, among other issues. Such hubris prompted John Connally, that year's Democratic gubernatorial candidate, to boast that Democrats would easily control the state for another half century. His prediction would prove to be wildly inaccurate.[1]

Southern residents were heeding conservatives' rippling criticism of President Kennedy and of what the Hays County GOP termed the "New Frontier's socialistic bills," particularly on civil rights. Kennedy did not strongly advocate for federal leadership in countering institutional discrimination, but he eventually committed to quelling violent outbreaks in the South. He acknowledged the situation in one speech: "One hundred years of delay have passed since President Lincoln freed the slaves, yet their heirs, their grandsons, are not totally free." The president further authorized the attorney general's office to initiate desegregation suits and withhold funding from federally supported programs that practiced discrimination. Mississippi Senator James Eastland argued that these measures amounted to totalitarianism.[2]

Among the more liberal pieces of legislation that rankled southern conservatives was a Kennedy-supported joint resolution to impose a constitutional ban on the poll tax in federal elections. At $1.50, Texas's poll

US congressional Texas delegation, Washington, DC, circa 1960. *Thornberry family collection.*

tax was the second highest in the country, with proof of payment required six months in advance in order to vote in primary elections. Thornberry joined five other Texas representatives (against the other sixteen) to vote for S. J. Res. 29, which would ban the tax in federal elections but not apply to state contests. The measure, which would become the Twenty-fourth Amendment, easily passed the House 294-86 on August 27, 1962, despite widespread southern opposition. (The amendment would be subject to ratification by each state in 1964.) Thornberry's "aye" vote signified a complete reversal in his thinking since his first session in Congress in 1949, when he joined a House majority and all but two Texas House members in voting down an identical measure.[3]

Thornberry was also the only southerner on the Rules Committee to regularly back the Kennedy administration, at the cost of some constituent support. "I was trying to support the [New Frontier] as best I could. That's of course when the turnaround came on civil rights, and I supported that. . . . And this Republican opposition developed, and I was not popular in this area [the Tenth District], as popular as I had been." A poll showed that Thornberry was not alone: Kennedy had already lost the support of roughly 4.5 million white voters strictly over civil rights.[4]

White backlash notwithstanding, Thornberry began paying more attention to black constituents leading up the 1962 election. Previously, he said, "I'd go into these communities, and I'd see a black, and I didn't know whether to shake his hand or not." He grew more comfortable after voting for the 1957 and 1960 Civil Rights Acts. "I did the first work with blacks, and it was an interesting experience for me because I got to know them, and they had come into their own by that time. . . . It had been developing, and I had known that."[5]

Even if not a racial hotbed like other former Confederate states, Texas cradled a deep-seated indignation toward desegregation in schools. The prevailing animosity was highlighted in Governor Allan Shivers's open invitation to fellow Texans to defy the Supreme Court's ruling in *Brown*. And although President Eisenhower defended desegregation in the Little Rock Nine incident, he acquiesced in Shivers's ordering the Texas Rangers to obstruct black children from entering Mansfield High School in 1956. The governor's pronouncement was especially impudent since Mansfield was Texas's first school district ordered to integrate by a federal court. The rangers were accompanied by Mansfield's mayor and police force, underscoring the systemic local support for the state's defiance. Emboldened by Mansfield, the Texas legislature passed a series of laws prohibiting integration unless local voters approved it. Following the Little Rock Nine in 1957, the legislature had closed a number of public schools and inventively redrew school zones to dodge federal intervention. The governor's office continued to reinforce segregation in the aftermath of Shivers's scandal-ridden tenure when conservative state senator Price Daniel defeated liberal attorney Ralph Yarborough in the 1956 gubernatorial primary and went on to win the general election. State leadership's segregationist yearnings were carried through by Daniel's successor, former US Navy Secretary John Connally, who openly criticized now senator Yarborough and the Kennedy administration on civil rights issues after his election in 1962. (Connally's defiance of the national party foreshadowed his defection to the Republican Party a decade later.) As of 1964—ten years after *Brown* had outlawed segregation—only 18,000 of the state's 325,000 black students were attending integrated schools.[6]

Although the state's political power structure was clearly shifting in one direction, Thornberry continued to push back. In addition to voting for the Civil Rights Acts of 1957 and 1960, he voted to increase the minimum wage in 1960 despite heavy resistance from the business class. Financial aid for the needy and for students and institutions of higher education remained priorities for Thornberry, as well. He helped introduce the ultimately enacted Housing Act of 1961, which provided lodging for low-income families, and he supported federal funding for student loans, medical schools, and colleges. During Kennedy's time in the White House, he also actively supported antitrust legislation, funding for the space program, and special assistance for deaf children.[7]

Thornberry was also instrumental in siting a new IRS data processing center in his district, fending off strong competition from Dallas and other cities. The center would be based in Austin and serve a five-state region (Arkansas, Louisiana, New Mexico, and Oklahoma, in addition to Texas) while employing about 1,500 people. "This is just another significant step in the continued phenomenal growth of the city of Austin," Thornberry said at the center's groundbreaking ceremony. Thornberry also viewed the adjoining IRS service center as an opportunity to boost black employment. Urged by Thornberry to promote the project's "policy of equal opportunity for employment," center director Robert Phinney circulated notices in black communities explicitly promoting the "Federal Civil Service Merit System on the basis of qualifications and without regard to race or religious belief."[8]

In the face of growing conservative backlash, Thornberry's lofty popularity remained largely intact over his fifteen years in Congress. Law partners Gene Fondren and Wilson Fox regularly hosted public appreciation barbecues in recognition of the congressman's service. The *Austin American* named both Thornberry and Fondren, who had served as general counsel for the Texas Senate General Investigating Committee to root out insurance scandals, as two of Austin's five "Newsmakers of the Year" in 1957. The two had met during Thornberry's first election to Congress in 1948 and the following year saw the kickoff of the barbecue tradition. What began as a small, informal affair held in Williamson County gradually expanded across the district over time, drawing hundreds of constituents each year.[9]

Republicans believed 1962 to be a turning point toward legitimate two-party representation in the state. The GOP entered an unprecedented twenty-two congressional candidates in sixteen Texas districts at their party's May 5 primary. Only six of Texas's twenty-two incumbent House members would run unopposed that year. Harris County, the state's most populous area, saw a record twenty-three candidates seek nomination among eighty-nine local offices. Inspired by US Senator John Tower's upset victory the previous year, Franklin County GOP chairman John Edwards declared, "We have a real powerhouse for the first time."[10]

Left to right: Wilson Fox, Senator Lyndon B. Johnson, and Thornberry at an appreciation barbecue in Taylor, Texas, 1957. *LBJ Library photo by Studtman Photo, Austin, Texas.*

The Republican lineup included Thornberry's first-ever opponent in a general election. Jim Dobbs was a thirty-eight-year-old former Hollywood actor once contracted by Warner Brothers as a featured player in US Navy training films. He also appeared in *Night and Day* with Cary Grant and *The Man I Love* with Ida Lupino. Dobbs subsequently worked as a Church of Christ minister in parts of central and east Texas, including the towns and cities of Crockett, Liberty, San Antonio, Pasadena, and Austin. Immediately before challenging Thornberry for his Tenth District seat, Dobbs had worked for a Houston-based public relations firm that organized lectures on Americanism (or anti-Communism) and conservatism.[11]

The prospect of unseating Thornberry was remote, but the Republicans' newfound momentum clouded the horizon for Democrats. Paul Stimson, an Austin educational consultant, was set to oppose Thornberry in the Democratic primary but withdrew once he determined he was no match.

Even a member of the opposition party—Republican House member Bob Wilson of California—publicly conceded that his party had "no hope or expectations" of defeating the incumbent. (A reprimanding by party bosses prompted him to revise his statement.) Nevertheless, a hunger for change was churning down South. The *Austin Statesman* editorial board was particularly displeased with the Eighty-Seventh Congress's Democratic majority, writing that "the Democrats often do not seem to know what they want" and that the "scratch-my-back and I'll-scratch-your-back has been strong." Real estate dealer Hal Hendrix, who lost to Dobbs in the Republican primary, bemoaned Stimson's surrender as a "loss to the voters." Hendrix further claimed that Thornberry's extended stay in Congress illustrated "the complete control held by an entrenched political group and hurts the public at large by taking away the privilege of a free choice among dissatisfied Democrats." A group of central Texas business and civic leaders called "Democrats for Dobbs" issued a statement that they were "dissatisfied with the manner in which the incumbent congressman has represented this district." Dobbs's own prediction that he would receive support from some "who never thought they'd ever vote for a Republican" would have sounded outlandish not so long ago. But the game had changed when a Catholic, liberal northerner had won the White House two years before.[12]

A self-declared "vigorous leader in the fight against socialism," Dobbs attacked the Kennedy administration and big government in general, denouncing the president and his allies as "Big Brother and his New Frontiersmen." Dobbs also advocated a more aggressive foreign policy against Communist China, which members of both parties considered a grave threat to western civilization. "We must not allow ourselves to think we can buy international friendship with giveaway programs," he proclaimed at a rally in San Marcos, south of Austin. A Dobbs campaign flyer branded Thornberry "a darling of the Americans for Democratic Action with a 91 percent Liberal voting record—an advocate of Medicare and every other wild spending scheme proposed by the . . . leadership of the Democratic Party for the past fourteen years." Fearmongering was becoming more common in Republican rhetoric, as one Dobbs pamphlet read, "1962 is not only your greatest opportunity—it may well be your last."[13]

Curiously, the hottest topic in the race was neither civil rights nor communism but rather dams. Flood damage had cost the region tens of millions of dollars over the century's first several decades—$61,400,000 from 1900 to 1913 alone, according to a US Army Corps of Engineers report. As a member of the House, Lyndon Johnson had helped procure federal funds to construct the Hamilton, Tom Miller, Austin, and Mansfield dams in the region. On top of preventing flood damage, these dams were credited with helping to spur Austin's mid-century commercial growth as well as projects like the Bergstrom Air Force Base and Robert Mueller Municipal Airport.[14]

Thornberry continued his predecessor's advocacy of dam construction in the interest of protecting lives and property. In 1960, he had introduced a resolution calling for the urgent completion of a US-Mexico reservoir along the Rio Grande. From the House floor, Thornberry argued that earlier completion of the project would have prevented $47.6 million worth of flood damage two years prior. Ensuing legislation was passed in both chambers and ultimately signed into law. Later, at the September 22, 1962, groundbreaking ceremony for the Somerville Reservoir, located one hundred miles east of Austin, Thornberry described water resources management as "one of the greatest problems of Texas today" because of its impact on regional industry, education, agriculture, and other fields. Earlier in the year, Thornberry pledged to help spearhead a $40 million public works bill for the construction of three dams in Williamson County along the upper San Gabriel River. According to the US Army's Board of Engineers for Rivers and Harbors, these projects would prevent floods; maintain a steady water supply; and preserve fish, wildlife, and recreational land.[15]

The Army engineers' findings notwithstanding, the damming of the San Gabriel had drawn intense opposition from a number of vocal Williamson County residents ever since the plan was first pitched twelve years before. A crowd of three hundred dam opponents showed up at a water commission meeting in May, making it the most heavily attended hearing in the commission's history. The group argued that the proposed dam would consume thousands of acres of prime real estate only to prevent flooding in roughly the same amount of territory in neighboring Milam County. Williamson County Judge Sam Stone, representing the protestors, said, "It's a matter of survival with us, and we would very definitely like to survive." Dobbs sided with the protestors, who opposed Thornberry's reelection. "To spend some $25 million to cover up over 13,000 acres of the finest blackland in Central Texas seems to me to be rather ridiculous," Dobbs told the *Austin American*. "We should be trying to work out a program to

HOMER THORNBERRY
The Man You Can COUNT *On!*

Born January 9, 1909 — Travis County. Parents taught at **Texas School for the Deaf.** Grandfather, Will T. Thornberry, was early **Methodist** preacher in Hays and Caldwell Counties. Homer is married to the former Eloise Engle. They have a daughter, Molly, 2.

When Homer was nine, his father died. It became necessary for him to help with family expenses.

To help support his mother, Homer worked at every kind of job. He sold newspapers, collected bills for a plumber, was a railroad freight clerk, worked with construction gangs. He worked his way through the University of Texas as chief deputy sheriff (a lot of responsibility at 21), and later as assistant to the county school superintendent.

He was graduated with a degree in business administration in 1932 and received his law degree in 1936.

In 1936, Homer Thornberry was elected to the Texas Legislature in the first primary over two opponents. In 1938 he was re-elected without an opponent. In 1940 he was elected District Attorney of Travis County and in 1942 was re-elected without an opponent.

In 1942, Homer had been deferred from the draft. However, at 33, he volunteered for service in the U. S. Navy, resigning his post as District Attorney to enter the armed services. He returned from service in 1946 to re-enter private law practice.

In a special election to fill a sudden vacancy on the Austin City Council, Homer Thornberry's name was filed and he was elected by a large majority in 1946. In 1947 his majority was again large in the regular election. He has been serving as Mayor Pro Tem of Austin.

CIVIC ACTIVITIES: Board of Directors, Kiwanis Club; former Chairman, Church Board; former Superintendent of Sunday School; active in Boy Scout work; member of Executive Council, U. of T. Ex Students Association.

Congressional campaign
collateral, 1962.
Thornberry family collection.

conserve this valuable land, not spend huge sums to flood it." Next to a "Weak Bridge Ahead" traffic sign along Interstate 35, Thornberry detractors staked a handmade version that read, "Weak Congressman Ahead."[16]

The San Gabriel project's opponents were outnumbered, however. The *Williamson County Sun* endorsed Thornberry's legislation because of its flood prevention measures and its conservation of water that would otherwise flow into the Gulf of Mexico. Claiming that "every extra gallon of water that can be held for Texas use will be of inestimable value," the newspaper predicted that in the future "the people [of Texas] can look back to the 1950s and 1960s and consider the vision of Williamson County people who fought hard for what so long seemed an illusion."[17]

Thornberry successfully guided the San Gabriel dams bill through the House. Although he spent most Octobers in Texas, he made an impromptu trip to Washington that month in 1962 to ensure it cleared a conference committee after it had passed in the Senate. (In so doing, he was forced to miss a banquet honoring his wife as Austin's "Woman of the Year," for which Thornberry was slated to speak. His longtime friend and former state legislature desk mate Herman Jones filled in for him.) The bill was folded into an omnibus flood control and public works bill that President Kennedy signed later that month. Following its passage, hundreds of Georgetown residents turned out to shake Thornberry's hand at several informal evening parties at the San Gabriel Center. With the election looming the next month, the *Williamson County Sun* endorsed Thornberry's candidacy for reelection, calling him "a man to whom the Tenth Congressional District is deeply indebted."[18]

When Election Day finally arrived, the 42,667 votes cast in Travis County were the highest ever in any county in the state. Thornberry soundly defeated Dobbs, thanks to 59 percent of Tenth District voters. Williamson County, the epicenter of the dam controversy, handed Thornberry a resounding 70 percent of its votes.[19]

While triumphant, Thornberry knew that his first contested general election would likely be his last. Johnson had previously promised to facilitate his friend's appointment to a federal judiciary position in Texas, pending an opening, yet Democratic leadership was loath to lose a trusted ally on the Rules Committee. Massachusetts Democrat John McCormack, Sam Rayburn's immediate successor as House Speaker, told a reporter, "We need Thornberry here because of other legislation. We have a number of other legislative matters on which we'll need his help. He can be extremely helpful in maneuvering and operating to get the administration's program passed." A worthy replacement on Rules was ultimately found in fellow moderate, Texan John Young, clearing one obstacle to Thornberry's exit.[20]

The second obstacle was hurdled in June 1963, when eighty-four-year-old Judge Ewing Thomason announced he would abdicate his judgeship in the Western District of Texas in El Paso. Acting on his promise to the late Sam Rayburn, Kennedy appointed Thornberry as Thomason's successor, officially announced on July 9, 1963. Syndicated columnist David Lawrence criticized the nepotistic nature of it all. "How can there be confidence in the federal judiciary if judgeships become a matter of political patronage?" Lawrence wrote, adding that Thornberry's selection undermined the "importance of moral integrity in the exercise of governmental powers, especially when judges are to be appointed." In a letter to future Watergate prosecutor Leon Jaworski, Thornberry confided, "As long as I have been in public service, one would think I could accept unfair attacks such as the one made by David Lawrence, but the truth is I was rather hurt by it." Any bruises to his pride were nursed by endorsements from both the American Bar Association and State Bar of Texas.[21]

Thornberry expected the Senate confirmation process to last several days; instead, it took four minutes. The matter was the Senate's first order of business on July 15, and its members unanimously confirmed Thornberry in "record-breaking time."[22]

Roughly 1,500 Tenth District residents threw one final barbecue for Thornberry on September 26. Fittingly, it took place in Taylor, Texas, on the banks of the San Gabriel River, where Thornberry's dam project had just entered its construction phase.[23]

Jake Pickle, executive director of the State Democratic Executive Committee in Austin, ran for Thornberry's seat in a special election. The two men had known each other ever since Pickle served as an administrative aide to then senator Lyndon Johnson. Pickle considered Thornberry his "very close and dear friend and who I had visited with on a personal basis probably more when he came to Austin than anybody else." Jim Dobbs ran again as the opposition candidate. Republican House member Ed Foreman, who served Texas's Sixteenth District, heralded the contest as "one of the most important races of 1963," adding that it was "time to get rid of the go-along-get-along kind of congressmen like this district has had." Pickle would have to contend with hotspots in the district where conservative backlash against civil rights reforms was intensifying. Using the small town of Brenham as an example, Pickle later remarked, "That's the old, old South. Civil rights didn't fit them at all. I don't think I could have survived it if Johnson hadn't been president."[24]

Pickle would not only win the special election but would keep his job in Congress until his retirement in January 1995 at age eighty-one. Clearly, he would not buckle under the rigors of which Thornberry had forewarned him:

> There are a lot of people that think there's a lot of glamour to it, but you remember, this is damned tough . . . It's a mean job, and the fun of being a congressman is a thing of the past. Everything that is going to be done from now on, you've got to choose sides, you've got to choose friends, you're going to be publicized, and it's going to be difficult.

Pickle would serve on the Ways and Means Committee, Social Security Subcommittee, and the Oversight and Unemployment Compensation subcommittees. He became best known for his crucial drafting of social security reforms to ensure the program's solvency. During his first term, he discovered "how much the members loved and respected him [Thornberry]. He kept his word. . . . He was sincere and earnest . . . a man of his own conviction who was his own man in spite of his close ties to Rayburn and Johnson." In honor of his predecessor, Pickle procured federal funding in 1989 to establish the Homer Thornberry Judicial Building in downtown Austin.[25]

Thornberry was two cars behind President Kennedy when he was assassinated in Dallas on November 22, 1963. Thornberry shared the vehicle with Vice President Johnson; Special Assistant to the President Larry O'Brien; and Democratic House members George Mahon and Jack Brooks, both from Texas. After the two shots rang out, Thornberry "could sense that something was wrong. . . . We kept going along and got more and more concerned about it—saw people running in this area below the textbook depository." Thornberry and the other passengers swarmed around Johnson to protect him. They saw Kennedy's car peel out down the street, and Thornberry instructed the driver to follow. After consulting a passerby near the Trade Mart, where Kennedy had been scheduled to speak, they proceeded to Parkland Memorial Hospital. "We couldn't see or talk to anybody. And we got out of the car and went to the door and asked somebody if they had seen anything," recalled Thornberry. "I went in the hospital, but I just stood in the corridor. I didn't feel like I should get in the way." Thornberry joined Johnson, his wife Lady Bird, Brooks, presidential aide Kenny O'Donnell, and several Secret Service agents in a small waiting room that was curtained off. Almost all members of the president's cabinet were concurrently en route to Tokyo following a series of conferences in Honolulu and could not be reached due to the hospital's poor communications services.[26]

Johnson, who "was just praying that everything was going to be all right," instructed Thornberry to take detailed notes of the afternoon's proceedings, which reporters would use to reconstruct that day's tragic chain of events. At her husband's behest, Mrs. Johnson checked on the First Lady and the Connallys. "I don't think I ever saw anyone so much alone in my life," Lady Bird wrote about Mrs. Kennedy. "It was a very tense, quiet time," recalled Thornberry. "Then about that time, somebody came to President Johnson and said, 'Mr. President, the President is dead.'" Then, Thornberry recalled, Johnson turned to him and said, "This is a time for prayer if there ever was one, Homer."[27]

After consulting with the Secret Service, Johnson and a small entourage exited the hospital and loaded into two police cars. Johnson sat in the back seat between Thornberry and a Secret Service agent with House member Albert Thomas in front. Mrs. Johnson and Brooks boarded a second vehicle behind them. Dallas Chief of Police Jesse Curry began to activate the lead car's siren before Johnson motioned that it was unnecessary. The cars headed to Dallas Love Field airport to board Air Force One. Thornberry described the mood before takeoff as "very quiet, very calm. There was still a great feeling of shock on the part of people who realized what had happened. . . . But it was also busy, the president was busy. He was talking to people on the plane and getting his statement together, finding out where members of the cabinet were."[28]

Thornberry and Brooks urged Johnson to take the oath of office as quickly as possible. Doing so would assure a restless population of a swift, seamless transition in leadership. Johnson asked Thornberry if he would administer the oath, but because he himself had yet to be sworn in as a judge, he was unqualified to do so. Federal District Judge Sarah Hughes, a Kennedy appointee in Dallas, was enlisted instead. With his wife and a composed Jackie Kennedy on either side of him, Johnson, "as calm and

Left to right: US Representative Jack Brooks, Vice President Lyndon B. Johnson, and Thornberry exiting Parkland Hospital after President John F. Kennedy is pronounced dead, 1963. *AP photo.*

collected" as Thornberry had ever witnessed, took the oath just over an hour after President Kennedy had been pronounced dead. (In the famously publicized photograph of Johnson taking his oath, Thornberry's face was obstructed by Johnson's left shoulder. "Homer, you never could get in the damn picture," Johnson chided him.)[29]

Thornberry rarely left Johnson's side in the days that followed. He went with Johnson to church service on the day after the shooting and followed him home as well. Thornberry then accompanied Johnson to the Oval Office for the entirety of his first full day as president, arriving early in the morning and leaving late in the evening. Thornberry joined Johnson and White House aide Bill Moyers at a 9:30 a.m. meeting with Secretary of State Dean Rusk, presumably to discuss the war in Vietnam. Johnson allowed photographers in the room briefly to again assure the public of a stable transition. Thornberry would stay by Johnson's side over the next several days. In a letter to Mrs. Thornberry, President Johnson wrote:

Vice President Lyndon B. Johnson taking the presidential oath of office aboard Air Force One in 1963. Standing alongside him are Lady Bird Johnson and Jacqueline Kennedy; Thornberry is visible beyond Johnson's left shoulder. *LBJ Library photo by Cecil Stoughton.*

> Homer has been such a comfort and strength to me. I don't know how I am going to get along without him when he finally leaves Washington to join all of you in El Paso. . . . All I know is I need all of you so much and wish so fervently that the Thornberrys were back in Washington by my side where they have been so long.

Writing to his parents-in-law, Thornberry reflected, "I suppose we will never completely recover from the shock and sadness of the tragedy which occurred when our president was killed. We can be thankful he served as he did and that we have a wonderful president who must carry on. He is doing a magnificent job."[30]

Thornberry harbored mixed feelings about leaving Washington at such a critical juncture, but an overflowing docket of court cases in El Paso beckoned. A local attorney had written Thornberry that "the backlog of civil cases is rather severe. . . . There are also several criminal cases which have stacked up. . . . If your appointment is delayed any great length of time, it is anticipated that the backlog of both civil and criminal cases will

increase rather tremendously." A quick farewell tour came first, starting with supper at the White House. The next day, he was feted at the
Texas delegation's regular Wednesday luncheon, where Johnson presented
Thornberry with his judicial commission. Afterward, Johnson "walked
with me down to the basement to where a car would pick me up to take
me back, and he said to me, 'You know that I don't want you to leave.' . . .
I said, 'I know that, Mr. President, but after all that has happened—I've
been nominated and confirmed—I don't believe it would be proper for
me to turn around.'"[31]

Thornberry was sworn in as a federal district judge on December 21,
1963, in El Paso. The courtroom was packed with dozens of attendees,
which included members of the state's supreme court, district courts, and
civil appeals courts. "I wish my mother were alive to see this," remarked
Thornberry. "I now have a good, steady job."[32]

CHAPTER 10

Storm Center (1964-1966)

T HE THORNBERRYS CHARTED THEIR COURSE FOR WEST TEXAS
around the same time that Bob Dylan released "The Times They Are
A-Changin'." Indeed, in all the important ways, their destination would
be Washington's polar opposite. Situated toward the northern perimeter
of the expansive Chihuahuan Desert, El Paso seemed stuck in a perpetual
heat wave. Homer's and Eloise's longstanding enjoyment of an extensive
social network evaporated upon arrival, and their children had to adjust to
new schools. "I didn't know but one person, and that was Judge Thomason
[Thornberry's predecessor]," Thornberry said. "I thought to myself, 'What
kind of a situation am I going to be in?'" Many of their new neighbors
and several city officials went to great lengths to make the new arrivals
feel welcome, but xenophobia gripped certain pockets of the community.
"There were a lot of lawyers in that district who thought probably somebody from El Paso should have been appointed rather than some fellow off
in Austin," Thornberry said. "There was some uneasiness about going to El
Paso." Indeed, a large number of locals had lobbied fiercely on behalf of former State Bar of Texas President William Kerr, a native El Pasoan, when
Thomason's judgeship was vacated. When an outsider was appointed
instead, some residents published their frustrations in letters to the *El
Paso Times*. One characterized Thornberry as a "stranger" undeserving of
a lifetime position there. Another claimed that the city had been "kicked
in the teeth" by the White House.[1]

In addition to facing local resentment, Thornberry inherited a substantial criminal docket. Given El Paso's proximity to the Mexican border, most
cases concerned narcotics smuggling and illegal immigration. Thornberry
was also forewarned by Thomason that some Hispanic lawyers used

deceptive Spanish, and he recommended that Thornberry hire a competent bilingual court reporter. The only staff members at his disposal were law clerk Sam Sparks, who was the son of a family friend, and Olga Bredt, who previously managed Thornberry's district congressional office. As Sparks put it, "We walked into a beehive."[2]

Thornberry responded with customary grit and determination. He went straight to work after being sworn in, working long hours, including weekends, and taking a break only to spend Christmas Day with his family. He dispensed with any and all recreation in order to process cases in obscure towns like Pecos and Del Rio.[3]

Located 208 miles east of El Paso, Pecos had one of the largest civil dockets in the country at the time, according to Sparks. Thornberry and he travelled frequently, working six days out of every week, and typically stayed in rundown inns like the Brandon Hotel for $3.50 per night. Thornberry characterized his Washington lifestyle versus his new one as "the highs and lows of life." As a result of a surgical procedure that removed part of his lung, Thornberry was particularly susceptible to West Texas's occasionally extreme cold weather. He drank a glass of Scotch after most workdays for what he claimed were medicinal purposes.[4]

Thornberry's new line of work, while arduous, afforded its share of benefits. Two decades had elapsed since he had last practiced law, and he found casework refreshing. He was also relieved of some of the burdens of elected officialdom, noting, "You don't have to be concerned about what people say or do about you [as a judge]." He also noticed a significant drop-off in the amount of hostile mail from extreme right-wing groups. "It's been delightful so far," he told the *Austin American* after his first few weeks. "I never did get used to that snow and sleet in Washington."[5]

At each stop in his district, Thornberry informed trial lawyers up front that he expected an efficiently run courtroom and a minimum of theatrics. Bemused by Thornberry's no-nonsense approach, attorneys joked that he acted like he was still running for Congress. Nevertheless, his priority remained the expeditious processing of a caseload brimming with sham mortgages, oil and gas issues, and workers' compensation disputes. Until Congress later relieved the federal court system of the latter, the hefty El Paso docket required outside assistance from judges like Sarah Hughes, who had sworn Johnson in aboard Air Force One.[6]

Thornberry strove for absoluteness with each ruling in the same fashion he approached each vote in Congress. He paced the hallways of his home at nights, wrestling with the legal and emotional implications of certain decisions. "It tears at you," he said. "Society must be protected, and wrongdoers must be punished as a deterrent to others, but it's always hard to separate persons from their families . . . to send people to prison." Interpreting ambiguously written laws presented additional challenges:

> At times it's a little hard to know just what Congress had in mind. . . . For me to use my own personal ideas of what should have been done was not appropriate. I had to stay by just exactly the plain meaning of the act or of the Constitution if that was what was before us.

According to Sparks, Thornberry was reversed only once by a higher court during his stint in West Texas. That instance was a guilty verdict he rendered in a bank robbery case, which the appellate court overturned after finding the defendant clinically insane.[7]

Thornberry had been at his new post for less than three months when Judge Ben Rice, a fellow district judge who had mostly served Austin and Waco since 1945, passed away at age seventy four. President Johnson solicited Thornberry's interest in returning to Austin to succeed Rice, which triggered mixed feelings. "Much of what I am I owe to the people of that area," Thornberry once wrote. "There I have personal ties and friendships which few men are privileged to experience. For more than a quarter of a century its people have loyally supported me in public service." Then again, he was loath to uproot his children again so soon after resettling in El Paso. "They weren't sure that their lives weren't going to get torn up again," recalled Thornberry. Johnson urged Thornberry to make the move because he considered Austin's concentration of state government litigation to hold greater importance. Thomason advised him, "That's where you've been elected by the people. . . . You need to go back." Thornberry ultimately concurred.[8]

A liberal outlier in Texas, Austin had roughly kept pace with the civil rights reforms coming out of Washington. Between 1964 and 1966, the Austin City Council created the Austin Equal Citizenship Corporation, Austin Equal Employment Opportunity Commission, and Austin Human Rights Commission, which collectively conducted outreach and research on preventing racial discrimination, processed complaints of racial prejudice, and recommended general policies for adoption by the council. In 1968, Austin would become the first city in Texas to pass a fair housing ordinance forbidding discrimination in property sales or rentals. But on the whole, integration was slow to develop. Following *Brown*, 104 black students enrolled in UT's entering class but mostly kept to themselves in East Austin, apart from the white majority. The Forty Acres Club, a private UT faculty club, had long remained segregated until President Johnson paid an unannounced visit in 1963 with several Washington aides, including assistant press secretary Andrew Hatcher, who was black. On the following day, the club announced its new policy of racial acceptance.[9]

Austin's legal sphere was not immune to discriminatory policies. According to Thornberry law clerk Joe Horrigan, Judge Rice had forbidden Andrew Jefferson, the black chief assistant to the US attorney for the Western District of Texas, from handling trials unless the defendant was also black. "Judge Thornberry put a stop to that immediately," recalled Horrigan. Thornberry also confronted the Travis County Bar Association when he learned that black attorneys were denied membership. "I want it changed," he told two bar board members over the phone. "I don't want to create a public spectacle out of it, and that's what it would be if I resigned and stated why I resigned." When the bar failed to comply, Thornberry summoned its directors into his chambers and convinced them to let their members decide the issue; they ultimately voted to lift the ban.[10]

Another hot topic pertained to conscientious objectors to the Vietnam War. Refusing to comply with the military draft, they roamed public spaces and riled local authorities. Most judges had indulged their wishes to be jailed as martyrs to their cause. But Thornberry saw little societal benefit in incarcerating nonviolent protestors at the taxpayers' expense. He thus concocted a more peaceable solution that entailed sentencing disruptive protestors to probation instead, prompting most to opt for joining the military in noncombat roles.[11]

President Johnson had long-term aspirations for Thornberry, and he wasted little time advancing the next part of his plan. Johnson had been unsuccessful in convincing Thornberry to return to Washington and serve on the powerful US Court of Claims, which heard claims against the federal government until its abolishment in 1982. As an alternative, he looked to move Thornberry to the Court of Appeals for the Fifth Circuit, whose jurisdiction was composed of six former confederate states including Texas.

"[The Fifth Circuit] is a different kind of court. It's hard, and I'm doing fine," Thornberry told Johnson over the phone. "You can find some other judge that can do a better job." Johnson made a second overture, which Thornberry again rebuffed: "Mr. President, I told you, I said I was not interested. I don't think I'm even really qualified for it." Johnson retorted, "You don't have any ambition." Thornberry countered, "Ambition is not what you use to go into court." The conversation ended there, but it spoke volumes about their differing valuations in power and glory.[12]

A third overture to convince Thornberry was made over the phone by Attorney General Ramsey Clark. "The president is really interested in appointing you to this court," said Ramsey. "He's the President of the United States, and I don't think you ought to turn him down." Thornberry responded, "I tell you what. If the president appoints me to serve on the court, I'll serve on it. I'm not applying for it. But I'll do the best I can."[13]

Senator Yarborough complained that his district was overdue for a native to receive such ennoblement. "Part of the Western District of Texas feels greatly aggrieved," Yarborough wrote Johnson in May of 1965. "I pledged over and over in the campaign of last fall that I would recommend for the next appointment . . . only persons from the Western part of the District." Johnson's commitment to elevating Thornberry's position, however, was ironclad.[14]

Thornberry officially joined the Fifth Circuit at the Johnsons' ranch in Stonewall, Texas, on June 3, 1965. "We didn't make it a big affair," claimed the humble new appellate judge. Roughly twenty relatives and friends, including President Johnson, attended the ceremony. Thornberry was sworn in by Travis County District Judge Herman Jones, his former law partner and desk mate in the Texas Legislature. In a brief address, the president stated:

> We hated to see him leave the legislative halls, but we are glad to see him preside in the temples of justice because we know that there is no more courageous person, no better and finer human being, and no man with a greater sense of justice and fairness and feeling of equality for all human beings, wherever they live, whatever their color, or whatever their religion, than Homer Thornberry.[15]

The Court of Appeals for the Fifth Circuit, one of the nine original circuits, was created in 1891 by an act of Congress to review appeals from federal district courts in Texas, Louisiana, Mississippi, Alabama, Georgia, and Florida. Two judges were appointed to the court initially, with additional

Thornberry, standing alongside President Lyndon B. Johnson, being sworn in to the Fifth Circuit Court of Appeals by Judge Herman Jones at the LBJ ranch, Stonewall, TX, 1965. *Thornberry family collection.*

judgeships created over time. Its caseload had historically gravitated toward maritime law because of activities in the region's Atlantic ports and the Gulf of Mexico. The court's bench had just increased by two members in 1961 following Chief Judge Elbert Parr Tuttle's urgent request for reinforcements. President Kennedy signed the Omnibus Judgeship Bill on May 20 of that year, adding seventy-one new positions to federal courts across the country, including the two requested for the Fifth. By then the Fifth Circuit was struggling to stay current with its burgeoning caseload as the South's population rose to just under 30 million, an increase of 33 percent since 1950 (the national average was closer to 25 percent). The Fifth was also anticipating a tidal wave of school desegregation cases in the contentious aftermath of *Brown*.[16]

Even before acquiring Thornberry, the Fifth Circuit leaned progressive on civil rights matters, quite the opposite inclination of most of the region's elected officials. Among its nine judges were "The Four," who included Tuttle and fellow civil rights reformists John Brown, Richard Rives, and John Minor Wisdom. Outgoing Circuit member Ben Cameron, a segregationist, crafted their collective nickname as an unflattering reference to the biblical Four Horsemen of the Apocalypse. Like many southern leaders, Cameron considered segregation a matter best guided by states' rights, which he considered "the bedrock of our constitutional system." In addition to The Four, existing Fifth members included Griffin Bell, Walter Gewin, Warren Leroy Jones, and James Coleman, who replaced Cameron at the same time that Thornberry was appointed. Civil rights leaders grew alarmed over Coleman's nomination for fear he would follow in his predecessor's footsteps. Their concern was warranted: as Mississippi's governor from 1956 to 1960, Coleman had committed black school teacher Clennon King to a state mental institution for trying to enroll at the University of Mississippi. A telegram from James Farmer, the national director of the Congress of Racial Equality, urged President Johnson not to appoint such an "ardent segregationist" to the bench, as it would represent "a serious setback to the Great Society." Johnson proceeded regardless, reasoning that replacing one conservative Mississippian with another would mitigate white reprisal.[17]

Between 1950 and 1960, the court's docket expanded from 408 appeals to 577, an incredible 41 percent jump. By the summer of 1963, the docket had reached 874. The average appellate judge handled sixty-nine cases a year versus ninety-seven for every Fifth Circuit member. By the time Thornberry came on board, the Fifth Circuit had the largest backlog of civil rights cases in the country and had become the busiest appellate court in American history.[18]

One of Thornberry's first cases concerned the constitutionality of the poll tax in Texas's state and local elections. The poll tax's origins dated back to the late 1800s, when the South witnessed resurgent conservatism, weakening populism, and proliferating Jim Crow laws. In order to further disenfranchise former slaves, many former Confederate states (and a few others) ignored the recently passed Fourteenth and Fifteenth Amendments, which guaranteed "privileges and immunities" and the right to vote to all US citizens. Federal enforcement of these two amendments was lax; furthermore, in 1883, the US Supreme Court struck down the Civil Rights Act of 1875, which had forbidden discrimination in public spaces. In addition to the poll tax, voting restrictions included literacy tests, grandfather clauses, and whites-only primaries. Thirteen years later, in the landmark

Plessy v. Ferguson, the high court upheld the constitutionality of state laws *requiring* racial segregation in public facilities—the infamous "separate but equal" ruling. In 1898, *Williams v. Mississippi* determined that states were permitted to employ poll taxes and literacy tests on the grounds that they applied to all citizens, a ruling upheld in *Breedlove v. Suttles* (1937) and *Pirtle v. Brown* (1941). Congress made periodic attempts to abolish the poll tax in state elections, but none were successful because of opposition from states' rights advocates. Franklin Roosevelt had publicly shamed conservative members of his party as upholders of "Polltaxia" during his presidency. He meanwhile surreptitiously pushed for poll tax abolishment on a state-by-state basis, but aside from Florida's repeal of the tax in 1937, his efforts were in vain. Even those blacks who paid the tax were often flunked by southern registrars on literacy tests or risked physical harm. An early version of the Voting Rights Act of 1965 included a provision prohibiting the application of poll taxes in state elections, but it was ultimately dropped in favor of a directive that the US attorney general challenge its use.[19]

Texas adopted its poll tax in 1902 and began restricting primaries to whites only in 1923. (The Supreme Court later eliminated white primaries in *Smith v. Allwright* in 1944, but the poll tax persisted in several states.) Texas's tax was born from a constitutional amendment overwhelmingly approved by voters (200,650 to 107,748). This outcome was attributed to the state's racist elements, weak populist presence, and relatively small black population. The tax ranged between $1.50 to $1.75, a prohibitive amount for many among the working classes and poor, which disproportionately affected blacks and Hispanics. Proponents of the tax justified its need as a revenue source for the state's public school system, when actually its contribution was ludicrously small. In the fiscal year ending August 31, 1954, poll tax revenue provided less than 1 percent of total public school funding in Texas—and no more than 2 percent in Alabama, Arkansas, Mississippi, and Virginia.[20]

Every Confederate state adopted its own poll tax around the same time as Texas, with slight variations in rates and payment deadlines (see Table 2). In Louisiana, the number of registered black voters had sharply declined from 130,344 in 1897 to a miniscule 730 in 1910. "The Negro should never be trusted with the ballot," Mississippi Governor James Vardaman stated in 1907. "He is different from the white man. He is congenitally unqualified to exercise the most responsible duty of citizenship." In 1947, the President's Committee on Civil Rights, created by President Truman, released a report titled *To Secure These Rights,* which concluded that in the 1944 presidential election, the poll tax contributed to a 10 percent voter turnout in seven states versus 49 percent in states without it. In 1962, Congress would pass the Twenty-Fourth Amendment, lifting poll taxes on federal elections, but five southern states—Arkansas, Louisiana, Mississippi, Texas, and Virginia—continued to impose the tax in state elections.[21]

Thornberry would help determine the fate of Texas's sixty-year-old poll tax in February 1966 in the case *United States v. Texas*. He was assigned as the lead member of a three-judge panel that included fellow Fifth Circuit Judge John Brown and Texas Western District Judge Adrian Spears. In 1949, Thornberry's first year in Congress, he had voted against repealing the poll tax in federal elections. Like Johnson and Rayburn, Thornberry had initially opposed major civil rights legislation partly to appease his constituent base and partly because he felt it was a subject that states should handle themselves. His stance shifted over time, beginning with his vote in favor of the 1957 Civil Rights Act's final version and for its 1960 follow-up. He was also among a handful of southern Democrats in 1962 to vote for the Twenty-Fourth Amendment banning the poll tax in federal elections.

Acting on the Civil Rights Act of 1964's directive to prosecute states using a poll tax as a precondition to voting, the US attorney general's office, serving as plaintiff in *United States v. Texas*, charged that the tax violated both the Fourteenth Amendment's Equal Protection Clause ("No State shall make or enforce any law which shall abridge the privileges or immunities of citizens of the United States . . .") and due process clause (". . . nor shall any State deprive any person of life, liberty, or property, without due process of law"). The attorney general also claimed that the tax violated the Fifteenth Amendment's prohibition on denying suffrage based on "race, color, or previous condition of servitude (such as slavery)." Moreover, the plaintiff argued that racial disparity in educational and economic opportunities made payment of the poll tax more burdensome for blacks, particularly in the context of their long-standing social and political suppression and ten other southern states' use of the tax to dissuade blacks from voting. The plaintiff cited a 12 percent disparity between the percentages of eligible white voters who paid the tax (57.3 percent) and eligible black voters who did likewise (45.3 percent).[22]

TABLE 2. Southern States with Poll Taxes on State Elections, Post-Civil War Era

STATE	LEGISLATIVE RATIFICA- TION YEAR	RATE (GENERAL ELECTIONS)[a]	PAYMENT DATES	POLL TAX IN STATE ELEC- TIONS REPEALED	RESCINDING AUTHORITY
Alabama	1901	$1.50	Oct. 1-Feb. 1 before election	1966	US Supreme Court (*Harper v. Virginia Board of Elections*)
Arkansas	1893, 1908[b]	$1.00	Jan. 1-July 1 of year before election	1905, 1964	Legislature (constitutional amendment approved by voters)
Florida	1889	$1.00	at least 30 days before election	1937	Legislature (constitutional amendment approved by voters)
Georgia	1877, 1908[c]	$1.00	by April 1 before election	1908, 1945	Legislature (constitutional amendment approved by voters)
Louisiana	1899	$1.00	by Dec. 31 before election	1934	Legislature (constitutional amendment approved by voters)
Mississippi	1891	$2.00	by Feb. 1 before election	1966	US Supreme Court (*Harper v. Virginia Board of Elections*)
North Carolina	1902	$1.29	by March 1 before election	1919	Legislature (constitutional amendment approved by voters)
South Carolina	1895	$1.00	at least six months before election	1949	Legislature (constitutional amendment approved by voters)
Tennessee	1890	$1.00	None	1953	Legislature (constitutional amendment approved by voters)
Texas	1902	$1.50	by Feb. 1 before election	1966	Fifth Circuit Court of Appeals (*US v. Texas*)
Virginia	1876, 1902[d]	$1.50	at least six months before election	1882, 1966	US Supreme Court (*Harper v. Virginia Board of Elections*)

TABLE 2

SOURCES: Jerrold G. Rusk, *A Statistical History of the American Electorate* (Washington, DC: CQ Press, 2001), 33-34; *Harper v. Virginia Board of Elections*, 383 US 363 (1966); *United States v. State of Texas*, 252 F. Supp. 234 (W.D. Tex. 1966).

NOTE: Other states, such as Kentucky and California, implemented a poll tax during parts of the twentieth century, but it had nothing to do with voting or discrimination against the poor or minorities. A blanket tax on voting, referred to as a head tax in these states, was instead tacked onto county tax bills. The state of Vermont implemented a poll tax in the amount of $2.00 (with no payment in advance required) from 1917 until its repeal in 1966 through a state constitutional amendment, but it was not considered discriminatory on account of the state's consistently high turnout rates.

[a] In some states, including Mississippi, Texas, and Tennessee, surcharges ranging from $0.25 to $1.00 were applied in certain cities, counties, and towns. The elderly, disabled, and military veterans were commonly exempted from the tax. Women were required to pay the tax once the Twentieth Amendment was ratified. Some states' poll taxes were cumulative (AL, GA , VA, and TN). That is, unpaid taxes were assessed retroactively based on how long an eligible voter had resided in the state. This practice further disenfranchised the poor and minorities.

[b] Arkansas's 1893 poll tax was declared invalid by a circuit judge on a technicality in 1905. The state legislature proposed a different poll tax amendment in 1907 that was approved by voters in 1908.

[c] Georgia's 1877 poll tax was replaced with a cumulative version in 1908.

[d] In 1902, Virginia reintroduced a poll tax with an "old soldier" clause, which excused war veterans and their descendants from paying.

As the defendant, the Texas attorney general's office countered that there was no evidence showing the poll tax to be discriminatory or violative of the Fifteenth Amendment. The defendant's case rested on a 1961 report by former US Attorney General Robert F. Kennedy that the United States Commission on Civil Rights did not receive a single complaint about voting discrimination in Texas and that the percentage of blacks who were registered to vote in Texas was roughly equivalent to the percentage of whites (the plaintiff disputed these estimates). The Texas attorney general's office also showed that neither the Constitution nor Congress could deny the right of states to levy taxes of any form. Furthermore, the defense called the $1.75 tax a "minute sum" costing "less than five cents a week in order to pay the tax" and brazenly contended that a person who could not afford the fee "is not intelligent enough or competent enough to manage the affairs of the government." The defense also cited the brusque Judge A. W. Terrell, who drafted many of the state's early election laws in the late 1800s. Terrell had called for "a system of election laws which will tend to diminish the depraved, the purchasable, and the reckless class of voters, and to increase the power of the patriotic, the interested, and the thoughtful class."[23]

In a plainspoken decision, Thornberry ruled that Texas's poll tax was un-
deniably unconstitutional. While detractors might have ascribed the former
politician's decision to judicial activism, Thornberry's explanation thoroughly
and dispassionately distilled the merits and demerits of each side's arguments.
Applying logic instead of moralizing about race, he rejected the plaintiff's argument that the 12 percent discrepancy in white and black poll tax payers
was a sufficient indicator of discrimination. Nor did he detect any evidence in
the last twenty years that showed the tax to be an overt means of singling out
blacks. Yet he disputed the defendant's argument that a poll tax was a necessary
registry device, given the availability of other options used in the forty-six
states without the tax. He also found it odd that for such a purportedly vital
source of revenue, it amounted to a voluntary tax on citizens of a limited age
range and did not apply universally. And rather than challenge the defense's
claim that $1.75 was a nominal amount, Thornberry instead zeroed in on its
claim that those who could not afford it were not "competent;" he pointed
out that the stated purpose of the tax had never been to "test" the intelligence
of voters. In the end, Thornberry rejected the plaintiff's claim that the poll
tax violated the Fourteenth Amendment's Equal Protection Clause but agreed
that it did violate the due process clause. He concluded simply, "If the State
of Texas placed a tax on the right to speak at the rate of one dollar and seventy-five cents per year, no court would hesitate to strike it down. . . . Yet
the poll tax as enforced in Texas is a tax on the equally important right to
vote." The Fifth's ruling would presage by six weeks the US Supreme Court's
decision in *Harper v. Virginia Board of Elections*, which abolished the poll tax in
any election in all states. "I don't think it's immodest for me to say [President
Johnson] was rather proud that I was the author of that opinion," Thornberry
later recalled.[24]

Total voter registration increased by roughly 13.7 percent in Texas following both *United States v. Texas* and the Voting Rights Act of 1965, while
actual turnout increased by a more modest 4.1 percent (see Table 3). The
somewhat lackluster latter figure can be partially ascribed to Texas's overall
historically low voter participation, as it has regularly ranked in the bottom
five states in that respect. In addition to voter suppression techniques like the
poll tax and whites-only primaries, historians have attributed Texas's weak
turnout figures to a restrictive annual voter registration (which was eliminated in 1971), property ownership requirements in certain localities for

TABLE 3. Registration and Turnout Percentages of Voting-Age Populations among States Whose Poll Taxes on State Elections Were Abolished between the 1964 and 1968 General Elections.

STATE	VOTER REGISTRATION		VOTER TURNOUT	
	1964	1968	1964	1968
Alabama	N/A	69.7%	36.0%	52.7%
Mississippi	N/A	63.1%	33.9%	53.3%
Texas	50.7%	64.4%	44.6%	48.7%
Vermont	90.8%	88.1%	70.3%	64.1%
Virginia	51.4%	55.6%	41.1%	50.1%

SOURCE: US Federal Election Commission[25]

some elections (eliminated in the 1970s), apathy caused by long-standing conservative hegemony, disinterest among the poor and uneducated, and large minority populations—particularly Hispanics—which tend to vote in fewer numbers.[26]

Three months after striking down his home state's poll tax, Thornberry would write the decision in another heated civil rights case, this time involving discrimination within the judicial system. In *Davis v. Davis*, the appellant, a black male convicted of first-degree murder, claimed that his conviction was rigged by systematic exclusion of blacks in grand and petit jury selection; a Louisiana district court had ruled against him. In *Scott v. Walker*, the Fifth Circuit had unanimously overturned a ruling by the same court and ruled en banc (all court members participated) that a jury commission's racial bias favoring whites in its selection of "qualified" jurors discriminated against blacks and was therefore unconstitutional. As he did in *United States v. Texas*, Thornberry wrote the lead opinion in *Davis* because Chief Justice John Brown sensed his new colleague's keen interest in civil rights matters. During the *Davis* proceedings, the typically unflappable Thornberry upbraided the defense for its poor preparation and ordered the state's assistant attorney general, who claimed to only work part-time, to find a more knowledgeable replacement. As with the *Scott* case, the

Fifth unanimously endorsed Thornberry's written opinion in *Davis v. Davis* that the petit and grand jury selection process in Louisiana's Acadia Parish was "constitutionally deficient." In both of the cases, the appellants were granted retrials under a reformed jury-selection procedure.[27]

In view of Thornberry's rulings in his first civil rights cases, the *New York Times* editorial staff depicted him as a fixture at the "storm center of the fight over equal rights for the Negro."[28]

The 1960s witnessed unprecedented civil rights gains that were precipitated by all three branches of the federal government. These included President Johnson's leadership on the Civil Rights Act of 1964 and Voting Rights Act of 1965, Congress's passage of the Twenty-Fourth Amendment, and the judiciary's abolishment of poll taxes in state elections. The Civil Rights Act of 1964 was especially noteworthy in comparison to its feeble predecessors. Among its provisions, the 1964 act prohibited racial and sexual discrimination in most public facilities and by employers and unions; withheld funds from federally supported programs that practiced discrimination; created the Equal Employment Opportunity Commission; and outlawed segregation in the workplace, schools, and public facilities. Roughly 94 percent of the 6 million voting blacks would cast their ballots for Johnson later that year.

At a private gathering in Austin's historic Driskill hotel following the announcement of the election results, President Johnson wondered aloud why Jake Pickle, the victor in the race for Thornberry's former Congressional seat, had fared better in his district than he himself had. Thornberry quipped that Pickle was simply more "favorably known" than Johnson. The jab drew howls from the group, which included Thornberry's wife and Governor Connally. Johnson was reportedly unamused.[29]

As they had with previous civil rights advances, white conservatives struck back. Until the mid-1950s, the two major parties shared virtually the same platform on civil rights, but the Democrats' internal conflicts swiftly changed that. After signing the Civil Rights Act of 1964, President Johnson famously told aide Bill Moyers, "We have lost the South for a generation." The Democratic South's dissolution, which could be traced back to Hubert Humphrey's daring pro-civil rights sermon at the 1948 primary, reached the point of no return when outspoken racist South

Carolina senator Strom Thurmond defected to the Republican Party in 1964. George Wallace soon left the party too to become the American Independent Party's presidential candidate in the 1968 race. Former Johnson protégé and Texas governor John Connally, who clashed with Johnson over the 1964 Civil Rights Act, would turn Republican in 1973.

Although Johnson won reelection in 1964 by a landslide, conservatives scored a consolation prize in the South. The Republican candidate, Arizona Senator Barry Goldwater, ran an overtly anti-civil rights campaign as part of his southern strategy to attract disaffected whites. He carried five southern states, an astounding feat for a Republican candidate at the time. The same election saw organized efforts by Texas Republicans to intimidate racial and ethnic minorities and deter them from voting. Texas's political transition was already underway following the shocking 1961 election of Johnson's successor in the Senate, John Tower, who was the first Republican senator elected by a former Confederate state since Reconstruction. Tower spearheaded conservative opposition to the 1964 Civil Rights Act and the 1965 Voting Rights Act. He was also the only Republican in the Senate to vote against ratifying the Twenty-Fourth Amendment.[30]

The South may have lost the Civil War, but resistance to civil rights for blacks remained unrelenting one century after the fact.

CHAPTER 11

Desegregation Redux (1966-1971)

A LTHOUGH SOUTHERN EDUCATION SYSTEMS WERE REQUIRED
to desegregate "with all deliberate speed" per *Brown* and its subsequent decree *Brown II*, the compliance rate over the ensuing decade was abysmal. A 1964 study conducted by the Department of Health, Education, and Welfare (HEW) showed only 2.14 percent of southern black children attending predominantly white schools in the ten years since the *Brown* ruling. *Brown* and *Brown II* had struck down segregation in principle, but they stopped short of ordering forced integration. The post-*Brown* "freedom of choice" mantra ostensibly permitted students to attend any school, but in actuality few children of either race selected schools dominated by a race different from their own. Furthermore, the court had provided little guidance on how to properly self-administer desegregation. It declined to set deadlines for compliance and relegated responsibility to uncooperative southern school authorities. The Supreme Court delegated oversight to district courts, many of which wound up reinforcing segregation, sometimes in defiance of circuit courts as well. Indeed, the Supreme Court had even refused to hear an appeal of a district court's 1963 ruling that had consented to the Gary, Indiana, school system's use of de facto segregation. Meanwhile, white parents enrolled their children in private schools or fled to suburbs rather than let them share classrooms with minorities. In sum, the school districts and white families alike found ways to circumvent *Brown*, and the court system had done little in response.[1]

Southern lawmakers persisted in rallying scholastic disobedience of *Brown*. The governors of Alabama, Arkansas, and Mississippi ordered law enforcement to physically obstruct black students from entering whites-only schools. Mississippi senator James Eastland had accused the Supreme

Court of trampling on the US Constitution and urged his constituents to reject *Brown*: "You are not required to obey any court which passes out such a ruling," Eastland announced to a crowd of followers. "In fact, you are obligated to defy it." In Texas, although the majority of residents supported desegregation, state legislators thwarted its implementation through a 1957 act requiring a referendum approval in each school district as a prerequisite to freedom of choice.[2]

The institution of segregation unquestionably limited accessibility to adequate educational opportunities for blacks. A *Newsweek* survey in 1963 showed that 59 percent of black parents believed their children received worse educations than whites. It also found that one out of five black families included a child who dropped out of high school, and one-third of these had done so for financial reasons. Numerous studies over time have shown that impaired access to a quality education is correlated with poverty, substandard housing, and limited social mobility. In *Brown*, the Supreme Court recognized that racially divided schooling also had detrimental psychological effects on the disaffected: "The policy of separating the races is usually interpreted as denoting the inferiority of the negro group. A sense of inferiority affects the motivation of a child to learn. Segregation with the sanction of law, therefore, has a tendency to [retard] the educational and mental development of negro children." In other words, segregation was not only unconstitutional, it was dehumanizing. "Preachers and writers have been preaching and writing for generations that we should do certain things for our brothers, and they have heard but not heeded," said liberal Fifth Circuit member Irving Goldberg, a recent Johnson appointee and Thornberry's closest friend on the court. "And that's where the courts come in."[3]

Practically, the Fifth assumed the active role of desegregating the South, a mantle that put its members at great personal risk. Race-related violence persisted, and the long-dormant Ku Klux Klan had reawakened after *Brown*. Certain members of the Fifth—particularly The Four (liberal judges Elbert Tuttle, John Brown, Richard Rives, and John Minor Wisdom)—received abusive phone calls and hate mail, and their families were harassed. Several received death threats. During a visit to the cemetery where their only son was buried, Judge Rives and his wife arrived to find his grave completely desecrated, an atrocity almost certainly motivated by racism. (If Thornberry received any threats, he did not disclose them to family members or peers. Living in Texas probably ensured greater personal safety than his

US Fifth Circuit Court of Appeals members, 1965; front row, left to right: John R. Brown, Richard Rives, Elbert P. Tuttle, Warren Jones; back row, left to right: Homer Thornberry, Walter Gewin, John M. Wisdom, Griffin Bell, James Coleman. *Courtesy Library, United States Court of Appeals, Fifth Judicial Circuit, New Orleans, Louisiana.*

colleagues from other southern states enjoyed.) But the Fifth's mission to effect the demise of "separate but equal" would not be derailed.[4]

Cases concerning desegregation in schools had begun trickling up to the Fifth Circuit around the time of Thornberry's arrival. He later characterized the environment:

It was a tough, tough area, a tough time. It was not easy to handle those cases because they were so unpopular. We had lawyers clamoring for rehearings. We had to have en banc sessions of the court, which required all judges of the court to meet. And there was not unanimity about these cases then. And it was not a pleasant experience to have people be concerned about civil rights, particularly in school cases.

A number of factors made school cases particularly thorny. First, these cases, which originated in the lower courts, were often decided by obstructionist district judges who displayed no interest in integrating the races. Second, many school desegregation plans that were presented to the Fifth lacked uniformity and were found to be "woefully inadequate" in addressing specific administrative problems. Third, most judges lacked expertise on the nuances of education systems, making remediation all the more arduous. Last and certainly not least, albeit empowered by *Brown*, the Fifth had received no external direction between the time of its first school desegregation ruling in 1956 (*Brown v. Rippy*) and the juncture a decade later when Congress and HEW finally got involved. Further, the Supreme Court never fully clarified the scope of obligations for lower district courts and school officials, nor did it establish desired ratios for student racial balance.[5]

The judges of the Fifth would need to be self-reliant, innovative, and tenacious in developing unitary school systems across the South. "We did a whole lot of winging it," recalled Joe Horrigan, Thornberry's law clerk during his first years on the Fifth. "That's where someone with [Thornberry's] approach was necessary." As of 1966, the Fifth had processed forty-one school cases—some of them more than once—while district courts had heard 128, all without uniform standards in place. Much work yet remained. At this time, Texas, at 17 percent, led all southern states in the percentage of black children enrolled in white schools. The middle of the pack—Arkansas, Florida, and Georgia—ranged between 1 and 10 percent. Alabama, Louisiana, and Mississippi brought up the rear with less than 1 percent.[6]

The landmark decision in *United States v. Jefferson County Board of Education* on December 29, 1966, which was heard by a three-judge panel that included Thornberry, marked the first time the court laid out a set of specific criteria by which schools must abide in crafting and executing desegregation plans. The new rules were informed both by the new "belated but invaluable" HEW standards and by pertinent court cases at all levels; they also fell within the scope of the 1964 Civil Rights Act. The Fifth's many criteria to achieve desegregation included (but were not limited to) the following:

- Student and teacher mixed-race ratios should meet those set forth by the HEW guidelines: 15 to 18 percent of a school system's pupil population should enroll in desegregated schools (a threshold considered "modest" by opinion author John Wisdom);

- HEW as well as local black and white school authorities should be consulted before proposing desegregation plans and transportation policies to the courts;

- Students would retain the right of transfer from segregated to mixed-race classrooms at other schools;

- Students should not be discriminated against or discouraged from participation in school activities such as organized sports;

- The proportions of teachers' races at a given school should approximate that of the entire school system;

- Racial discrimination in the hiring of new faculty members was prohibited;

- Beyond the classroom, segregation would not be permitted in school services, facilities, activities, and programs;

- The quality of schools should be equalized such that existing inferior institutions (which had been predominantly black) would be closed in favor of mandatory annual freedom of choice plans;

- Sensible geographic zones and new transportation routes should be established to deliver blacks and whites from segregated neighborhoods to integrated schools; and

- The courts would have the last word on determining the adequacy of a school system's desegregation plan.

The newfound clarity and uniformity established by *Jefferson* had at last explicated *Brown II*'s order to precipitate desegregation, even if not "with all deliberate speed" as originally intended. Thornberry's ruling in support of Wisdom's definitive opinion would prove vital in the case, for the third member of the *Jefferson* panel, Mississippi District Judge William Harold Cox, was an established obstructionist and dissented as expected.[7]

While useful, the HEW guidelines alone were not sufficient to make the average desegregation plan stand on its own two feet. On one hand, per Wisdom's opinion in *Jefferson*, "The guidelines present the best system available for uniform application, and the best aid to the courts in evaluating the validity of a school desegregation plan and the progress made under that plan." On the other hand, Wisdom continued, the HEW standards "have the vices of all administrative policies established unilaterally without a hearing." The guidelines' limitations were evident in *Davis v. Board of School Commissioners of Mobile County* (March 12, 1968), whose three-judge panel also included Thornberry. The case marked the second time the Fifth had reviewed the Mobile County school district's desegregation plan after rejecting its first attempt two years before. The school district contended that its new plan now met the HEW guidelines. The guidelines required districts to have between 15 and 18 percent of their student populations enrolled in desegregated schools; Mobile claimed to far exceed the minimum with 38 percent. However, as Thornberry's opinion read, "The percentage of total students in biracial schools is superficially acceptable, but beneath the surface the picture is not so good." In *Mobile*, Thornberry applied an important takeaway from *Jefferson* that "school desegregation can first be measured quantitatively, using percentages as a rough rule of thumb, but ultimately must be measured qualitatively." Although the Mobile public school system was technically in compliance with the HEW standards, the fact that only 6.5 percent of the county's black children were receiving biracial education flunked the court's qualitative assessment. Far fewer were enrolled in schools with more than a handful of white students. Moreover, the district had failed to explain the rationale behind its redrawn geographic zones, which required "objective criteria such as landmarks and safety factors" in order to create a "unitary racially nondiscriminatory system." Like many others, the case was remanded to a lower court to try again.[8]

Some districts took more extreme actions to circumvent the court system and HEW guidelines. Such measures included closing entire schools rather than integrating them, delegating control of public schools to governors or state legislators to dodge court orders, subsidizing enrollment in segregated schools through tuition grants, denying state funds to integrated public schools, criminalizing teaching or attendance at integrated schools, and firing teachers who supported desegregation efforts. One school superintendent objected to a Fifth desegregation ruling on the dubious grounds that it did not include a definition for "Negro." Such subterfuges had been partially curtailed by the "carrot and stick" effect of the 1964 Civil Rights Act's Title VI, which revoked federal funds to public schools and other programs that practiced forms of discrimination, including segregation. Further, the 1964 Civil Rights Act empowered the court system to have the final say in these unprecedented desegregation cases, resulting in the Fifth's pioneering use of injunctions in civil rights cases. (Injunctions empowered judges to render appropriate remedies in the absence of a jury and enabled citizens to bring suits.) Whereas the injunction had been abused by the courts in the early twentieth century to quash progressive legislation, the Fifth would repurpose it to facilitate civil rights rulings.[9]

On top of the controversial nature of school cases, their sheer quantity threatened to overwhelm the nine members of the Fifth. The court thus began consolidating cases concerning districts that were in close proximity. Some school districts objected to getting bundled, arguing that each district had unique issues that should be addressed separately. At least one Fifth judge agreed: in his tautly worded dissent in *Jefferson*, Cox wrote, "Judicial haste and impatience cannot justify this Court in equating integration with desegregation." (Wisdom's opinion in that case asserted that the terms "integration" and "desegregation" were interchangeable, a delineation not made in *Brown*.) The newly Republican White House sided with Cox: after being elected in 1968, President Nixon had urged that integration be postponed, calling any immediate action "extremist."[10] But most members of the Fifth believed that the need for uniformity and administrative expediency superseded any excuses for further delays. In *Alexander v. Holmes County Board of Education*, a three-judge Fifth Circuit panel that included Thornberry ordered the aggressive integration of thirty-three school districts in Mississippi. The case prompted Nixon to pressure HEW Secretary Robert Finch and the Justice Department to compel the Fifth to temporarily postpone the order, marking the first time the federal government had supported a stay on desegregation activity. (Supreme Court Associate Justice Hugo Black, the supervisory justice for the Fifth, viewed this as an act of reciprocation rewarding southern whites won over by Nixon's use of Barry Goldwater's race-baiting southern strategy, which helped seal his election.) Fifth Circuit Chief Judge John Brown complied with Finch's order, a decision he would come to deeply regret. Following the delay, however, the Fifth consolidated and processed desegregation cases with remarkable efficiency. In the roughly nine months between December 12, 1969, and September 24, 1970, the court issued an incredible 166 school desegregation orders—a rate of four per week.[11]

Brown was now bearing fruit by the bushels thanks to the Fifth, but voices on both sides of the debate decried the use of "forced busing," the pejorative term for court-ordered biracial student public transportation.

Some argued that such social engineering would disrupt communities and draw attention away from improving the quality of education. The 1963 *Newsweek* survey had found that 71 percent of black parents preferred mixed schools, yet just 51 percent supported the new busing system, with 30 percent fearing the hardship it would incur upon their children. (To the contrary, a defining 1996 Harvard University report on desegregation contended that racial and ethnic minorities overwhelmingly supported busing upon its first being implemented.) Alas, the majority of Fifth Circuit judges sensed that in the absence of a perfect solution, mandatory busing was the only option for correcting what Thornberry described in his *Mobile* decision as the "vexing, continuing problem" of segregation. Not until the 1971 case *Swann v. Charlotte-Mecklenburg Board of Education* did the Supreme Court take up (and sanction) involuntary busing. Fifth Circuit Judge Griffin Bell, who nonetheless supported civil rights, was against busing as part of any solution, and he clashed with Wisdom on the subject in several cases. Thornberry himself had mixed feelings but was convinced of its necessity:

> There were cases where you can't be sure about even now—what we did to the public schools—almost tearing them up and making them change to accept black children, but it was inevitable. And I don't have any apologies for my part making those decisions.[12]

While it gave Fifth members fits, forced busing provided a hot-button issue for Texas conservatives in both parties to exploit. The Republican-backed Austin Anti-Busing League drummed up twenty thousand signatures for a petition to Washington. Democrat Lloyd Bentsen broadcast his opposition to mandatory busing en route to unseating Senator Ralph Yarborough in the 1970 primary. Republican Senator John Tower proposed a constitutional amendment to ban it and rode it during his successful 1972 reelection campaign against moderate Democrat Barefoot Sanders, who would become best known for desegregating the Dallas Independent School District as a federal district judge. Despite its detractors, mandatory busing enabled redrafted school district plans to end segregated education.[13]

The Fifth's effective desegregation of southern public school systems was the culmination of decades of work by progressive minds in all three federal branches. As a congressman and judge, Thornberry had contributed to legislation and rulings at critical junctures that upheld basic civil liberties like the right to a quality education.

Brown's initial shortcomings notwithstanding, the high court deserves credit for enabling the Fifth Circuit to terminate "separate but equal" on the ground—precipitating hundreds of desegregation orders. The high court also recognized that equalizing educational opportunities had the transformational ability to empower the disadvantaged as well as instill greater compassion for different ethnicities among those at impressionable ages. In other words, integrated education was key to harmonizing the races, a notion upon which Chief Justice Earl Warren exquisitely expounded in *Brown*:

> [Education] is the very foundation of good citizenship. Today it is a principal instrument in awakening the child to cultural values, in preparing him for later professional training, and in helping him to adjust normally to his environment. In these days, it is doubtful that any child may reasonably be expected to succeed in life if he is denied the opportunity of an education. Such an opportunity, where the state has undertaken to provide it, is a right which must be made available to all on equal terms. . . . To separate [pupils] from others of similar age and qualifications solely because of their race generates a feeling of inferiority as to their status in the community that may affect their hearts and minds in a way unlikely ever to be undone.[14]

A SUPREME OPPORTUNITY

Chief Justice Warren's decision to step down from the Supreme Court in June of 1968 set off a chain reaction which would return Thornberry to the political battlegrounds. Originally named to the court in 1965 by Johnson, Associate Justice Abe Fortas, who as Johnson's attorney had saved his client's career following his hotly disputed election to the Senate in 1948, was Johnson's choice to succeed Warren. Deputy Attorney General Warren Christopher advised the president to cast a wide net before selecting his nominee to take Fortas's existing place, but Johnson had already made up his mind.[15]

Thornberry was attending a party at Texas Supreme Court Chief Justice Robert Calvert's house when he received an urgent phone call from the president. Johnson told Thornberry he wanted him to become the first member of the Fifth Circuit Court of Appeals to ever serve on the Supreme Court. Thornberry had heard rumors to this effect but did not take them seriously until this point. Thornberry hesitated at first but, well-schooled in Johnson's tenacity, gave his consent.[16]

Thornberry and Johnson, along with their families, had grown apart since Thornberry's Fifth Circuit appointment three years before. The Johnson daughters were both married in the late 1960s, and only the younger one, Luci, remained in Texas. Thornberry had paid intermittent visits to Johnson in the interim, sometimes staying overnight at the White House. But the nature of their day jobs distanced their relationship both for geographic reasons and out of deference to the ethical boundary between their respective branches. "He [Johnson] recognized that as a federal judge I had certain limitations, and he was very careful about it," Thornberry recalled. "It has been very remarkable how very careful he was about talking to me about my duties as a judge. . . . [He] never made any suggestions [about particular court cases]."[17]

With Thornberry's consent, Johnson went about rallying support with his customary tactics. In an illustrative phone call to frequent antagonist Senator Yarborough, Johnson played up Thornberry's popularity, credentials, life story, and character (with some exaggeration)—whatever it took to get his support:

> This boy [Thornberry] was a close friend of Kennedy's, and Kennedy liked him. . . . The Supreme Court people who associate with him tell me he's one of the best members of any circuit court in the country. Now, these conservatives been raising hell all the time about wanting somebody with legal experience, with courtroom experience, with judicial experience. Well now, I don't know how much more judicial [experience] you can have but on a federal district court and on a circuit district court on the roughest one in the country. . . . And he's a church man. And he's a family man. Everyone in Austin always voted for him because he was a good person. Couldn't talk until he was five years old because his mother and father were both deaf mutes. . . . His neighbors taught him to talk. He sold newspapers . . . for years to help support his mother.[18]

Johnson particularly needed to win over Dick Russell of Georgia, the acknowledged leader of the southern Democratic delegation in the Senate. Johnson was well familiar with that chamber's machinations and knew that if he could win over Russell on both the Fortas and Thornberry appointments, other southern senators would fall in line. Johnson's cause was aided by the fact that Russell and Thornberry had spent time duck hunting together. "When you sit in a duck blind all day with a man," Russell said, "you really get to know him." Russell had called Thornberry "a good man, an able man, and a fair man." After securing Russell's support, Johnson, over dinner with him, called Thornberry to inform him of his official nomination to the Supreme Court.[19]

As expected, Johnson's ambitions of elevating Thornberry and Fortas drew enemy fire. Republican Senator Robert Griffin of Michigan denounced the dual appointments as a "smack of cronyism at its worst—and everyone knows it." Despite having no objections initially, Republican Senate Minority Leader Everett Dirksen joined roughly half of the Republican senators in plotting a filibuster against both nominations. One of many letters from disgruntled citizens to the White House accused Johnson of having "arbitrarily chosen two members of the 'club' without caring what the rest of the country desires, what the incoming president might desire, or what Congress might desire. . . . It seems that in high places friendship is the overriding consideration, not ability. It appears that *who* you are is far more important than *what* you are." Another read, "It is indeed a shame in your lame-duck position that you should drag the robes of justice through the mire of liberalism once again and place untold business on the American people."[20]

Some detractors felt that Thornberry was underqualified. He had indeed served fewer than five years as a judge, but judicial inexperience was not unusual among US Supreme Court justices. (As of the 1998-99 term, among the 108 men and women who have ever served on the High Court, only twenty-four had more than ten years of judicial experience at the state or federal level, and forty-three—including eight chief justices—had no experience at all.) Regardless, according to Johnson, Chief Justice Warren had told him the court "needed somebody . . . that had legislative experience. None of [the justices] had it, and they always had to look at what the Congress intended, background and everything . . . [Thornberry will] give a good balance to that court . . . particularly on law and order. That's what I want." Not all insiders were convinced, however. Larry Temple, special counsel to the president from 1967 to 1969, believed Johnson's overconfidence in Thornberry's broad appeal clouded his assessment: "He [Johnson] started to chastise me about it, saying in effect that my political judgment wasn't very good." Johnson Senate liaison Mike Manatos recalled a member tellling him:

I can go along with Abe Fortas. But I served with Thornberry over in the House, and he just isn't qualified to be a member of the Supreme Court. . . . Of course, I'm going to swallow hard and vote for him, but that's a mistake.[21]

Johnson had anticipated opposition but was certain that Thornberry's fan base would help overcome it. Marvin Jones, senior judge on the US Court of Claims, sent a personal note to Johnson on the court's behalf that read:

He [Thornberry] possesses unusual qualities as a lawyer, has a distinguished record both in Congress and in the judiciary, and enjoys the confidence of all who know him. He is a diligent student of the United States government and is familiar with all three of its branches. We regard his qualifications as outstanding.

In a letter to Attorney General Ramsey Clark, who had also endorsed Thornberry, American Bar Association Chair Albert Jenner cited unanimous support from his organization's members, who deemed Thornberry "highly acceptable from the viewpoint of professional qualifications." Charles Alan Wright, a University of Texas at Austin law professor and authority on federal courts, wrote a letter to the editor published by the *New York Times* that endorsed Thornberry. An excerpt reads:

To his great ability and his broad experience Judge Thornberry adds the most important attribute of any judge of justice—a keen humanity. We are fifty states, but we are 200 million people, and Supreme Court decisions affect the very real individuals who are parties to the litigation, and all of the rest of us as well. Judge Thornberry is constantly conscious of this.

The *Times* editorial staff concurred:

Judge Thornberry demonstrated the firmness of his dedication to the constitutional guarantees of equal treatment long before he left Congress to accept a Kennedy appointment. . . . He has fought segregation in the schools, in bar associations and in many other areas. . . . Clearly, his credentials go beyond the fact that he is the man Lyndon Johnson used to describe as "my congressman."

Endorsements also came from the *Washington Post*, *Washington Evening Star*, and *Washington Daily News*.[22]

Thornberry expected rough patches during the confirmation process but kept his composure, recalled former congressional aide Bill Wiley. In the worst-case scenario, he would retain the privilege and prestige of sitting on the Fifth Circuit. "This is not a bad day's work," he told law clerk Tippie Newton. Privately, Thornberry was reasonably confident about his chances and prepared his family for the likelihood of relocating back to Washington. He later reflected, "I always felt . . . that if there had been a vacancy and my name came up, I would have been confirmed."[23]

As part of the appointment process, Thornberry was summoned to appear before the predominantly conservative Senate Committee on the Judiciary. Since Thornberry's record reflected no softness on crime, combative members focused on civil rights. North Carolina Democrat Sam Ervin, a respected constitutional lawyer, criticized Thornberry for abolishing Texas's poll tax: "Frankly I don't understand the opinion although I've read it backwards and forwards many times." Thornberry responded only with a smile. He also kept mum about his personal ideology, preferring to let his record speak for itself. "For a judge, separate and apart from the court, to spend his time discussing the case or apologizing for it is not proper," Thornberry later explained. "Whatever reasoning for it [a given ruling] was there in black and white." He deftly ducked leading questions about hypothetical cases, responding, "It's not appropriate for me to pass on something that's not before me now and might come before me." Although not a member of the panel, Republican Senator John Tower of Texas vowed to block Thornberry if and when a vote arose, marking the first time ever that a senator opposed the appointment of a US Supreme Court nominee from his own state. Of greater concern was a group of senators led by Strom Thurmond who contemplated filibustering the joint nominations.[24]

The confirmation hearings drew the attention of the major television networks. A CBS story quoted Senator Ervin discrediting Thornberry as a judicial activist who "interprets the Constitution not by what it says but by what it would have said if he had written it." CBS correspondent Roger Mudd reported that many liberals were not all that enamored with Thornberry, either. CBS anchor Tom Dunn reported that a conservative activist group, on the other hand, considered Thornberry "decidedly liberal by their standards." In late July, *NBC News* noted that the hearing process was taking longer than normal and risked spilling over into early election season. (Stalling

By JACK BUCHANAN

"Think we'll ever get those robes?"

Jack Buchanan cartoon, 1963. *Courtesy of the* Dallas Morning News. *Reprinted by permission.*

the hearing process until after the elections worked to the Republicans' advantage since they expected to retake the White House and all but erase Thornberry's candidacy.)[25]

The Fortas nomination presented additional headaches for Johnson. The first wave of objections to the Fortas appointment consisted of standard partisan ammunition (too liberal, too soft on crime). Then Russell withdrew his support for Fortas when Johnson dithered over the appointment of Alexander Lawrence, a good friend of Russell who had been mentioned as a candidate for a federal district judgeship in southern Georgia. (Senators close to the president customarily recommended candidates for judgeships in their own states, and their counsel was usually heeded.) Russell suspected Johnson was using Lawrence as leverage to gain his support for Fortas, and he eventually lost patience. According to Temple, Johnson felt betrayed by his former mentor's reversal after having worked through their many differences over the years, including their disagreements on civil rights.[26]

Then concerns about Fortas's character took over the debate. Revelations surfaced that he had been secretly receiving $20,000 annually from a foundation set up by a former client convicted of securities violations. He had also taken $15,000 from American University for a nine-week series of lectures he delivered—an unusually large amount for such a short period, equating to roughly 40 percent of an associate justice's annual salary at the time. While not illegal, the fees nevertheless drew questions about Fortas's ethical standards, particularly after it was discovered that he was paid not by the university but by former clients and businessmen. Additional concern was raised over Fortas's divulgence to the White House of private discussions he had with other Supreme Court members, which bothered even his strongest supporters. Prior to Russell's retraction, Johnson had rallied approximately seventy pledges for Fortas (sixty-seven were needed to overcome a filibuster), but his vessel of support capsized once Fortas's misdeeds became exposed. Several defectors, including Dirksen, dropped the vote to bring cloture on the filibuster to 45-43—well short of the necessary two-thirds majority needed to overcome it. Fortas eventually withdrew himself from consideration. He would resign from the court altogether in 1969 when he was discovered to have received yet another questionable payment on the side.[27]

Fortas's aborted appointment effectively quashed Thornberry's shot at reaching the pinnacle of his profession. "He [Thornberry] never really came up to bat," Larry Temple said. "He was in the dugout waiting his turn, and his turn never came." Fleeting consideration was given to naming Thornberry directly to the chief justice vacancy. According to Temple, it was an idea that at least Senator Russell could get behind; for although they had philosophical disagreements in Congress, he thought so highly of Thornberry that he would be Russell's top choice for chief justice were he himself president of the United States. However, most agreed that rerouting Thornberry's path to the high court in this way was simply unfeasible so soon after the Fortas firestorm. "I think the same fight would have erupted . . . and the same consequence," said White House press secretary George Christian.[28]

Word around the Capitol held that under less volatile circumstances Thornberry would have sailed through the rest of the confirmation process. Recently retired Supreme Court Associate Justice Tom Clark disagreed, believing that Johnson's relationship to Thornberry doomed his chances from the start. Had he been in Johnson's shoes, he would have packaged Fortas with a distinguished Republican lawyer. "But he was very fond of Homer Thornberry . . . and, by God, he was going to see it through this way."[29]

Johnson was completely distraught over the outcome of the Fortas-Thornberry saga. In his retirement years, Johnson would write to Thornberry, "I do always remember [Texas District] Judge [Benjamin Harrison] Powell said being on the Supreme Court was the greatest honor a man could have—greater even, he felt, than being president, and I wish it could have happened to him or to you."[30]

CHAPTER 12

Court Unpacking (1972-1980)

D ESEGREGATION OF SCHOOLS, AMONG OTHER CIVIL RIGHTS
triumphs of the 1960s, was followed by decades of concerted efforts to undo it. Richard Nixon's presidential bid owed part of its success
to stoking white fervor on issues like integration and mandatory school
busing, and reciprocation was in order. On his watch, Nixon filled Supreme Court vacancies with conservative justices whose disregard for
racial quotas in schools motivated their decisions in important cases like
Keyes v. School District No. 1 (1973), *Milliken v. Bradley* (1974), and *Regents
of the University of California v. Bakke* (1978). The lower federal courts'
own dwindling support for integration—as well as widespread white
flight to suburbs—fueled the growth of de facto segregation in school
systems during the 1980s and 1990s. Studies would show that segregated schooling resulted in lower test scores, higher dropout rates, less
well-prepared teachers, and lower percentages of students who went on
to attend and complete college. A Harvard University study on the unraveling of desegregation showed that a student in a predominantly black
or Latino school was fourteen times more likely to receive a substandard
education than a student in a school that was over 90 percent white.
De facto segregation was also found to exacerbate the self-perpetuating
cycle of poverty and low-quality education. The southern strategy's legacy further tightened Republicans' grip on the southern electorate while
the national Democratic Party took heat from conservative governors
over federal initiatives like urban social and welfare programs and voting
protections.[1]

Notwithstanding recent de facto resegregation in some schools, the Supreme Court's *Brown* ruling and the Fifth Circuit's desegregation efforts were

not in vain. A January 2003 report from the Harvard Project on School Desegregation concluded that "Desegregation did not fail. . . . Minority high school graduates increased sharply and the racial test score gaps narrowed substantially until they began to widen again in the 1990s." Beyond spurring racial reconciliation, *Brown* also helped galvanize the women's liberation movement in lifting a sexual caste system in schools, communities, and the workplace. Wisdom's and Thornberry's ruling on *United States v. Jefferson County* had not only transformed school desegregation law but supplied the constitutional *raison d'être* for affirmative action. Mississippi Senator James Eastland, who had encouraged public retaliation to *Brown*, implied in a 1979 interview that he shared former US Attorney Ramsey Clark's assessment that "the Fifth Circuit had done something that the Supreme Court couldn't do—that they brought racial integration to the Deep South a generation sooner than the Supreme Court could have done it."[2]

Eventually the volume of desegregation suits before the Fifth would be replaced by an influx of employment discrimination cases, another new area of the law in which the Fifth would establish precedent. These cases questioned the fairness of common hiring practices involving aptitude tests and seniority systems that put certain demographics at a disadvantage. The Fifth had established that aptitude tests administered to job applicants were permitted under Title VII of the Civil Rights Act of 1964 so long as certain criteria were met. Then, in *United States v. Georgia Power Company* (1973), the Fifth ruled that employers had to show the necessity of such tests if more blacks were denied employment than whites. In his decision on *Bing v. Roadway Express, Inc.* (1973), Thornberry explained the courts' deference to the "rightful place theory" to assess the constitutionality of a seniority-based hiring system: "Thus blacks confined by discrimination to certain positions must be given the opportunity to transfer into the formerly 'white' positions as vacancies occur in order to assume their 'rightful place.'"[3]

The Fifth added new members during the 1970s in an ultimately vain attempt to keep pace with its snowballing caseload. Its judgeships numbered fifteen for much of the decade, nearly double its membership twenty years prior. Meanwhile, in 1974, the quantity of appeals filed with the court exceeded three thousand for the first time ever, triple those filed in the preceding decade. Of the total appeals filed with all eleven appeals courts at this time, the Fifth processed a disproportionate 20 percent. The mushrooming caseload was attributed to a growing regional population, mounting federal legislation and regulation, and greater sentiment that the court system was the guarantor of individual rights. "There was a great deal of agitation from the time it became fifteen judges [in 1968] that the court ought to be split," Thornberry recalled, "and there was a great deal of dissension among the judges themselves." A familiar method of expediting adjudication had been to assign cases to three-judge panels consisting of at least two Fifth Circuit judges (one of whom presided over each case) and a local district judge to fill the third spot if needed. But this arrangement provided only limited relief.[4]

As of 1961 (before Thornberry joined), the Fifth Circuit's judgeships had reached nine, which was considered the optimum number (the Supreme Court has maintained nine justices since 1869). A membership exceeding this figure, the theory went, would impair the court's collegiality and efficiency, while en banc proceedings would become unmanageable. Nonetheless, Tuttle, who preceded Brown as chief judge, argued that such sacrifices were inevitable if the court was to avoid drowning.[5]

The federal judiciary's Court Administration and Case Management and Judicial Statistics committees were summoned in September of 1963 to evaluate the needs of the courts, including Tuttle's request for more judgeships. The respective chairs of these committees—Third Circuit Chief Judge John Biggs Jr. and Eighth Circuit Chief Judge Harvey Johnsen—subscribed to the theory of nine, which dampened Tuttle's hopes of expansion. Upon convening at the United States Judicial Conference, both committees came to an impasse, acknowledging the need for additional judgeships but skirting the touchy subject of court division. Tuttle proposed the creation of an ad hoc committee to investigate the ramifications of realigning the court. Earl Warren, the Supreme Court Chief Justice at the time, paid special attention to the matter because, as the author of the *Brown* opinion, he took special interest in the Fifth on account of its growing civil rights record. Warren appointed all members of the Committee on Court Administration to the special panel, called together the Special Committee on the Geographic Organization of the Courts, and instructed Biggs to head it. Tuttle realized that although Warren had taken action on the matter, years could pass before a resolution would be reached. The court needed immediate attention, he believed. A compromise was eventually meted out in 1964, when four temporary judgeships were created. They would become permanent within two years, and by 1968 two more were added, bringing the total to fifteen.[6]

An alternative to continually increasing judgeships was to cleave the court in two. But the idea of splitting up the court—proposed as early as 1950—was sternly opposed by those like Thornberry who feared the consequences, both foreseen and not foreseen. For example, he and other opponents of carving out a circuit that served just Texas and Louisiana fretted that the docket would get overrun with oil and gas interests from the former state and depress the acceptance rate of cases from the latter. Thornberry hence sided with liberal Judges Brown and Goldberg and the ultraconservative Judge Thomas Gee against the split. No court had been apportioned since the Eighth Circuit's division in 1929, but as a stumped Brown ultimately conceded, he and his colleagues were "at the end of our rope. We cannot, consistent with the quality of work demanded by our consciences, the public interest, the litigants, and the historical reputation of the Fifth Circuit, do more."[7]

The matter would be placed before the Senate Judiciary Committee. Senator James Eastland, the committee chair since 1956, supported realignment only because it would remove liberal judges in Texas and Louisiana from presiding over his home state of Mississippi, a changeover he hoped would stunt desegregation efforts. But Brown urged the committee to experiment with a larger judiciary just as the Ninth Circuit had recently done. After lengthy deliberations in both the House and Senate, the Omnibus Judgeship Act of 1978 was signed into law by President Jimmy Carter, ballooning the number of judges on the Fifth from fifteen to twenty-six. It was now the largest English-speaking court in the world. And yet, the relentless avalanche of cases could not be contained for long. The court's underachievement convinced Thornberry and other purists to change their minds.[8]

With the Fifth's ultimately unanimous blessing, Carter signed the Fifth Circuit Court of Appeals Reorganization Act, which on October 15, 1980, bisected the court "to enhance the court's ability to deliver consistent, fair, and expeditious justice," in his words. The downsized Fifth would encompass only Texas, Louisiana, and Mississippi, while the new Eleventh Circuit would strictly serve Alabama, Florida, and Georgia. The severance was emotional for many judges, who were sad to part with many of their colleagues who together had presided over some of the most challenging and controversial court cases of the twentieth century. But the old Fifth's subdivision proved a fruitful transition: caseloads in the region became much more manageable, and travel requirements were reduced significantly. Eleventh Circuit Chief Judge John Godbold, appearing before the Senate Subcommittee on Courts on March 7, 1984, reported that the new arrangement was an "unqualified success."[9]

FALLEN GIANT

Thornberry was visiting the LBJ Ranch in November of 1967 when President Johnson took him aside and confided that he would not be seeking reelection. Thornberry was both "surprised and sad" over his friend's decision, which Johnson would not make public until the following April.[10]

The 1968 election was not kind to the Democratic Party, whose convention in Chicago is best remembered for bloody demonstrations by antiwar protestors. Although the popular vote was close, Nixon had won the electoral vote by a decisive margin of 301 to Hubert Humphrey's 191. As former Thornberry congressional aide Bill Wiley put it, the general election that year was "payback time for a lot of Republicans."[11]

Johnson spent most of his remaining years at the ranch. His retirement first involved working with former staff members on a series of memoirs. Despite his plentitude of free time and financial security, Johnson was habitually disconsolate in private, having little urge to travel or seek out popular forms of entertainment. "The man I saw in his retirement had spent so many years in pursuit of work, power, and individual success that he had no inner resources left to commit himself to anything once the presidency was gone," wrote former White House aide Doris Kearns Goodwin. Johnson's health and energy level declined considerably in 1970 as he began experiencing chest pains. He nonetheless retained his competitive streak, writing Thornberry after a vacation, "Keep those dominoes handy. I'm back in Texas and about to get in the mood for just such a diversion. . . . I might even be big about it if you 'happened' to win a time or two."[12]

Johnson would stay retired for only five years. On January 22, 1973, he suffered a fatal heart attack during an afternoon nap at his ranch. Johnson's death came two days after President Nixon was inaugurated into his second term and five days before he signed the Paris Peace Accords to end US

Left to right: Eloise Thornberry, Lady Bird Johnson, Lyndon B. Johnson, and Thornberry at the LBJ ranch, 1968. *LBJ Library photo.*

involvement in Vietnam, Johnson's great undoing. Several Great Society programs would be dismantled by Nixon and subsequent administrations.

Historians would struggle to accurately appraise Johnson's legacy in light of his paradoxical persona, extraordinary savvy and ambition, impressive number of domestic policy achievements, and disastrous wartime decisions. In *Flawed Giant*, presidential scholar Robert Dallek cited the inconclusive results of a 1996 survey among US history scholars about Johnson's presidency: fifteen considered him near-great, twelve thought him average, and five felt he was an outright failure. Renowned biographer Robert Caro concluded that for much of his career, Johnson allowed ambition to supersede compassion whenever the two were at odds. Other authors countered that Caro placed too much importance on Johnson's careerism and underappreciated his "profound kinship for the underdog in society."[13]

Enigmatic though he was, Johnson's legacy on civil rights is certain. With each step up the political ladder, he became a stronger advocate of racial liberation until becoming, in his time, its most impactful establishment champion. His leadership in both the Senate and White House influenced Thornberry, Sam Rayburn, and other southern officials to spearhead meaningful civil rights legislation, with many enduring applications. He also recognized the need for constant vigilance. "Sometimes, I think we've come a long way on race, and sometimes I just don't know," Johnson had lamented toward the end of his presidency. At a 1972 civil rights symposium at his presidential library, six weeks before he died, Johnson informed the audience that the preservation of civil liberties was far from over:

> So let no one delude themselves that our work is done. By unconcern, by neglect, by complacent beliefs that our labors in the field of human rights are completed, we of today can seed . . . our future with storms that would rage over the lives of our children and our children's children.[14]

Before Johnson was buried at his ranch, thirty-two thousand people stood in line to pay their respects at an Austin library named for him where his casket was on temporary display. An estimated 60 percent of them were black, one of whom was overheard to say, "People don't know it, but he did more for us than anybody, any president, ever did." Namely, the Voting Rights Act of 1965, one of Johnson's crowning achievements, is credited with helping to boost the number of black elected officials in the South. They numbered roughly seventy at the time of its passage before increasing to five hundred by 1970, twenty-five hundred by 1980, and forty-eight hundred by 1990.[15]

Before a joint session of the Sixty-Third Texas Legislature, Thornberry exalted the legacy of the man responsible for facilitating his rapid ascendancy through the federal judiciary and involvement in momentous civil rights cases:

> Other presidents had dreams and aspirations which momentarily seemed lost in defeat. Abraham Lincoln dared to believe in a viable citizenship for the enslaved. Woodrow Wilson envisioned nations banded together in a quest for peace; he was scorned by his own countrymen.
>
> Always there are those who would doubt, deny, or diminish. We have seen and heard indications that the Great Society is no longer viable. The Great Society is no tangible, visible institution which can be closed down overnight. It exists in the hearts of us all—never to be forgotten. Like a seed which germinates to full fruition, the Great Society will continue its undying influence.[16]

CHAPTER 13

Semiretirement (1981-1995)

T HORNBERRY BEGAN SERVING IN A REDUCED CAPACITY ON THE
Fifth Circuit as a senior judge beginning in 1978, the same year he
entered grandparenthood. He continued to hear oral arguments, prepare
cases, and write opinions, but he would no longer be saddled with internal
administrative or emergency matters. But the Fifth's cleavage in 1980 provided only so much relief, as the court had to borrow more district judges
and rely more on senior members like Thornberry.[1]

The vacancy left from Thornberry's semiretirement would be filled by
Judge Reynaldo Garza, the first Hispanic member of the Fifth Circuit. The
following year, on August 3, 1979, Florida Supreme Court Chief Justice
Joseph Hatchett became the first black judge to join the Fifth. Judge Elbert
Tuttle, who had taken senior status in 1967, drove almost six hours that
morning to Jacksonville, Florida, to attend the ceremony. He described the
milestone as "the complete turn of the wheel."[2]

Thornberry had recently reached a milestone of his own in 1974 when
he became one of twenty-four people in US history—and the second from
Texas (the other being his El Paso predecessor, Judge Ewing Thomason)—
to serve at least ten years in each of the legislative and judicial branches of
the federal government (see Table 4). By the conclusion of his active service on the court, Thornberry had earned the esteem of a great many colleagues, law clerks, and attorneys on account of his thorough preparation,
reasoning skills, deference to the law, and longevity in public service. He
was perceived more as a practical arbiter than as a legal theorist, explained
former law clerk Joe Horrigan:

> [Thornberry] stood apart because some of those judges . . . wanted to
> debate things from a philosophical standpoint or get pretty esoteric in their

decision-making process or views. The Judge just cut through that. . . . He just looked at things in a broader spectrum than the other judges. His starting point was "What was the fair thing to do?"

Thornberry also abstained from associating socially with lawyers in order to preserve impartiality in his courtroom should their paths ever cross there. Befitting his gentility, he steadfastly refrained from criticizing others ("Sometimes he would roll his eyes, but that would be the most I would ever see," said former law clerk Charles Schwartz). Fellow Fifth Circuit Judge Carolyn King remembered how Thornberry set an enduring example for newer judges:

Homer Thornberry's political views didn't dominate his decisions. . . . That made him a good mentor for me. . . . He had incredible integrity. You would think that in this line of work everyone would have integrity. . . . You get into some of these cases, and you're not too sure where to go. . . . But I could always rely on him to decide on a case the way he thought the law required him to.[3]

To the end, Thornberry remained mindful that he served the taxpayers foremost and strived to ensure they got their money's worth. He often asked his law clerks what was on their minds "besides the rent," urging them to prioritize the public good over personal matters while on the clock.[4]

While Thornberry remained productive in the twilight of his judgeship, his active participation in court proceedings naturally began to wane. "He's more of a listener than a questioner," one lawyer recorded in the 1991 *Almanac of the Federal Judiciary*. Another added, "He's old and tired, but his mind is still good."[5]

The Fifth Circuit followed the Supreme Court's rightward drift as conservative newcomers replaced the old guard. As a result, the Fifth grew less sympathetic to jury verdicts, class action suits, and civil rights complaints entering the 1980s. Such ideological divergence was on display in the 1989 case *Waltman v. International Paper Co.*, one of the nation's first sexual harassment lawsuits. (In addition to the 1964 Civil Rights Act's protections of racial and ethnic minorities' civil liberties, Title VII forbade sexual harassment at the workplace, which the court system subsequently affirmed in cases like *Chrapliwy v. Uniroyal, Inc.* (1982) and *Meritor Savings Bank, FSB v. Vinson* (1986). Title IX of the Education Amendments of 1972 later nixed federal funding for public schools that practiced sex discrimination.) Sue

TABLE 4. Statistics on Members of the Federal Legislative and Judicial Branches, 1776-2009

US Congress members (distinct)	12,350[a]
US federal judges (distinct), all levels	3198
Members with experience in each branch	194
Members with at least 10 years experience in each branch (as of Jan. 1974, Thornberry's 10-year mark; includes Thornberry)	24
Members with at least 10 years experience in each branch (through Dec. 2009)	29
Members, 10+ years in each branch, from Texas (through Dec. 2009)	2[b]

SOURCES: US Federal Judicial Center, US Congressional Biographical Directory

[a] Estimated

[b] Ewing Thomason (1931-1947 in Congress; 1947-1963 in the judiciary) and Thornberry (1949-1963 in Congress; 1964-95 in the judiciary)

Waltman, a paper mill employee, was victimized by her coworkers but was denied reparations by a district judge. Hearing the appeal was a Fifth Circuit three-member panel of Judges Thornberry, King, and Edith Jones, who received their appointments from Presidents Johnson, Carter, and Reagan, respectively. Despite compelling evidence of the appellees' misconduct ("To say that she was harassed was an understatement," King later remarked), the panel lacked consensus. During oral arguments, Jones reasoned that Waltman's supervisor had already absolved his company by apologizing, negating the basis for a punitive award. A startled Thornberry, who had kept silent up to that point, turned to her and replied, "It doesn't matter." Thornberry and King ruled in favor of the appellant, with Jones dissenting. The ruling would be cited frequently for its precedent in similar cases.[7]

Texas, like the rest of the South, had become a Republican-majority state by late in the twentieth century. Whites remained overrepresented at the polls relative to burgeoning racial and ethnic minority populations, who tended to vote Democratic. With his election in 1978, Bill Clements became Texas's first Republican governor since Reconstruction. George W. Bush's

Thornberry in his federal courthouse chambers, circa 1987. *Thornberry Family Collection.*

surprise gubernatorial victory over Ann Richards in 1992 dealt another blow to the Texas Democratic Party. Republicans' share in the legislature also escalated to the point of supremacy, reinforcing the Democrats' complete reversal of fortune since the heyday of the civil rights movement.[8]

Austin had remained the state's liberal anomaly, but its class structure followed the statewide trend of socioeconomic polarization. It had evolved from a struggling city at the time Thornberry was born—when education and government constituted its dominant industries—into a commercial haven. Austin's business presence had been rising since the end of the Second World War. In 1963, it was recognized by the Bureau of Business Research at the University of Texas as having the "up-swingingest" growth rate in the state. At that time, Austin's population stood at 67,500, about one-tenth of what it would become by the turn of the century, when Austin ranked among *Forbes* magazine's top-ranked places to work in the country. The influx of technology companies in the 1970s greatly expanded employment opportunities as IBM became the first major high-tech manufacturer there, followed in time by Texas Instruments, Motorola, and Dell Inc.[9]

Thornberry wasn't exactly overjoyed by the extreme makeover his hometown had undergone over the century. In a 1984 interview, he bemoaned,

> It's so many people, too big. . . . Not many people know each other. . . . I could go into any bank in the thirties and forties, and I'd know people. You could see the president sitting there and . . . you'd go and shake hands. You don't see the officials of the bank [nowadays], and you don't know the people who work there.

He presumably found solace when the overcrowded downtown district welcomed the Homer Thornberry Judicial Building in 1993.[10]

LOVE AND DEATH

By the mid-1980s, Thornberry had written roughly 1,600 opinions and the majority opinion on 625 of them. In 1989, he celebrated his eightieth birthday in the presence of 150 friends, relatives, lawyers, and judges at Austin's University of Texas Club. "If I had known I was going to live to be eighty years old, I would have taken better care of myself," he told them. The party itself wasn't a surprise, but the announced creation of an endowed Presidential Scholarship in Law at the University of Texas in Thornberry's name was. "I'm taken aback. Overcome. It's one of the most wonderful things that has ever happened to me," he said, fighting back tears. Lady Bird Johnson and her daughters, Lynda Johnson Robb and Luci Baines Johnson, had joined several of Thornberry's former law clerks to seed the fund.[11]

Three months following the soiree, Eloise Engle Thornberry, his wife of forty-four years, passed away in her sleep. She had given no indication of failing health, and because no autopsy was performed, the cause of death was never known. (Relatives suspected heart attack or stroke.) Her lively marriage to Homer endured three relocations, the responsibilities of a congressional spouse, a live-in mother-in-law, three children, and two grandchildren, Homer Ross Tomlin and David Dalton Tomlin. By extension, she too was a public servant, interfacing with constituents and fulfilling various civic obligations like serving the deaf. She did the disciplining in the household so that the children would not harbor negative feelings about their father. Eloise also fought alcohol and codeine addictions and twice underwent rehabilitation, for the most part successfully. Despite her demons, the

Thornberry celebrating his eightieth birthday with son David and, seated
left to right, daughter Molly, wife Eloise, and daughter Kate, Austin, Texas, 1989.
Thornberry family collection.

popularity that she and Homer accrued in their social circles owed as much
to her charm and gregariousness as it did to his stature and affability. On
the morning of her death, as paramedics removed her body, the judge was
heard to say, "So long, baby. We had a great marriage."[12]

Bachelorhood did not suit Thornberry despite the regular companion-
ship of friends and neighbors. His disposition improved the following year
when he reunited with longtime acquaintance Marian Harris. Harris had
known Thornberry since their days of rationing out thirty-five-cent shrimp
cocktails among friends during the Depression. One of her sisters, Bess, was
married to longtime friend Judge Herman Jones, with whom Thornberry
had served in the Texas legislature in the 1930s. Harris had been widowed at
age twenty-eight with two small children. Forty-five years later their paths
began crossing in serendipitous fashion. A smitten Thornberry began coor-
dinating outings together and double dates with the Joneses. Thornberry
blundered badly when he brought the wrong tickets to a UT Longhorn
football game. Instead of spectating from his customary first-row seats at
midfield, the pair was forced to scale the stadium's steep concrete steps

Thornberry with grandchildren Homer Ross Tomlin (left) and David Dalton Tomlin, Houston, Texas, circa 1987. *Thornberry family collection.*

into the nosebleed section. Harris was a good sport about the mix-up, but Thornberry kicked himself repeatedly for potentially sabotaging his grand plan to win her over.[13]

Meanwhile several widows wasted little time competing for Thornberry's attention. Their courtship often took the form of donated casseroles and other homemade foodstuffs that packed Thornberry's refrigerator, contained in matching sets of Tupperware vessels conspicuously labeled with their donors' names. But the judge had his heart set on the one that played hard to get.

Harris continued to see the judge socially following the football misstep, but had no interest in remarrying. Thornberry proposed anyway. She rejected his first overture, then another two. She finally relented on his fourth attempt. A delighted Thornberry chose February 24, 1990, as their wedding date. Upon hearing the news, his eldest child Molly reminded him that the date coincided with the anniversary of his first marriage. Embarrassed over his absent-mindedness, he asked Harris if she wanted to switch the date. She shot him a "funny look" but otherwise did not object.[14]

Four years after Congressman Jake Pickle and Senator Lloyd Bentsen successfully secured funding, the Homer Thornberry Judicial Building opened its doors in early 1993. It housed several courtrooms and judges' chambers and would be used primarily to process bankruptcy cases. The dedication ceremony drew hundreds of attendees and several reporters. Thornberry would office out of his new building for his remaining days, and federal district Judge Sam Sparks, Thornberry's first law clerk, joined him. Thornberry sometimes took circuitous routes on downtown errands to get visual confirmation that his name had not been removed.

Calamity struck in the summer of 1995 when Thornberry's townhouse was burglarized in broad daylight. An intruder caught Homer, Marian, and their longtime housekeeper Kathy Williams off-guard early one morning and bound them separately with rope. In the process, the burglar knocked Marian to the ground. The judge was enraged but powerless to do anything. The perpetrator made off with jewelry and other valuables. Marian, who eventually untied herself and the others, would be hospitalized with three broken bones, but otherwise there were no serious injuries among them. The incident was eerily reminiscent of a break-in one year earlier at the residence of civil rights icon Rosa Parks, while she was present. The eighty-one-year-old Parks was struck in the face and robbed of fifty-three dollars. But unlike Parks's assailant, the Thornberry robber was never apprehended. Thornberry was never himself again. Even after the installation of a security alarm system, his demeanor was noticeably cloudier, and his patience dwindled.[15]

Thornberry had been diagnosed with colon cancer several years before, and although it had gone into remission, it returned around the time of the break-in. He finally succumbed to the disease on December 12, 1995, one month shy of his eighty-seventh birthday. A crowd of three hundred mourned his passing at University United Methodist Church, where he had been a longtime member. Attendees included Lady Bird Johnson, Jake Pickle, and numerous judicial colleagues. Speaking at the ceremony, Fifth Circuit Chief Justice Henry Politz described Thornberry as a "peacemaker" who promoted level-headedness and consideration of multiple perspectives when deciding difficult cases. Fellow eulogist and Fifth Circuit Court

Homer and Marian Thornberry, Austin, Texas, circa 1990. *Thornberry family collection.*

member Thomas Reavley, who had known Thornberry since his time in Congress, told how Thornberry was as valuable to Lyndon Johnson's and Sam Rayburn's aspirations as they were to his. He also recalled how Thornberry endeared himself to those from many walks of life: "He was as equally at home with the people on the porch in front of the store in Dime Box [a small rural Texas community] as he was in the Oval Office at the White House." Thornberry's survivors would disobey one of his final wishes that his obituary be kept brief.[16]

Congressman and Judge Homer Thornberry was often made out to be the epitome of the American dream. His life story was indeed remarkable, especially considering what he overcame in his youth. And, in his various roles in public service, he fought to offset for others the kind of misfortune that he had inherited.

In truth, Thornberry himself could not have become the proverbial self-made man without some assistance. His ascension was buoyed by parental guidance, access to a good education, powerful friends, and other advantages facilitated by his race and gender. If not for an unexpected invitation to work for the Travis County Sheriff, he might have stayed in the oil and gas business. If not for his mother's encouragement, he might not have completed college, where his interest in public affairs was first piqued. His first pursuit of elected office came at the suggestion of a family friend who was also willing to pay the filing fee. When he entered the US House of Representatives, a paternalistic Sam Rayburn accelerated his rise to become one of its most influential members. Rayburn also arranged for President Kennedy to appoint him to the federal judiciary. His quick advancement to the appellate level—and very nearly to the nation's highest court—was enabled by his close friend Lyndon Johnson, who happened to be the president of the United States. The eternally grateful Thornberry often mentioned that he owed his life to the Democratic Party.

Yet for all the benefaction Thornberry received, he seized these opportunities less for self-gain than out of a commitment to serve, often assuming high-pressure positions under grueling circumstances. Indeed, subverting a centuries-old racial caste system through political and legal channels was no small undertaking. Actualizing the most radical social policy reforms since the Emancipation Proclamation required the audacious leadership of Thornberry and others serving those parts of the country most heavily steeped in prejudice.

Thornberry's name emblazons the side of an important edifice not only because of his accomplishments but also because of his morality, integrity, and honesty. This was a man who once paid his clients' parking tickets himself, rather than dissolve them through unscrupulous means. He combated poisonous cultural biases, both internal and external, in the interest of social justice and at the risk of professional and personal safety. In his worldview, a fully functional social order required a foundation of moral principles and conduct, the security of equal rights and opportunities, and the capacity for individual responsibility and drive. In this light, the Homer Thornberry Judicial Building serves as a standing testament that helping others to help themselves can lead to liberty and justice for all.

My Most Unforgettable Character

H ER FATHER FROWNED AT HER FOR REACHING ACROSS THE table to grab some food. Whereupon, she jumped up, ran to fetch the broom, and returned to hit him over the head. A few days before this episode, she watched her grandmother milk a cow with great interest. The grandmother sat the little girl down and tried to teach her how to milk, and when she made a mistake, her grandmother corrected her. Furious, the child grabbed up the pail of milk and threw it in her grandmother's face.

This was my mother at eight years of age. She was totally deaf and had neither heard nor uttered a word since an illness in infancy. She had been born in a rural section of Texas into a large family who spoiled her, and she was allowed to grow up almost without restraint or discipline.

It was not until she began to commit the more serious breaches of conduct that her parents would agree to a separation. A family friend persuaded them that Mary's best interests lay in attending a school for the deaf in Austin, the capital. Having reached the difficult decision to part with this child whom they loved so much, they embarked upon the 200-mile trip by horse and buggy. My mother never forgot that trip. She told me many times of the nights they camped out and of her first sight of the school now known as the Texas School for the Deaf.

It was summer vacation, but arrangements were made to leave her in the care of her first teacher, Miss Emily Lewis, whose memory is still beloved by many deaf people in Texas. The hour came for parting. Tearful and fearful, the parents prepared to surrender their daughter to strangers and to dark hours of homesickness. They were incredulous to discover her happily poring over a book with her new teacher, learning the alphabet of the sign language. There were no tears in her eyes, only the dawning of new comprehension as she blissfully bade them goodbye. There were times later, of course, when she would be homesick and long to see her family, but this was the real beginning of her life. She was at the threshold of knowledge and communication.

For all of her eighty-five years, my mother faced a life of obstacles with great courage and optimism. Apparently, never having heard the word "defeat" she was unwilling to accept it.

After she graduated from the Texas School for the Deaf she married my father, who was one of its teachers. My father had also lost his hearing in infancy, and because of his deafness did not learn to talk. Twelve years later I was born. Their joy was unbounded upon learning that my hearing and speech were normal. Because they could not hear me cry in the night, they took turns, each sitting up half the night by my crib in dim lamp-light.

I learned to "talk" to them using my hands at an early age. My mother claims that at eight months I would crawl to her, tug at her skirt when someone knocked at the door. In fact, for the first three years of my life I did not speak; I could only talk in sign language on my hands. But at that time my parents resorted to every opportunity to see that I learned to talk orally. They invited a young girl cousin to come live with us, and she taught me the use of my voice and ears. At the same time, they saw to it that I associated early in life with kind and understanding neighbors who helped me learn to speak.

One neighbor related many times how she would teach me to talk. One example was to say to me, "Homer, get me the broom." While I knew in sign language how to name a broom, I was at a loss to know what she meant. She then would show me the broom, and from then on I would understand the word spoken and signed simultaneously.

When I started school I encountered the problem of learning to read. One evening at home as I was studying my reading lesson, I ran across the word "town"—the pronunciation or meaning of which I did not know. I showed it to my father. I was unable to grasp its meaning by the word he used in sign language. He then drew for me on paper, as best he could, a picture of a town. I still did not grasp the word. It was only the next day at school when one of my classmates pronounced the written word for me that I understood it.

Some of the problems experienced by deaf parents may be illustrated by three incidents from my childhood. On one occasion I had been quite ill all day. Finally, I dropped off to sleep. My parents kept waking me up every few minutes to inquire how I felt. Each time they awakened me I began to cry. Finally in desperation during the night, they brought our nearest neighbor, Mrs. Simon Gillis, over to ask me why I continued to cry. My answer was, "I'm all right! If they would just leave me alone I could sleep!"

Another time, I climbed up on the buffet in our dining room but could not climb down. When mother missed me she ran through the house clapping her hands, as was her habit to call me. Each time she came through the dining room I could see her and I would hold out my arms, crying to her. But I was partially hidden by an open door, and she never thought to look for me on the buffet! She frantically summoned Mrs. Gillis, who promptly located me by my shrieks. According to Mrs. Gillis, the reunion which occurred between my mother and me was very touching.

My mother told me of her embarrassment when once we visited old friends of the family in another city and were invited to dinner. Apparently at the table I used profane words, unaware of the meanings. The friends understood the problem and explained to my mother. She then endeavored to make me understand that I could not use those words. As a result, as proficient as I came to be in the use of the sign language, I never knew and do not know now if profane or obscene words exist in the language.

From the time I first remember my father, he was in poor health. In 1918 he died in the influenza epidemic which swept the country, leaving my mother with an unfinished home, a mortgage and other debts all past due, and the responsibility of rearing and caring for a nine-year-old son. This responsibility she fiercely pursued all of her life even unto the day I had become a middle-aged man, married and the head of a family, enjoying the confidence of the people who had sent me to the Congress of the United States.

When my father died, many people could see little hope for the two of us except to suggest that we move back to my aged grandmother's small farm.

My mother did not for a moment consider this suggestion. She was determined that we would remain in Austin where she felt there existed the opportunity for me to obtain the education and background she desired.

When thoughtful, good people raised the question as to how we would live, she simply said that she would succeed my father in teaching and that she would rely upon friends to help her obtain the position. Her will and determination proved to be stronger than the obstacle of her lack of a college education, for surely enough, friends did see that she was placed on the teaching staff of the Texas School for the Deaf. This position she held for twenty-six years.

Soon after my father died I recall going with her, dressed in black, to the bank to explain that she could not pay a past-due note of my father's but would do so as soon as possible. I can still see the look of dismay on her face as I translated that the note was not the only one, that there was another one outstanding as well.

With great determination she set to the task. She began teaching, and gradually over the years the debts were paid. Yet at the beginning of each summer it would be necessary to borrow money from the bank to tide us over for the three months' vacation period. This amount she would then repay during the next school year.

Through all of these years she was vigorous, cheerful, and in sturdy good health. She could spade up her own garden where she spent many happy hours; she would do the washing every week in a black pot of boiling water in the back yard (for some reason, we always ate cabbage on wash days); and she would walk the three mile round trip to school every day regardless of the weather. She was an excellent cook, and a host of people today fondly recall her chicken and dumplings, peach cobbler, biscuits, fried chicken, and lemon pies. When she cooked it was with abandon, and pausing frequently to talk with her hands, she would drop flour or raw dough all over the floor, cabinets, and into drawers—much to the consternation of any woman in the kitchen.

When I was twelve I began to supplement the income by selling newspapers and delivering milk. At fourteen years of age I became a page in the Texas legislature. With the money from this job, my mother and I had our eleven-year-old home wallpapered and painted for the first time.

My mother never allowed deafness, the inability to talk, poverty, adversity, or temporary setbacks to stop her in a determination to live a useful life and to provide for her son opportunities which she had seen denied to others under more favorable circumstances. From the beginning, there was no doubt in her mind but that I would obtain a college education. She was also a firm disciplinarian and did not spare the rod. She was scrupulous regarding my Christian education in the Methodist church of our neighborhood, and she herself was always active in numerous groups.

From her, too, I received a most valued heritage: that of recognizing the importance of friends. All of my life she emphasized to me our need for friends; she, herself, acquired hundreds of them during her lifetime—both among the hearing, as well as among the deaf. She was always loyal to them, and they, to her. Over a period of seventy years she knew the clerks in the grocery stores and the salesladies in Austin's shops, and, always, she would pause to have a visit by means of tablet and pencil. She would walk down the streets with a half-expectant smile, searching for a familiar face. When she saw a friend, a beatific expression would spread over her countenance, and she would stop to visit.

At length, I received my BBA and LLB degrees from the University of Texas and immediately found myself elected to the state legislature, subsequently to the office of district attorney, and later to the city council of Austin, Texas.

My mother had won her game.

When war was declared and I left home for the first time for duty in the navy, she was nearly seventy years old. And yet, she continued to exhibit the same ability to adapt herself to changing circumstances as readily as she had as a school girl of eight years. She had retired from teaching by this time, but she consented to substitute during the war years in my absence.

At the close of the war when I brought my bride home to live with us, my mother welcomed her gracefully and with love. She was even enthusiastic about the renovating and remodeling into which we plunged her house and furnishings! And she was ready for all of the other new experiences: her first grandchild and namesake was born when she was seventy-three years old. Absolute adoration! A short time thereafter we moved to a new home and sold the only one I had ever known. I could not hold back a few tears on moving day as I left the house that had meant so much to my mother and me. Dry-eyed, she never glanced backward.

Following my elections to Congress, I moved my family to Washington, DC. This change, too, she took in stride and with equanimity made her first plane trip to a strange city, far away from her lifelong friends and surroundings. She made new friends, of course, and found former ones who were now associated with Gallaudet College, the only college for the deaf in the world. With interpretation, she discovered the delights of television, and sightseeing in this part of the country never failed to thrill and excite her.

But the crowning event of her life was her three grandchildren whom she idolized and helped care for. When visitors came, no sooner would greetings be exchanged than she would write on her note pad, "What do you think of my three lovely grandchildren?" The grandchildren in turn loved her devotedly and used the sign language at very early ages.

One interesting facet of my mother's character was her keen awareness in the field of politics. She read the paper completely through each day. I remember her going to vote the first time women were permitted to do so. She was always an ardent and loyal Democrat. Having an appreciation for what needed to be done for the less fortunate, she believed in the programs of the Democratic Party. Franklin D. Roosevelt she admired tremendously and she could not help but appreciate the fighting qualities of Harry S. Truman. She thought Dwight D. Eisenhower had a good face and asked me many times how he could be a Republican.

She loved Mr. Sam Rayburn and Lyndon Johnson. Both men knew her well and expressed their admiration for her many times.

As much interest as she took in politics, she never quite became accustomed to the vicissitudes of her son's political career. She would spell out on her hands, "I wish Homer would get a good, steady job."

One of the most rewarding events in her life was my appointment by our beloved friend, Speaker Sam Rayburn, to the Board of Directors of Gallaudet College, previously cited as the only senior college for the deaf in the world. During the years I have served in this capacity, the college has experienced a building expansion program and will soon accommodate three times the number of students from all parts of the globe as it formerly did. I am grateful that I have been able to participate in this contribution to the education of the deaf. Today, there stands on the campus of that great institution the Mary L. Thornberry Speech and Hearing Research Center. As its dedicated and expertly trained personnel seek to find ways to brighten the future for handicapped infants and adults, it serves as a living memorial to my mother.

Throughout her long life, my mother seemed to be indestructible. In the face of every adversity she looked to the future with strength and resolution. Even with a fractured hip at the age of eighty-four that preceded her last year-and-a-half on this earth, she held on with a tenacity which was characteristic of her entire life. Never did she abandon her courage against overwhelming odds, her faith in her friends, nor her belief that if we but do the right, all else in life will turn out satisfactorily. On this earth, she had a serene belief in the goodness of God, and now in His heaven she is gathered with His angels in all of their glory.

JUDGE HOMER THORNBERRY

Notes

INTRODUCTION

1. Editorial, "Voter IDs on Trial," *NewYork Times*, July 13, 2012, http://www.nytimes.com/2012/07/14/opinion/voter-ids-on-trial-in-texas.html?_r=2&hp (accessed June 28, 2014); "Map of Shame, Map of Hope," Lawyers' Committee for Civil Rights Under Law, http://www.lawyerscommittee.org/page?id=0042 (accessed June 28, 2014); Joe Holley, "Holder Calls Texas Voter ID Law a 'Poll Tax,'" *Houston Chronicle,* July 10, 2012, http://www.chron.com/news/houston-texas/article/Holder-calls-Texas-voter-ID-law-a-poll-tax-3697707.php (accessed June 28, 2014).
2. "Poll: A Leadership Deficit," *U.S. News &World Report,* October 31, 2005: 80.

CHAPTER 1

1. Pamela Ward, "Repackaged Post Office is Renamed," *Austin American-Statesman*, January 10, 1993: B1.
2. Dale M. Simmons, "Downtown Post Office Renovations Planned," *Austin American-Statesman*, September 15, 1989, final edition: B3; Ward, "Repackaged Post Office is Renamed," B1.
3. Ward, "Repackaged Post Office is Renamed."
4. Ward, "Repackaged Post Office is Renamed"; Pamela Ward, "Judge Recalled as Quiet Leader," *Austin American-Statesman*, December 15, 1995: B1+.

CHAPTER 2

1. Anthony M. Orum, *The Making of Modern Austin, TX: Power, Money, and the People* (Austin, TX: Texas Monthly Press, 1987), 6, 18-19. 21; Amelia Barr, *All the Days of My Life: An Autobiography, the Red Leaves of a Human Heart* (New York, NY: D. Appleton and Company, 1913), 196.
2. L. Tucker Gibson Jr. and Clay Robison, *Government and Politics in the Lone Star State: Theory and Practice,* 2nd ed. (Englewood Cliffs, NJ: Prentice-Hall, Inc., 1995), 37, 47; Randolph B. Campbell, *Gone to Texas: A History of the Lone Star State* (New York, NY: Oxford University Press, 2003), 471.

3. Campbell, *Gone to Texas*, 326, 337; Chandler Davidson, *Race and Class in Texas Politics* (Princeton, NJ: Princeton University Press, 1990), 9-10.

4. Orum, *The Making of Modern Austin, TX*, 29-31, 188; Emmett Shelton Sr., *My Austin* (Boston, MA: American Press, 1994), 33-35; Eliot M. Tretter, "Austin Restricted: Progressivism, Zoning, Private Racial Covenants, and the Making of a Segregated City" (Austin, TX: Institute for Urban Policy Research and Analysis, 2012), 10, 19.

5. Orum, *The Making of Modern Austin, TX*, 31; Shelton, *My Austin*, 8, 16, 39-40, 44, 66, 69.

6. Shelton, *My Austin*, 13, 15; Emmett Shelton Sr., self-interview, August 20, 1978, Tape #880, Oral History Collection, Austin History Center, Austin Public Library, Austin, TX; Texas School for the Deaf, *Handbook of information* (1941), 4, 11, 13, 55-57.

7. Emmett Shelton Sr., self-interview, August 22, 1977, Tape #913, Oral History Collection, Austin History Center, Austin Public Library, Austin, TX; Shelton, *My Austin*, 10, 69; Kevin W. Fisher, "A Profile of the Life and Career of Judge William Homer Thornberry," *Fifth Circuit Reporter* 13.3 (1996): 7; Homer Thornberry, interview by Anthony Orum, February 28, 1984, transcript, Austin History Center, Austin, TX.

8. Molly Thornberry, interview by author, May 8, 2010; Fisher, "Judge William Homer Thornberry."

9. J.A. Arlow, "Communication and character: A clinical study of a man raised by deaf-mute parents," *Psychoanalytic Study of the Child* 31 (1976): 139-63; H.S. Wagenheim, "Aspects of the analysis of an adult son of deaf-mute parents," *Journal of the American Psychoanalytic Association* 33, no. 2 (1985): 413-435; U. Harbriech, "Influence of deaf-mute parents on the character of their offspring," *Acta Psychiatra Scandinavica* 59, no. 2 (1979): 129-38.

10. Homer Thornberry, interview by Brian Davis, August 20-21, 1992, transcript, United States Court of Appeals Library, Fifth Judicial Court, New Orleans, LA; Homer Thornberry, "My Most Unforgettable Character," unpublished story, 1962.

11. Thornberry, interview by Brian Davis; Kate Thornberry Hill, interview by author, August 20, 1999.

12. "From the Hornet's Nest," unknown source, 1948(?), "AF-Biography Homer Thornberry" file, Austin History Center, Austin Public Library, Austin, Texas; Shelton, self-interview, August 20, 1978, Tape #880.

13. Lynette Lezzoni, *Influenza 1918: The Worst Epidemic in America History* (New York, NY: TV Books, 1999), 7, 9, 11, 15-17, 113, 192, 202; Jeffrey Taubenberger, "Revisiting the 1918 Flu," interview by Elizabeth Farnsworth, PBS, March 24, 1997.

14. Kevin W. Fisher, "Judge William Homer Thornberry," 7.

15. Thornberry, "My Most Unforgettable Character;" "Hellen Keller Biography," American Federation for the Blind, http://www.afb.org/section.aspx?FolderID=1&SectionID=1&TopicID=129&DocumentID=1351 (accessed June 22, 2014).

16. Thornberry, "My Most Unforgettable Character."

17. Texas School for the Deaf, *Handbook of information* (1941), 11, 32, 35, 40 ,42, 51.

18. Thornberry, "My Most Unforgettable Character."

19. Ibid.

20. Ibid.

CHAPTER 3

1. Thornberry, interview by Anthony Orum, February 28, 1984, transcript, "AF-Biography Homer Thornberry" file, Austin History Center. Austin Public Library, Austin, TX; Anita Brewer, "Distinguished Alumnus Homer Thornberry," *Alcalde, The University of Texas Alumni Magazine*, January 1966: 11; Hill, interview by author.

2. Brewer, "Distinguished Alumnus Homer Thornberry," 10.

3. Joe B. Frantz, *The Forty Acre Follies* (Austin, TX: Texas Monthly Press, 1983), 7; Alex Murphree, "Texas Re-Discovers Its University," *Texas Weekly* 10, no. 15, April 14, 1934: 8; Jake Pickle and Peggy Pickle, *Jake* (Austin, TX: University of Texas Press, 1997), 21; Margaret Catherine Berry, *UT History 101: Highlights in the History of the University of Texas at Austin* (Austin, TX: Eakin Press, 1997), 79-80; Homer Thornberry, speech at University of Texas Distinguished Alumni Dinner, Austin, TX, October 22, 1965, transcript, Personal Papers of Homer Thornberry, Box 10, LBJ Presidential Library, Austin, TX.

4. Brewer, "Distinguished Alumnus Homer Thornberry," 11; "A comprehensive look at UT history: Students' Association Presidents," UT History Central, University of Texas at Austin, http://www.texasexes.org/uthistory/atoz.aspx?letter=S (accessed June 22, 2014).

5. Brewer, "Distinguished Alumnus Homer Thornberry," 11; Thornberry, interview by Anthony Orum; Bess Jones and Marian Thornberry, interview by author, December 12, 1999.

6. Frantz, *The Forty Acre Follies*, 5, 199; Campbell, *Gone to Texas*, 361, 369-70.

7. Shelton, self-interview, August 22, 1977, Tape #913; Brewer, "Distinguished Alumnus Homer Thornberry," 10; "Youngest Deputy Sheriff in Texas Represents New Type of Law Enforcement," *Austin Statesman*, August 8, 1930: 5; Seth Kantor, "When Homer Finally Takes a Steady Job, It Is to Be a Dilly," *Houston Press*, July 3, 1963: 4.

8. "Youngest Deputy Sheriff in Texas Represents New Type of Law Enforcement," 5; Thornberry, interview by Anthony Orum.

9. "Youngest Deputy Sheriff in Texas Represents New Type of Law Enforcement," 5; Thornberry, interview by Brian Davis.

10. Thornberry, interview by Brian Davis; Kantor, "When Homer Finally Takes a Steady Job, It Is to Be a Dilly," 4.

11. Thornberry, interview by Brian Davis; Brewer, "Distinguished Alumnus Homer Thornberry," 11.

CHAPTER 4

1. "Homer Thornberry for Legislature," *Austin American*, February 9, 1936: 5.

2. Shelton, self-interview, August 22, 1977, Tape #913.

3. Texas Legislature election returns (1936, 1938), Lorenzo de Zavala State Archives and Library, Texas State Library and Archives Commission, Austin, TX; "Thornberry Scores Complete Victory; Lee Allen Sheriff," *American-Statesman*, July 26, 1936: 1+.

4. "Legislators and Leaders: Homer Thornberry," Legislative Reference Library of Texas, http://www.lrl.state.tx.us/legeLeaders/members/memberDisplay.cfm?memberID=

1749&searchparams=chamber=H~city=~countyID=227~RcountyID=~district=
~first=~gender=~last=Thornberry~leaderNote=~leg=45~party=Democrat~
roleDesc=~Committee= (accessed June 23, 2014); Thornberry, interview by
Brian Davis.

5. "Rep. Thornberry Secures Funds for Placement Officer," *Modern Silents*, July 1937: 23;
Gallaudet College, press release on Mary Lillian Thornberry Scholarship Loan Fund,
January 5, 1959.

6. Thornberry, interview by Brian Davis; Richard Morehead, *50 Years in Texas Politics: from
Roosevelt to Reagan, from the Fergusons to Clements* (Burnet, TX: Eakin Press, 1982), 19-
26; Homer Thornberry, interview by Anthony Orum.

7. Texas Legislature election returns (1936, 1938), Lorenzo de Zavala State Archives
and Library, Texas State Library and Archives Commission, Austin, TX; Gary A. Keith,
Eckhardt: There Once Was a Congressman from Texas (Austin, TX: University of Texas Press,
2007), 82; Morehead, *50 Years in Texas Politics*, 28-29, 35; "Great Depression," Texas
State Historical Association, https://www.tshaonline.org/handbook/online/articles/
npg01 (accessed September 10, 2014).

8. Leslie Carpenter, "Federal District Court Bench Is Logical Step for Homer Thornberry," *Corpus Christi Caller-Times*, August 4, 1963; Jones and Thornberry, interview by
author; Thornberry, interview by Brian Davis; Dan Murph, *Texas Giant: The Life of Price
Daniel* (Austin, TX: Eakin Press, 2001), 46-47.

9. Murph, *Texas Giant: The Life of Price Daniel*, 46, 53-54; Keith, *Eckhardt: There Once Was a
Congressman from Texas*, 100.

10. V. O. Key Jr., *Southern Politics in State and Nation* (Knoxville, TN: University of Tennessee Press, 1949), 3-4, 270-271, 294.

11. Campbell, *Gone to Texas*, 406; Robert Caro, "My Search for Coke Stevenson," *New
York Times*, February 3, 1991: section 7, 1+; Robert Caro, *The Years of Lyndon Johnson:
Means of Ascent* (New York, NY: Alfred A. Knopf, 1990), 170; Keith, *Eckhardt: There Once
Was a Congressman from Texas*, 100; Key, *Southern Politics in State and Nation*, 254, 259;
Chandler Davidson, *Race and Class in Texas Politics* (Princeton, NJ: Princeton University
Press, 1990), 9-10.

12. U.S. Navy annual qualifications questionnaire for Homer Thornberry, November 24,
1964, Homer Thornberry Personal Papers, LBJ Presidential Library, Austin, TX; Homer Thornberry to Travis County Bar Association, March 17, 1986, Homer Thornberry Personal Papers, LBJ Presidential Library, Austin, TX.

13. Thornberry, interview by Anthony Orum; Thornberry, interview by Brian Davis;
Jones and Thornberry, interview by author; Bess Jones, interview by author, May 23,
1999.

14. Morehead, *50 Years in Texas Politics*, 26; Kenneth E. Hendrickson Jr. and Michael L.
Collins, eds., *Profiles in Power: Twentieth-Century Texans in Washington* (Arlington Heights,
IL: Harlan Davidson, Inc., 1993), 71-76.

15. "Lawmaker Tells of Misery Found on Tour of Area," *Austin American*, January 24, 1938:
1+; Curran Douglass, *Austin Natural and Historic: An Introductory Guide to Austin History,
Natural History, Points of Interest, and More* (Austin, TX: Nortex Press, 2000), 136.

16. Robert Dallek, *Lone Star Rising: Lyndon Johnson and His Times 1908-1960* (Oxford, UK: Oxford University Press, 1991), 125-130, 142.

17. Dallek, *Lone Star Rising*, 35; Albin Krebs, "War Shattered Johnson's Dream," *Dallas Morning News*, January 23, 1973, 10A; Homer Thornberry, interview by Joe B. Frantz, December 12, 1970, transcript, AC 78-94, Interview 1, LBJ Presidential Library Oral Histories, LBJ Presidential Library, Austin, TX, http://transition.lbjlibrary.org/items/show/70971 (accessed June 28, 2014); Wright Patman, interview by Joe. B. Frantz, August 11, 1972, transcript, AC 74-97, Interview 1, LBJ Presidential Library Oral Histories, LBJ Presidential Library, LBJ Presidential Library, Austin, TX, http://transition.lbjlibrary.org/items/show/71024 (accessed June 28, 2014).

18. Orum, *The Making of Modern Austin, TX*, 131; Dallek, *Lone Star Rising*, 171-174, 177-178.

19. Irwin Unger and Debi Unger, *LBJ: A Life* (New York, NY: John Wiley & Sons, Inc., 1999), 126; Orum, *The Making of Modern Austin, TX*, 88, 113, 119, 128.

20. Thornberry, interview by Joe B. Frantz; Robert Caro, *The Years of Lyndon Johnson*, 948; Doris Kearns Goodwin, *Lyndon Johnson and the American Dream* (New York, NY: St. Martin's Press, 1976), 91; Thornberry, interview by Brian Davis.

21. Douglas L. Smith, *The New Deal in the Urban South* (Baton Rouge, LA: Louisiana State University Press, 1988), 33, 91-92, 126; Dewey W. Grantham, *The South in Modern America* (New York, NY: HarperCollins Publishers, 1994), 91-92, 116, 126.

22. Grantham, *The South in Modern America*, 125-126; Smith, *The New Deal in the Urban South*, 187; Richard Wormser, *The Rise & Fall of Jim Crow: The African-American Struggle Against Discrimination, 1865-1954* (New York, NY: Franklin Watts, 1999), 111-112; "Good Neighbor Commission," Texas State Historical Commission, http://www.tshaonline.org/handbook/online/articles/mdg02 (accessed on August 11, 2014).

23. Key, *Southern Politics in State and Nation*, 3-4, 299; Grantham, *The South in Modern America*, 22.

24. Frederic D. Ogden, *The Poll Tax in the South* (Birmingham, AL: The University of Alabama Press, 1958), 2-3; Smith, *The New Deal in the Urban South*, 189, 208, 233, 259; Key, *Southern Politics in State and Nation*, 301, 315, 329, 388.

25. Smith, *The New Deal in the Urban South*, 248, 259; Wormser, *The Rise & Fall of Jim Crow*, 111-112.

CHAPTER 5

1. Homer Thornberry, campaign speech for Travis County district attorney, transcript, 1940, Homer Thornberry Personal Papers, LBJ Presidential Library, Austin, TX; U.S. Naval Reserves annual qualifications questionnaire for Homer Thornberry; "Committee Decides Next Week on Vote Recount," *Austin Statesman*, August 8, 1940: 13.

2. "Patterson Undecided on Meeting Date," *Austin Statesman*, August 9, 1940: 1; "Committee Decides Next Week on Vote Recount," 13.

3. US Department of Justice questionnaire for Homer Thornberry, 1963, Homer Thornberry Personal Papers, LBJ Presidential Library, Austin, TX.

4. Thornberry, interview by Brian Davis; Homer Thornberry to Eloise Thornberry, September 23, 1944, Homer Thornberry Personal Papers, Box 6, LBJ Presidential

Library, Austin, TX; Homer Thornberry to Eloise Thornberry, September 29, 1944, Homer Thornberry Personal Papers, Box 6, LBJ Presidential Library, Austin, TX.

5. Fisher, "Judge William Homer Thornberry," 8; US Naval Reserves annual qualifications questionnaire for Homer Thornberry; Debbie Hiott, "Retired Jurist Herman Jones, 'the Gentleman of the Courts,' Dies at 83," *Austin American-Statesman*, October 28, 1994: B1; Jones, interview by author; Thornberry, interview by Brian Davis.

6. Orum, *The Making of Modern Austin, TX*, 145, 158; Campbell, *Gone to Texas*, 411.

7. Campbell, *Gone to Texas*, 411; Key, *Southern Politics in State and Nation*, 257; Keith, *Eckhardt: There Once Was a Congressman from Texas*, 96.

8. Orum, *The Making of Modern Austin, TX*, 134, 145; "Gillis Post to be Filled at Election," *The Austin Statesman*, April 4, 1946: 1; "Petitions Ask Thornberry on City Council," *Austin American*, March 10, 1946: 10; "Thornberry's Name Filed." *Austin Statesman*. May 21, 1946: 1+; Thornberry, interview by Anthony Orum.

9. City of Austin election history, May 7, 1946, http://www.ci.austin.tx.us/election/byrecord.cfm?eid=94 (accessed June 24, 2014); "City Candidates List Views on Bonds," *Austin American*, May 22, 1946: 9; Thornberry, interview by Anthony Orum; Orum, *The Making of Modern Austin, TX*, 185.

10. "City Candidates List Views on Bonds," 9; "Thornberry Wins City Council Post," *Austin American,* June 4, 1946: 1.

11. "Thornberry May Push Ordinance," *Austin American*, June 6, 1946: 1; "Thornberry Sworn In," *Austin Statesman*, June 6, 1946: 1+; Thornberry, interview by Anthony Orum.

12. Austin City Council meeting minutes, October 3, 1946, Austin, TX, http://www.austintexas.gov/edims/document.cfm?id=88177 (accessed June 28, 2014), 713; Austin City Council meeting minutes, May 22, 1947, Austin, TX, http://www.austintexas.gov/edims/document.cfm?id=88616 (accessed June 28, 2014), 1296; Austin City Council meeting minutes, December 23, 1947, Austin, TX, http://www.austintexas.gov/edims/document.cfm?id=88660 (accessed June 28, 2014), 1831-1832; Austin City Council meeting minutes, March 31, 1948, Austin, TX, http://www.austintexas.gov/edims/document.cfm?id=88713 (accessed June 28, 2014), 223-229.

13. "Council Hears Plea on Vet Beer Permit; Miller, Thornberry Clash on Zoning," *Austin American*, October 18, 1946: 17; Austin City Council meeting minutes, October 10, 1946, Austin, TX, http://www.austintexas.gov/edims/document.cfm?id=88178 (accessed June 28, 2014), 718; Austin City Council meeting minutes, January 9, 1947, Austin, TX, http://www.austintexas.gov/edims/document.cfm?id=88626 (accessed June 28, 2014), 877.

14. Austin City Council meeting minutes, January 30, 1947, Austin, TX, http://www.austintexas.gov/edims/document.cfm?id=88629 (accessed June 28, 2014), 929-930.

15. Tretter, "Austin Restricted," 5; Fisher, "Judge William Homer Thornberry," 8; Morris Polsky to the family of Homer Thornberry, December 16, 1995, Homer Thornberry Personal Papers, LBJ Presidential Library, Austin, TX; Austin City Council meeting minutes, April 3, 1947, Austin, TX, http://www.austintexas.gov/edims/document.cfm?id=88606 (accessed June 28, 2014), 1141; Austin City Council meeting minutes, April 10, 1947, Austin, TX, http://www.austintexas.gov/edims/document.cfm?id=88607 (accessed June 28, 2014), 1153.

16. Orum, *The Making of Modern Austin, TX*, 185, 190; Austin City Council meeting minutes, June 12, 1947, Austin, TX, http://www.austintexas.gov/edims/document. cfm?id=88620 (accessed June 28, 2014), 1351; Austin City Council meeting minutes, January 23, 1947, morning meeting, Austin, TX, http://www.austintexas.gov/edims/document.cfm?id=88634 (accessed June 28, 2014), 910-911; Austin City Council meeting minutes, August 21, 1947, Austin, TX, www.austintexas.gov/edims/document.cfm?id=88666 (accessed June 28, 2014), 1551-1552.

17. Hill, interview by author, August 20, 1999; Kate Thornberry Hill, interview by author, August 30, 2000; Molly Thornberry, interview by author, August 16, 2014.

18. Hill, interview by author, August 20, 1999; Homer Thornberry to John W. Washington, March 17, 1945, Homer Thornberry Personal Papers, Box 12, LBJ Presidential Library, Austin, TX.

19. Homer Thornberry to Eloise Thornberry, September 29, 1944, Homer Thornberry Personal Papers, Box 8, LBJ Presidential Library, Austin, TX.

20. Mary Thornberry to Homer Thornberry, January 2, 1945, Homer Thornberry Personal Papers, Box 12, LBJ Presidential Library, Austin, TX; Thornberry, interview by Brian Davis; Carpenter, "Federal District Court Bench Is Logical Step for Homer Thornberry"; Sarah McClendon, "Mrs. Thornberry in 'Perfect' Role," *Austin American*, May 6, 1957: 1.

21. Thornberry, interview by Joe B. Frantz; Patrick Cox, *Ralph W. Yarborough, the People's Senator* (Austin, TX: University of Texas Press, 2001), 91; Homer Thornberry, speech, Rotary Club meeting, San Marcos, TX, 1950, Homer Thornberry Personal Papers, Box 25, LBJ Presidential Library, Austin, TX.

CHAPTER 6

1. Orum, *The Making of Modern Austin, TX*, 210; Thornberry, interview by Anthony Orum.

2. Key, *Southern Politics in State and Nation*, 10; Thornberry, interview by Anthony Orum, "AF-Biography Homer Thornberry"; Robert Caro, "My Search for Coke Stevenson," section 7, 1+.

3. Thornberry, interview by Anthony Orum.

4. "Texas Voters have Their Say In Vote Today," *Austin American,* November 2, 1948: 1; "Johnson Rolls In As Demos Sweep States," *Austin American,* November 3, 1948: 1; "Odyssey of Homer," *Time,* July 5, 1968: 15.

5. Thornberry, interview by Brian Davis.

6. Ibid.

7. Pickle and Pickle, *Jake*, 183-85; Thornberry, interview by Brian Davis.

8. David McCullough, *Truman* (New York, NY: Simon & Schuster, 1992): 53-4, 586; Robert Mann, *The Walls of Jericho: Lyndon Johnson, Hubert Humphrey, Richard Russell, and the Struggle for Civil Rights* (New York, NY: Harcourt Brace & Company, 1996), 20.

9. Homer Thornberry to Eloise Thornberry, December 30, 1949, Homer Thornberry Personal Papers, Box 12, LBJ Presidential Library, Austin, TX.

10. Homer Thornberry to Eloise Thornberry, October 2, 1949, Homer Thornberry Personal Papers, Box 6, LBJ Presidential Library, Austin, TX; Thornberry, interview by

Joe B. Frantz; Homer Thornberry to Eloise Thornberry, December 30, 1949, Homer Thornberry Personal Papers, Box 12; Kate Thornberry Hill, interview by author, June 28, 2011.

11. Thornberry, interview by Brian Davis; Hill, interview by author, August 20, 1999; Thornberry, interview by Joe B. Frantz; Thornberry, speech, Rotary Club meeting.

12. Homer Thornberry, interview by Anthony Champagne, transcript, January 4, 1980, Sam Rayburn Library and Museum, Bonham, TX; "Rayburn Is Dead; Served 17 Years As House Speaker," *New York Times*, November 17, 1961: 1+; Thornberry, interview by Brian Davis.

13. Thornberry, interview by Brian Davis; Civil Service Retirement Act, H.R.4295, 81st Cong., 1st sess., *Congressional Record* 95 (April 14, 1949): 4699; Social Security Act, H.R.5118, 82nd Cong., 1st sess., *Congressional Record* 97 (October 4, 1951): 12621; H.R.6102, 81st Cong., 1st sess., *Congressional Record* 95 (August 24, 1949): 12104; H.R.244, 82nd Cong., 1st sess., *Congressional Record* 97 (May 21, 1951): A2961; floor remarks by Homer Thornberry, 82nd session, 1st sess., *Congressional Record* 97 (February 5, 1951): A567.

14. Veterans' Educational Assistance Act, H.R.7656, 82nd Cong., 2nd sess., *Congressional Record* 98 (June 2, 1952): 6366; H.R.5893, 82nd Cong., 2nd sess., *Congressional Record* 98 (February 18, 1952): 1090; Defense Production Act, H.R.3871, 82nd Cong., 1st sess., *Congressional Record* 97 (July 5, 1951): 7658; H.R.4914, 82nd Cong., 1st sess., *Congressional Record* 97 (August 10, 1951): 9813; editorial, "'Full Mobilization,' Thornberry plea," The Editor's Notebook, *Austin American* (December 15, 1950), 4.

15. Floor remarks by Homer Thornberry, 83rd Cong., 1st sess., *Congressional Record* 99 (January 26, 1953): 578-579; floor remarks by Homer Thornberry, 83rd Cong., 1st sess., *Congressional Record* 99 (June 8, 1953): 6202-6203; J. H. Carmical, "New Regime Faces Farm Prices Riddle," *New York Times* (January 25, 1953), F1; "Commodity Letter: A Special Staff Report on Price and Production Trends Affecting Industry," *Wall Street Journal* (January 6, 1953), 1; "Farm Employment Hits Lowest Seasonal Level Since 1925, U.S. Reports," *Wall Street Journal* (January 14, 1953), 18; floor remarks by Homer Thornberry, 83rd Cong., 1st sess., *Congressional Record* 99 (June 8, 1953): 6202-6203; H.R.2960, 81st Cong., 1st sess., *Congressional Record* 95 (July 12, 1949): 9320; US Department of Agriculture Economic Research Service, *History of Agricultural Price-Support and Adjustment Programs, 1933-84* (Washington, D.C.: 1985): 20-21; Agricultural Act of 1949, H.R.12, 84st Cong., 1st sess., *Congressional Record* 101 (May 4, 1955): 5668.

16. Mann, *The Walls of Jericho*, 121; Cox, *Ralph W. Yarborough, the People's Senator*, 91; H.R.2032, 81st Cong., 1st sess., *Congressional Record* 95 (April 27, 1949): 5161; H.R.2032, 81st Cong., 1st sess., *Congressional Record* 95 (May 4, 1949): 5597.

17. Thornberry, speech, Rotary Club meeting; Thornberry, interview by Anthony Orum.

18. Dallek, *Lone Star Rising*, 314; Unger and Unger, *LBJ: A Life*, 126; Keith, *Eckhardt: There Once Was a Congressman from Texas*, 82-83.

19. D. B. Hardeman and Donald C. Bacon, *Rayburn: A Biography* (Austin, TX: Texas Monthly Press, 1987), 351; Homer Thornberry, speech, "Heritage of the School Children of Texas," floor of US House of Representatives, Washington, DC, July 27, 1951, *Con-*

gressional Record 97 (July 27, 1951): 9088-90, Submerged Lands Act, H.R.4484, 82nd Cong., 1st sess., *Congressional Record* 97 (July 30, 1951): 9088-9089; Submerged Lands Act, H.R.4198, 83rd Cong., 1st sess., *Congressional Record* 99, (April 1, 1953): 2637.

20. McCullough, *Truman*, 587, 651; The President's Committee on Civil Rights, *To Secure These Rights*, December 1947.

21. Smith, *The New Deal in the Urban South*, 259; Key, *Southern Politics in State and Nation*, 5; Grantham, *The South in Modern America*, 199-200; Mann, *The Walls of Jericho*, 43.

22. Mann, *The Walls of Jericho*, 47, 59, 64-65.

23. H.R.3199, 81st Cong., 1st sess., *Congressional Record* 95 (July 26, 1949): 10248; Fair Employment Practice Act, H.R.4453, 81st Cong., 2nd sess., *Congressional Record* 96 (February 22, 1950): 2301; Hill, interview by author, August 20, 1999.

24. Sam Rayburn to Mr. and Mrs. Norris Head, February 10, 1948, Sam Rayburn Papers, Box 3R340, Dolph Briscoe Center for American History, Austin, TX; Fair Employment Practice Act, H.R.4453, 81st Cong., 2nd sess., *Congressional Record* 96 (February 22, 1950): 2206; Fair Employment Practice Act, H.R.4453, 81st Cong., 2nd sess., *Congressional Record* 96 (February 23, 1950): 2301.

25. H.R.3199, 81st Cong., 1st sess., *Congressional Record* 95 (July 25, 1949): 10099-10100.

26. Homer Thornberry, speech, Committee for Poll Tax Amendment meeting, Austin, TX, October 18, 1949, Homer Thornberry Personal Papers, Box 24, LBJ Presidential Library, Austin, TX; Homer Thornberry, transcript, anti-poll tax address, November 1949, Homer Thornberry Personal Papers, Box 24, LBJ Presidential Library, Austin, TX.

27. Remarks by Homer Thornberry, "Heritage of the School Children of Texas," *Congressional Record* 97 (July 27, 1951), 9089; H.R.3199, 81st Cong., 1st sess., *Congressional Record* 95 (July 25, 1949): 10106; H.R.3199, 81st Cong., 1st sess., *Congressional Record* 95 (July 26, 1949): 10248.

28. Thornberry, interview by Anthony Champagne; Hardeman and Bacon, *Rayburn: A Biography*, 123.

29. "Rayburn Is Dead," 1+.

30. Ibid; Thornberry, interview by Anthony Champagne; Anthony Champagne, *Congressman Sam Rayburn* (New Brunswick, NJ: Rutgers University Press, 1984), 159.

31. Eric Sevareid, "Sam Rayburn Believed Implicitly in America's Strength, Rectitude," *The Sunday Bulletin,* October 15, 1961: 2 VB; "Rayburn Is Dead," 1+; Robert Allen Rutland, *The Democrats: From Jefferson to Clinton* (Columbia, MO: University of Missouri Press, 1995), 241; Thornberry, interview by Brian Davis; Hardeman and Bacon, *Rayburn: A Biography*, 98.

32. Thornberry, interview by Anthony Champagne; Thornberry, interview by Joe B. Frantz; James W. Riddlesperger Jr. and Joanne Connor Green, "Texans in Congress: The Changing Nature of the Texas Congressional Delegation," Anthony Champagne and Edward J. Harpham, eds., *Texas Politics: A Reader* (New York: W.W. Norton & Company, 2nd ed., 1998), 34.

33. Hill, interview by author, August 20, 1999; Marj Whiteman, "Thornberry Given Okay," *Austin American*, July 16, 1963: 1+.

CHAPTER 7

1. Homer Thornberry, interview by Anthony Champagne; "Homer's Party Huge Success," *Williamson County Sun*, October 23, 1958: 1+.

2. "About the Committee on Rules—History and Processes," US House Committee on Rules, http://rules.house.gov/about (accessed June 28, 2014).

3. Homer Thornberry, interview by Brian Davis; Rep. Young Will Be Named to Rules Panel; "Texas Democrat Expected to Back Kennedy," *Wall Street Journal*, July 10, 1963: 7.

4. *Fair Labor Standards Act*, H.R.7214, 84th Cong., sess. 1, *Congressional Record* 101, (July 20, 1955): 11087; *Social Security Act*, H.R.7225, 84th Cong., 1st sess., *Congressional Record* 101 (July 18, 1955): 10798-99; H.R.12, 84th Cong., 1st sess., *Congressional Record* 101 (May 4, 1955): 5668; H.R.3822, 84th Cong., 1st sess., *Congressional Record* 101, pt. 5 (July 6, 1955): 9989; Felix Belair, "President on Way to Mexico Talks," *New York Times*, February 19, 1959: 10.

5. Grantham, *The South in Modern America*, 210; Cox, *Ralph W. Yarborough, the People's Senator*, 104, 107, 122; Campbell, *Gone to Texas*, 418.

6. Key, *Southern Politics in State and Nation*, 255, 259; Grantham, *The South in Modern America*, 201-203; Davidson, *Race and Class in Texas Politics*, 161-164; Dallek, *Lone Star Rising*, 500.

7. Dallek, *Lone Star Rising*, 417; Cox, *Ralph W. Yarborough, the People's Senator*, 98; Randall B. Woods, *LBJ: Architect of American Ambition* (New York, NY: Free Press, 2007, c. 2006), 279; Davidson, *Race and Class in Texas Politics*, 161.

8. Keith, *Eckhardt: There Once Was a Congressman from Texas*, 119; Thornberry, interview by Anthony Champagne; Davidson, *Race and Class in Texas Politics*, 163-164.

9. Dallek, *Lone Star Rising*, 500; Davidson, *Race and Class in Texas Politics*, 163-164.

10. Mann, *The Walls of Jericho*, 166, 184; Lyndon Baines Johnson, *The Vantage Point: Perspectives of the Presidency 1963-1969* (New York, NY: Holt, Rinehart and Winston, 1971), 155; Hardeman and Bacon, *Rayburn: A Biography*, 112, 331-332; Sam Rayburn to Victor H. Smith, March 12, 1948, Sam Rayburn papers, Dolph Briscoe Center for American History, Austin, TX.

11. Thornberry, interview by Anthony Orum; Hill, interview by author, August 20, 1999; Orum, *The Making of Modern Austin, TX*, 71.

12. Thornberry, interview by Brian Davis; Mann, *The Walls of Jericho*, 168; Thornberry, interview by Joe B. Frantz.

13. Mann, *The Walls of Jericho*, 167-168.

14. William S. White, "Democrats Spur Civil Rights Vote," *New York Times* (August 20, 1957), 1+; Mann, *The Walls of Jericho*, 170; C. P. Trussell, "Civil Rights to Go to Floor of House," *New York Times* (May 22, 1957), 22.

15. Civil Rights Act of 1957, H.R.6127, *Congressional Record* 103 (May 6, 1957): 8488, 8503; Civil Rights Act of 1957, H.R.6127, *Congressional Record* 103 (May 18, 1957): 9518.

16. William S. White, "Civil Rights Compromise Set to Pass House Today," *New York Times* (August 27, 1957), 1; Civil Rights Act of 1957, H.R.6127, *Congressional Record* 103 (August 27, 1957): 16112-16113; Unger and Unger, *LBJ: A Life*, 215; J.J. "Jake" Pickle,

"Homer Thornberry, My Congressional Role Model," *Texas Law Review* 74, no. 5, April 1996: 944.

17. White, "Democrats Spur Civil Rights Vote," 1+; Mann, *The Walls of Jericho*, 223.

18. Dave Shanks, "Lawmaker at Home," *Austin American*, November 1, 1955: 17; Jon Ford, "Congressman Visits All Spots in District," *San Antonio Express*, September 25, 1955: 3B; "Congressman To Be Feted On October 4," *Williamson County Sun*, September 20, 1962: 2; "Bastrop Chicken Fry to Honor Thornberry," *American-Statesman*, October 7, 1962: A4; "Thornberry Boosters to Honor Congressman Thursday," *Williamson County Sun,* October 25, 1962: 6.

19. Bill Hamilton "New Job's No Snap," *Austin American*, January 19, 1964: 1+; editorial, "Thornberry for Fortas," *New York Times,* June 27, 1968, late city ed.: 42; Sam Houston Johnson, interview by Michael L. Gillette, March 31, 1978, LBJ Presidential Library Oral Histories, LBJ Presidential Library, Austin, TX; Sam Houston Johnson, interview by Michael L. Gillette, June 9, 1976, LBJ Presidential Library Oral Histories, LBJ Presidential Library, Austin, TX.

20. "Homer's Party Huge Success," 1+; Don Scarbrough, editorial, "A Texan in Washington—Thornberry Wields Power as Rules Member," *Williamson County Sun*, January 7, 1960: 3; Walter Hornady, "A Texan in Washington—Thornberry Wields Power as Rules Member," *Dallas Morning News*, December 28, 1959: 8.

21. Saul Alinsky, *Rules for Radicals* (New York, NY: Vintage Books, 1989, c. 1971), xvii; Leslie Carpenter, "Those Juicy Plums on the Federal Bench," *Austin American*, June 22, 1965: 4; Thornberry, interview by Joe B. Frantz.

22. Pickle, "Homer Thornberry, My Congressional Role Model," 943-946; Thornberry, interview by Anthony Champagne.

23. Thornberry, interview by Anthony Orum; Hardeman and Bacon, *Rayburn: A Biography*, 431-432.

24. Hardeman and Bacon, *Rayburn: A Biography*, 431-432; Labor-Management Reporting and Disclosure Act, H.R.8342, *Congressional Record* 105, pt. 12 (August 14, 1959): 15882-15892; Hill, interview by author, August 20, 1999; Thornberry, interview by Anthony Champagne.

25. Hill, interview by author, August 20, 1999.

26. Goodwin, *Lyndon Johnson and the American Dream*, 39; Thornberry, interview by Joe B. Frantz.

27. "Rayburn Is Dead," 1+; Mann, *The Walls of Jericho*, 76, 95, 107, 200.

28. Cox, *Ralph W. Yarborough, the People's Senator*, 121; Jack Valenti, *This Time, This Place: My Life in War, the White House, and Hollywood* (New York, NY: Harmony Books, 2007), 5-6.

29. John W. Gardner, *On Leadership* (New York, NY: The Free Press, 1993, c. 1990), 59.

30. Mann, *The Walls of Jericho*, 282.

31. Thornberry, interview by Anthony Orum.

CHAPTER 8

1. Grantham, *The South in Modern America*, 30, 33.

2. Wormser, *The Rise & Fall of Jim Crow*, 72-73; Key, *Southern Politics in State and Nation*,

5; Davidson, *Race and Class in Texas Politics*, 9-10; Harvard Sitkoff, *The Struggle for Black Equality, 1954-1992*, rev. ed. (New York, NY: Hill and Wang, 1993, c. 1981), 14; Grantham, *The South in Modern America*, 203.

3. Grantham, *The South in Modern America*, 12; Campbell, *Gone to Texas*, 326, 337, 365-366; Orum, *The Making of Modern Austin, TX*, 191; Cox, *Ralph W. Yarborough, the People's Senator*, 136-137.

4. Orum, *The Making of Modern Austin, TX*, 175-176, 184, 189-190, 192.

5. Ibid, 61, 145, 169.

6. Campbell, *Gone to Texas*, 411; Orum, *The Making of Modern Austin, TX*, 198; Thornberry, interview by Anthony Orum; Frantz, *The Forty Acre Follies*, 206.

7. Kevin Brown, *Race, Law, and Education in the Post-Desegregation Era* (Durham, NC: Carolina Academic Press, 2005), 168; Mann, *The Walls of Jericho*, 227; Campbell, *Gone to Texas*, 427; Wormser, *The Rise & Fall of Jim Crow*, 132.

8. Caro, *The Years of Lyndon Johnson*, 772; Grantham, *The South in Modern America*, 199.

9. Grantham, *The South in Modern America*, 210; Mann, *The Walls of Jericho*, 245; Arthur M. Schlesinger Jr., *A Thousand Days: John F. Kennedy in the White House* (New York, NY: Fawcett Premier Books, 1992, c. 1965), 855-856; Civil Rights Act of 1960, H.R.8601, 86th Cong., 2nd sess., *Congressional Record* 106, (March 24, 1960): 5453-5454.

10. Mann, *The Walls of Jericho*, 248-249; Civil Rights Act of 1960, H.R.8601, 86th Cong., 2nd sess., *Congressional Record* 106, (March 24, 1960): 5453-5454, 5459-5460.

11. Mann, *The Walls of Jericho*, 249, 256; "Civil Rights Bill Ready for House," *New York Times* (April 20, 1960), 24; Civil Rights Act of 1960, H.R.8601, 86th Cong., 2nd sess., *Congressional Record* 106 (April 21, 1960): 8509-8510.

12. Mann, *The Walls of Jericho*, 260; "Civil Rights Act of 1960 signed," African American Registry, http://www.aaregistry.org/historic_events/view/civil-rights-act-1960-signed, accessed on September 23, 2014; Sitkoff, *The Struggle for Black Equality*, 75.

13. *Congressional Quarterly Almanac* 15-18 (Washington, DC: Congressional Quarterly Service, 1959-1962).

14. Thornberry, interview by Joe B. Frantz; Thornberry, interview by Brian Davis; Dallek, *Lone Star Rising*, 576; Valenti, *This Time, This Place*, 65.

15. Thornberry, interview by Joe B. Frantz; Thornberry, interview by Brian Davis.

16. Dallek, *Lone Star Rising*, 588; Thornberry, interview by Joe B. Frantz.

17. Schlesinger, *A Thousand Days: John F. Kennedy in the White House*, 849; Sitkoff, *The Struggle for Black Equality*, 75.

18. "Thornberry Defeats Dobbs for 8th Term in Congress," *Austin American*, November 7, 1962: 17; *Congressional Quarterly Almanac* 9-18 (Washington, DC: Congressional Quarterly Service, 1949-1962); "Random Notes in Washington: Travel Likely for G.I. Families," *New York Times*, January 29, 1962, late city ed.: 12; Thornberry, interview by Anthony Orum.

19. "Rep. Young Will Be Named to Rules Panel; Texas Democrat Expected to Back Kennedy," *Wall Street Journal*, July 10, 1963: 7; "JFK Appoints Thornberry Judge, Keeps Promise to Sam Rayburn," *Austin American*, July 10, 1963: 13; Thornberry, interview by Brian Davis; vote to increase membership of House Rules Committee, 87th Cong.,

1st sess., *Congressional Record* 107 (January 31, 1961): 1589; "Young Republicans Rap Rayburn as 'Traitor,'" *Dallas Morning News*, February 26, 1961, early city ed., sec. 1:9.

20. Schlesinger, *A Thousand Days: John F. Kennedy in theWhite House*, 858-859, 865-866, 871.

21. Caro, *TheYears of Lyndon Johnson*, 1009.

22. Carpenter, "Federal District Court Bench Is Logical Step for HomerThornberry"; Hill, interview by author, August 20, 1999; "JFK Appoints Thornberry Judge, Keeps Promise to Sam Rayburn," 13; Thornberry, interview by Brian Davis.

23. Thornberry, interview by Brian Davis.

24. Ibid.

25. Thornberry, interview by Joe B. Frantz.

26. Thornberry, interview by Anthony Champagne; Edward Allen, *Sam Rayburn: Leading the Lawmakers* (Chicago, IL: Encyclopedia Britannica Press, 1963), 188-189.

27. Allen, *Sam Rayburn: Leading the Lawmakers*, 190; Sevareid, "Sam Rayburn Believed Implicitly in America's Strength, Rectitude," 2 VB; remarks by Homer Thornberry, *Congressional Record* 108 (January 18, 1962): 492.

28. Hill, interview by author, August 20, 1999; Kate Thornberry Hill, interview by author, August 20, 2000; "Life on the Ranch: A Day at Home with LBJ," *U.S. News &World Report*, April 13, 1964: 67-68.

29. KateThornberry Hill, interview by author, April 29, 2004; "Friend Meets Girl's Uncle on Phone—It WasTHE Lyndon," *El Paso Herald*, November 27(?), 1963: sec. B, 5.

30. Thornberry, interview by Joe B. Frantz; ScottWright, "Austinite with Gift for Justice Dead at 86," *Austin American-Statesman*, December 13, 1995: A1+.

31. Colin Barnes, Geof Mercer, andTom Shakespeare, *Exploring Disability: A Sociological Introduction* (Cambridge, UK: Polity Press, 1999), 204.

32. H.R.5246, 83rd Cong., 1st sess., *Congressional Record* 99 (May 25, 1953): 5486-5487; H.R.5246, 83rd Cong., 1st sess., *Congressional Record* 99 (May 26, 1953): 5585; H.R.5246, 83rd Cong., 1st sess., *Congressional Record* 99 (August 1, 1953): 10833.

33. "Life and Labors ofThomas H. Gallaudet," *The North American Review* 87, no. 181 (October 1858): 517-532; Katharine A. Jankowski, *Deaf Empowerment: Emergence, Struggle, and Rhetoric* (Washington, DC: Gallaudet University Press, 1997), 20.

34. Jankowski, *Deaf Empowerment*, 23, 68-69, 71.

35. Barnes, Mercer, and Shakespeare, *Exploring Disability: A Sociological Introduction*, 112; US House Committee on Education and Labor hearing on H.R.6655, transcript, May 5, 1954 (US Printing Office, 1954): 8-9; Myron Uhlberg, *Hands of My Father: A Hearing Boy, His Deaf Parents, and the Language of Love* (NewYork, NY: Bantam Books, 2009, c. 2008), 33.

36. H.R.6655, 83rd Cong., 2nd sess., *Congressional Record* 100 (June 10, 1954): 7850-7851, 7857; US House Committee on Education and Labor hearing on H.R.6655, transcript, May 5, 1954 (US Printing Office, 1954): 8-9.

37. US House Committee on Education and Labor hearing on H.R.6655, transcript, May 5, 1954 (US Printing Office, 1954): 8-9, 24-26.

38. Bradshaw Mintener, "A New Era at Gallaudet," speech, Gallaudet University, Washington, DC, February 5, 1957, reprinted in *Congressional Record* 103 (February 20, 1957):

A1325; H.R.11901, 86th Cong., 2nd sess., *Congressional Record* 106 (April 25, 1960), 8659; H.R.12699, 86th Cong., 2nd sess., *Congressional Record* 106 (July 2, 1960): 15764.

39. "Honorary Degree Recipients," Gallaudet University, http://www.gallaudet.edu/academic_affairs/honorary_degrees/honorary_degree_recipients.html, accessed on July 3, 2014; Homer Thornberry, "The American Opportunity," speech, Gallaudet University, Washington, DC, June 3, 1963, reprinted in *Congressional Record* 109, June 5, 1963: 10227.

40. Thornberry, interview by Joe B. Frantz; Hugo F. Schunhoff to Lyndon Johnson, June 15 1965, Office Files of John Macy: "Homer Thornberry 12/4/63-12/31/65" folder, LBJ Presidential Library, Austin, TX; "Uninvited Guest Named Johnson is Graduation Speaker for Deaf," *New York Times,* June 14, 1966: 44; "LBJ Cited for Service to the Deaf," *Austin Statesman,* March 24, 1967: 9; Ernestine Wheelock, "Austinite Receives Prestigious Appointments," *Austin American-Statesman*, January 26, 1969: C2.

41. Wheelock, "Austinite Receives Prestigious Appointments," C2.

42. Elizabeth Carpenter, "Her Actions Are Her Words," *American-Statesman,* May 31, 1953: B-1; "Mrs. Thornberry Marks 80th Milestone Today," *Washington Post,* May 24, 1953: 115; Lyndon Johnson to Mary L. Thornberry, March 16, 1957, LBJA Congressional File: "Thornberry, Homer," Box 56, LBJ Presidential Library, Austin, TX.

43. Hill, interview by author, August 20, 1999; David Thornberry and Molly Thornberry Schiller, interview by author, July 26, 2013; "Ex-Teacher Dies in Washington; Funeral Here," *Lone Star* 80, no. 1, September 15, 1958: 1+.

44. Kantor, "When Homer Finally Takes a Steady Job, It Is to Be a Dilly," 4; Blake Clark to Homer Thornberry, May 11, 1962, Homer Thornberry Personal Papers, LBJ Presidential Library, Austin, TX.

45. Lyndon Johnson to Homer Thornberry, July 11, 1958, LBJA Congressional File: "Thornberry, Homer," Box 56, LBJ Presidential Library, Austin, TX; Leonard M. Elstad, interview by David G. McComb, February 14, 1969, LBJ Presidential Library Oral Histories, LBJ Presidential Library, Austin, TX.

46. Phil Casey, "$475,000 Gallaudet Center Opens," *Washington Post*, October 20, 1959: A14.

47. Gallaudet College, news release, March 18, 1959; William Holland, "2 Buildings Honor Artist, Teacher," *Evening Star*, May 16, 1969; "Thornberry Attends Ceremonies," *Austin American*, May 18, 1969; Gallaudet College, press release, January 5, 1959.

48. US General Accounting Office, *Educating Students at Gallaudet and the National Technical Institute for the Deaf: Who Are Served and What Are the Costs?*, report to US Senate Subcommittee on the Handicapped, Committee on Labor and Human Resources, March 22, 1985.

49. Jankowski, *Deaf Empowerment: Emergence, Struggle, and Rhetoric*, 132; Suzanne Goldenberg, "'Not deaf enough' university head is forced out," *The Guardian*, October 30, 2006, http://www.theguardian.com/world/2006/oct/31/usa.highereducation, accessed on July 3, 2014; "Gallaudet's board ousts president," *Washington Times*, October 30, 2006, http://www.washingtontimes.com/news/2006/oct/30/20061030-122608-4001r/?page=all, accessed on July 3, 2014.

50. Sara Collins, "A Time Capsule Found at a Demolished Mary Thornberry Building," *SIGNews* 7, no. 6, June 2009: 17+; "Mary Thornberry Building Dedication," Gallaudet University, http://www.gallaudet.edu/gts/video__gallaudet/around_campus/mary_thornberry_building_demolition.html, accessed on September 20, 2014; Khera Allen to author, September 10, 2014.

51. "Gallaudet Regional Centers," Gallaudet University, http://www.gallaudet.edu/Outreach_Programs/Regional_Centers_.html, accessed on July 3, 2014; Lisa Jacobs to author, July 29-30, 2013.

CHAPTER 9

1. Garth Jones, "Texas GOP Pins Hope in Primary," *Austin American,* February 15, 1962: 3; "Texas Demos Could Lose Labor Support," *Austin Statesman,* September 19, 1962: 3; "Connally Says GOP Not Needed in Texas," *Austin Statesman,* June 27, 1962: 3.

2. "GOP in Hays County Fires Salvo at Court," *Austin American,* May 15, 1962: 19; Sitkoff, *The Struggle for Black Equality*, 145-147.

3. Key, *Southern Politics in State and Nation*, 581, 586-587; S J RES 29, 87th Cong., 2nd sess., *Congressional Record* 108 (August 27, 1962): 17670; H.R.3199, 81st Cong., 1st sess., *Congressional Record* 95 (July 26, 1949): 10248.

4. Thornberry, interview by Anthony Orum; Schlesinger, *A Thousand Days: John F. Kennedy in the White House*, 883.

5. Thornberry, interview by Anthony Orum.

6. Campbell, *Gone to Texas*, 427; Cox, *Ralph W. Yarborough, the People's Senator*, 136-137, 189.

7. H.R.12677, 86th Cong., 2nd sess., *Congressional Record* 106 (June 30, 1960): 15190; Constituent letters to Paul Kilday, Paul Kilday Papers, Box 9/R1, "Labor - Minimum Wage Law Legis. (Fair Labor Standards Amendments)" folder, Dolph Briscoe Center for American History, Austin, TX; Housing Act, H.R.6028, *Congressional Record* 107 (June 22, 1961): 10890, 11142; S.R. 2393, 87th Cong., 1st sess., *Congressional Appeal* 107 (September 18, 1961): 20040; "Thornberry Voting Record That Of Moderate Liberal," *The Commercial Appeal,* June 29, 1968: 8; Sherman Antitrust Act, H.R.3659, 84th Cong., 1st sess., *Congressional Record* 101, pt. 3 (March 29, 1955): 3941; H.R.7007, 86th Cong., 1st sess., *Congressional Record* 105 (May 20, 1959): 8634; H J RES 507, 86th Cong., 1st sess., *Congressional Record* 105, pt. 13 (August 25, 1959): 16951.

8. Homer Thornberry, speech, IRS Data Processing Center groundbreaking, Austin, Texas, October 18, 1962, Homer Thornberry Personal Papers, Box 24, LBJ Presidential Library, Austin, TX); Robert Phinney, Internal Revenue Service public service announcement, August 1, 1963, Vice Presidential Masters, Box 272 "T," LBJ Presidential Library, Austin, TX; Homer Thornberry to Fagan Dickson, June 13, 1962, Homer Thornberry Personal Papers, LBJ Presidential Library, Austin, TX.

9. "Those Who Write the News Honor Those Who Make It," *Austin American*, December 17, 1957: 17; Gene Fondren, interview by author, December 5, 2000; "'Hi, Homer,'" *Austin American,* October 5, 1962: 21.

10. "Republicans Believe '62 to be THE Year," *Austin Statesman,* February 15, 1962: A13.

11. "Jim Dobbs Repub. Nominee," *American-Statesman*, May 6, 1962: A1+.

12. Robert E. Ford, "Republicans Stage Run at Democrats," *Austin American*, February 7, 1962: 5; Jones, "Texas GOP Pins Hope in Primary," 3; Sarah McClendon, "Report by Towers Alters GOP Guess," *Austin American*, July 21, 1962: 1+; "A Curious Congress," *Austin Statesman*, September 6, 1962: A6; "Hendrix Lashes at Democrats," *Austin American*, February 8, 1962: 38; "'Democrats for Dobbs' Formed by Centexan," *Austin Statesman*, October 6, 1962: 5; "Dobbs Says He's Gaining Staunch Demo Votes," *Austin Statesman*, October 2, 1962: 12.

13. "Jim Dobbs For US Congressman," political campaign flyer, 1962, Homer Thornberry Personal Papers, LBJ Presidential Library, Austin, TX); "Giveaways Draw Fire of Dobbs," *Austin American*, March 28, 1962: 5.

14. Orum, *The Making of Modern Austin, TX*, 33, 45, 53, 88, 113, 119, 128, 131.

15. H.R. 12263, 86th Cong., 2nd sess., *Congressional Record* 106 (June 9, 1960): 12274; Homer Thornberry, speech, Somerville Reservoir groundbreaking ceremony, Somerville, TX, September 22, 1962, Homer Thornberry Personal Papers, Box 24, LBJ Presidential Library, Austin, TX; "Centex Solons Support Dams on San Gabriel," *Austin American*, February 1, 1962: A29; "Dam at Laneport is Recommended," *Williamson County Sun*, February 1, 1962: 1.

16. "Reception for Thornberry Turns Into 'Dam Party,'" *Williamson County Sun*, October 18, 1962: 1+; "Dam at Laneport is Recommended"; "Laneport Project Is Blasted at Austin Hearing Monday," *Williamson County Sun*, May 3, 1962: 1; "San Gabriel Dams Hurdle One Hump," *Williamson County Sun*, October 4, 1962: 1; "Three-Dam Program Now Issue in Politics," *Austin American*, February 8, 1962: 19; Fondren, interview by author.

17. "Dams! A Flood of Dams!" *Williamson County Sun*. October 11, 1962: 2.

18. "Thornberry Flies to Washington to Push Public Works Measure," *Austin Statesman*, October 8, 1962: 7; "JFK Signs Bill For Dams," *Williamson County Sun*, October 25, 1962: 1; "Another Party For the Thornberrys," *Williamson County Sun*, October 11, 1962: 2; "Reception for Thornberry Turns Into 'Dam Party'"; "The SUN Endorses . . . " *Williamson County Sun*, November 1, 1962: 2.

19. "Thornberry Defeats Dobbs For 8th Term in Congress," 17; "County Vote Follows Trend Set in Texas," *Williamson County Sun*, November 8, 1962: 1.

20. Thornberry, interview by Joe B. Frantz; Thornberry, interview by Brian Davis; "JFK Appoints Thornberry Judge, Keeps Promise to Sam Rayburn," 13; "Rep. Young Will Be Named to Rules Panel," 7.

21. David Lawrence, "Thornberry's Nomination Called Reward from JFK," *Houston Chronicle*, July 13, 1963: sec. 6, 2; Homer Thornberry to Leon Jaworski, July 19, 1963, Homer Thornberry Personal Papers, LBJ Presidential Library, Austin, TX; "Thornberry to Return to Texas as US Judge," *Bastrop Advertiser*; July 11, 1963: 1; Robert E. Baskin, "Rep. Thornberry Tested in Service, Found Strong," *Dallas Morning News*, July 10, 1963, early city ed.: sec. 1, 14.

22. Whiteman, "Thornberry Given Okay," 1.

23. "Rep. Thornberry Resigns House Effective Dec. 20," *El Paso Times*, September 27, 1963: 1-A.

24. J. J. "Jake" Pickle, interview by Joe B. Frantz, May 31, 1970, transcript, LBJ Presidential Library Oral Histories, LBJ Presidential Library, Austin, TX; Glen Castlebury, "Foreman Warns GOP to Solidify," *Austin Statesman,* October 6, 1963: F1; Nancy Mathis, "Six Decades of Politics, Pickle-Style," *Houston Chronicle,* April 9, 1994: 1A.

25. Pickle, interview by Joe B. Frantz; Pickle, "Homer Thornberry, My Congressional Role Model," 944.

26. Thornberry, interview by Brian Davis.

27. Thornberry, interview by Joe B. Frantz; Lady Bird Johnson, *A White House Diary* (New York, NY: Holt, Rinehart and Winston, 1970), 4-5; "Odyssey of Homer," 15; Steven M. Gillon, *The Kennedy Assassination: 24 Hours After* (New York, NY: Basic Books, 2009), 65.

28. Thornberry, interview by Joe B. Frantz.

29. Gillon, *The Kennedy Assassination: 24 Hours After*, 108; Thornberry, interview by Joe B. Frantz; "Johnson Names 2 to Appeals Court," *New York Times,* June 18, 1965: 18L; Thornberry, interview by Brian Davis; Charles Schwartz, interview by author, March 12, 2004.

30. "Will Homer Skip Court?" *Austin Statesman,* November 25, 1963: A1+; Gillon, *The Kennedy Assassination: 24 Hours After*, 205-206; Lyndon Johnson to Eloise Thornberry, December 11, 1963, Office Files of John Macy, Homer Thornberry file, Lyndon B. Johnson Lib., Austin, TX; Homer Thornberry to George and Kate Engle, December 13, 1963, Homer Thornberry Personal Papers, LBJ Presidential Library, Austin, TX.

31. Frank L. Hunter to Homer Thornberry, May 27, 1963, Homer Thornberry Personal Papers, LBJ Presidential Library, Austin, TX; Thornberry, interview by Joe B. Frantz; Thornberry, interview by Brian Davis.

32. "Thornberry to Take Oath on Dec. 21," *San Antonio Express*, December 4, 1963, final ed.: 8B; Audio recording of swearing-in of Homer Thornberry to US District Court, Western District of Texas, December 21, 1963, Audiovisual Materials, LBJ Presidential Library, Austin, TX; Fisher, "Judge William Homer Thornberry," 9.

CHAPTER 10

1. Thornberry, interview by Brian Davis; Chris Fox to Homer Thornberry, May 22, 1963, Homer Thornberry Personal Papers, LBJ Presidential Library, Austin, TX; W. J. Turner, letter to the editor, *El Paso Times,* May 29, 1963; W. J. Hooten, letter to the editor, *El Paso Times,* May 22, 1963.

2. Ewing Thomason to Homer Thornberry, 1963, Homer Thornberry Personal Papers, LBJ Presidential Library, Austin, TX; James Noel to Homer Thornberry, November 8, 1963, Homer Thornberry Personal Papers, LBJ Presidential Library, Austin, TX; Bill Hamilton, "New Job's No Snap," *Austin American,* January 19, 1964: 1+; Sam Sparks, interview by author, March 4, 2004.

3. Hamilton, "New Job's No Snap," A1+.

4. Sparks, interview by author, March 4, 2004; Sam Sparks, interview by author, June 9, 2012.

5. Sparks, interview by author, June 9, 2012; Hamilton, "New Job's No Snap," A1+.

6. Thornberry, interview by Brian Davis; Sparks, interview by author, March 4, 2004;

Sam Sparks, interview by author, June 19, 2012; Hamilton, "New Job's No Snap," A1+.

7. Brewer, "Distinguished Alumnus Homer Thornberry," 12; Thornberry, interview by Brian Davis; Sparks, interview by author, March 4, 2004.

8. Homer Thornberry to Harvey Payne, undated, Office Files of John Macy, "Homer Thornberry 12/4/63-12/31/65" folder, LBJ Presidential Library, Austin, TX; "JFK Appoints Thornberry Judge, Keeps Promise to Sam Rayburn," 13; Thornberry, interview by Brian Davis; Sparks, interview by author, June 9, 2012.

9. Austin Equal Citizenship Corporation Board of Directors, untitled report on investigating discrimination complaints, June 9, 1967, Austin Equal Citizenship Corporation Records, call #AR.2012.006, Austin History Center, Austin Public Library, Austin, TX; Ordinance to create Austin Equal Opportunities Commission, Pickle Papers, Box 95-112/67, Dolph Briscoe Center for American History, Austin, TX; "Austin Equal Citizenship Corporation Records, Administrative History," Dolph Briscoe Center for American History, http://www.lib.utexas.edu/taro/aushc/00257/ahc-00257.html, accessed on July 4, 2014; Glen Castlebury, "Housing Law Is Approved," *Austin-American Statesman*, May 18, 1968: 1; Frantz, *The Forty Acre Follies*, 206, 211, 214.

10. Joseph Horrigan, interview by author, July 18, 2012; Thornberry, interview by Joe B. Frantz.

11. Sparks, interview by author, June 19, 2012.

12. Sam Sparks, interview by author, June 20, 2012; Thornberry, interview by Joe B. Frantz; Thornberry, interview by Brian Davis.

13. Thornberry, interview by Brian Davis.

14. Thornberry, interview by Joe B. Frantz; Ralph Yarborough to Lyndon Johnson, May 18, 1965, Office Files of John Macy, "US Court - Appeals - 5th Circuit" folder, LBJ Presidential Library, Austin, TX.

15. Thornberry, interview by Joe B. Frantz; Lyndon Johnson (speech, Homer Thornberry swearing-in ceremony to Fifth Circuit Court of Appeals, June 3, 1965, Stonewall, TX), reprinted in White House press release, July 3, 1965, Office Files of John Macy, "US Court - Appeals - 5th Circuit - Georgia, Florida . . ." folder, LBJ Presidential Library, Austin, TX.

16. Deborah J. Barrow and Thomas G. Walker, *A Court Divided: The Fifth Circuit Court of Appeals and the Politics of Judicial Reform* (New Haven, CT: Yale University Press, 1988), 2-5; Jack Bass, *Unlikely Heroes* (Tuscaloosa, AL: The University of Alabama Press, 1981), 155.

17. Bass, *Unlikely Heroes*, 23; Jack Bass, "The 'Fifth Circuit Four,'" *The Nation,* May 3, 2004: 30; James Farmer to Lyndon Johnson, May 4, 1965, Office Files of John Macy, "U.S. Court - Appeals - 5th Circuit - Georgia, Florida . . ." folder, LBJ Presidential Library, Austin, TX; Fred P. Graham, "Coleman Picked For Court Post," *New York Times,* May 13, 1965: 24; Drew Pearson, "Will LBJ Bow to Sen. Eastland?" *Washington Post.* December 16, 1964: B21.

18. Barrow and Walker, *A Court Divided*, 2-5; Bass, *Unlikely Heroes*, 3-4; Graham, "Coleman Picked for Court Post," 24.

19. Campbell, *Gone to Texas*, 337; "Canonizing the Civil Rights Revolution," *Northwestern University Law Review* 103, no. 1 (2009): 71-73; "The Voting Rights Act of 1965," U.S. Department of Justice, http://www.justice.gov/crt/about/vot/intro/intro_b.php, accessed on July 5, 2014.

20. Ogden, *The Poll Tax in the South*, 19, 55-56.

21. Bass, *Unlikely Heroes*, 264-267; Ogden, *The Poll Tax in the South*, 111.

22. *United States v. State of Texas*, 252 F. Supp. 234 (W.D. Tex. 1966).

23. Ibid; defendant trial brief, *United States v. State of Texas*, 252 F. Supp. 234 (W.D. Tex. 1966), Appendix F, 29-31, National Archives at Fort Worth, Fort Worth, TX.

24. *United States v. State of Texas*, 252 F. Supp. 234; *Harper v. Virginia Board of Elections*, 383 U.S. 363 (1966); Thornberry, interview by Joe B. Frantz.

25. "Voter Turnout in the 1964 Presidential Election by State;" "Voter Turnout in the 1968 Presidential Election by State."

26. "Voter Turnout in the 1964 Presidential Election by State," US Federal Election Commission, http://www.fec.gov/pages/rat64.htm, accessed on July 5, 2014; "Voter Turnout in the 1968 Presidential Election by State," US Federal Election Commission, http://www.fec.gov/pages/rat68.htm, accessed on July 5, 2014; Thomas Patterson, *The American Democracy*, 10th ed. (College Station, TX: Texas A&M University Press, 2011), 529-535.

27. *Davis v. Davis*, 361 F. 2d 770 (5th Cir. 1966); *Scott v. Walker*, 358 F. 2d 561 (5th Cir. 1966); Horrigan, interview by author, July 18, 2012; Joseph Horrigan, interview by author, January 12, 2012.

28. Editorial, "Thornberry for Fortas," 42.

29. Sitkoff, *The Struggle for Black Equality*, 154, 172; Jake Pickle, interview by author, October 24, 2003.

30. Anthony Champagne and Edward J. Harpham, "The Changing Political Economy of Texas," *Texas Politics: A Reader*, ed. Anthony Champagne and Edward J. Harpham (New York, NY: W. W. Norton & Company, 1998), 10; Davidson, *Race and Class in Texas Politics*, 234-235; George R. Green and John J. Kushna, "John Tower," *Profiles in Power: Twentieth-Century Texans in Washington*, eds. Kenneth E. Hendrickson Jr. and Michael L. Collins (Arlington Heights, IL: Harlan Davidson, Inc., 1993), 197, 200-201.

CHAPTER 11

1. Brown, *Race, Law, and Education in the Post-Desegregation Era*, 158; Sitkoff, *The Struggle for Black Equality*, 23; Trina Jones, "Brown II: A Case of Missed Opportunity?" *Law and Inequality: A Journal of Theory and Practice* 24, no. 1 (winter 2006): 13; *Bell v. School City of Gary, Indiana*, 213 F. Supp. 819 (N.D. Ind. 1963); Dara N. Byrne, ed., *Brown v. Board of Education: It's Impact on Public Education, 1954-2004* (Brooklyn, NY: Thurgood Marshall Scholarship Fund, 2005), 74-75.

2. Bass, *Unlikely Heroes*, 17; Richard B. Morehead, "Texas Racial Bars Tumbling Down," *The Dallas Morning News*, May 10, 1964: sec. 1, 16.

3. "Definitions of Discrimination," in "The Negro in America," special issue, *Newsweek*, July 29, 1963: 18; *Brown v. The Board of Education of Topeka, Kansas*, 347 U.S. 483 (1954); Bass, *Unlikely Heroes*, 328.

4. Jack Bass, "The 'Fifth Circuit Four,'" *The Nation,* May 3, 2004: 30; Jack Bass, *Unlikely Heroes*, 79.

5. Thornberry, interview by Brian Davis; *United States v. Jefferson County Board of Education*, 372 F. 2d 836 (5th Cir. 1966); *Browder v. Gayle*, 142 F. Supp. 707 (5th Cir. 1956); Bass, "The 'Fifth Circuit Four,'" 30; Harvey C. Couch, *A History of the Fifth Circuit 1891-1981* (Bicentennial Committee of the Judicial Conference of the United States, 1984), 154.

6. *United States v. Jefferson County Board of Education*; Horrigan, interview by author, July 18, 2012.

7. *United States v. Jefferson County Board of Education*; Bass, *Unlikely Heroes*, 270.

8. *United States v. Jefferson County Board of Education*; *Davis v. Board of School Commissioners of Mobile County*, 393 F.2d 690 (5th Cir. 1968).

9. Brown, *Race, Law, and Education in the Post-Desegregation Era*, 168; Couch, *A History of the Fifth Circuit 1891-1981*, 49-50; *United States v. Jefferson County Board of Education*; Jack Bass, *Taming the Storm: The Life and Times of Judge Frank M. Johnson, Jr. and the South's Fight over Civil Rights* (New York, NY: Doubleday, 1993), 135; Bass, *Unlikely Heroes*, 327.

10. *United States v. Jefferson County Board of Education*; *Davis v. Board of School Commissioners of Mobile County*; Bass, *Unlikely Heroes*, 314.

11. Bass, *Unlikely Heroes*, 312-313, 315; *Alexander v. Holmes County Board of Education*, 396 U.S. 19 (1969); Bob Woodward, *The Brethren: Inside the Supreme Court* (New York, NY: Simon & Schuster, 1979), 36-37.

12. "Complete Equality, Nothing Less," in "The Negro in America," special issue, *Newsweek*, July 29, 1963: 19-21; Gary Orfield and Susan E. Eaton, *Dismantling Desegregation: The Quiet Reversal of Brown v. Board of Education* (New York, NY: The New Press, 1996), 109; Bass, *Unlikely Heroes*, 317; Thornberry, interview by Brian Davis.

13. Davidson, *Race and Class in Texas Politics*, 236-237.

14. *Brown v. The Board of Education of Topeka, Kansas*, 347 U.S. 483 (1954).

15. Warren Christopher, interview by T. Harri Baker, October 31, 1968, transcript, LBJ Presidential Library Oral Histories, LBJ Presidential Library, Austin, TX.

16. Thornberry, interview by Joe B. Frantz; Thornberry, interview by Brian Davis.

17. Thornberry, interview by Brian Davis; Thornberry, interview by Joe B. Frantz.

18. Recording of Telephone Conversation between Lyndon B. Johnson and Ralph Yarborough, June 25, 1968, 5:35 p.m., Citation #13141, Recordings and Transcripts of Conversations and Meetings, LBJ Presidential Library, Austin, TX.

19. Mark Silverstein, *Judicious Choices: The New Politics of Supreme Court Confirmations* (New York, NY: W.W. Norton & Company, 1994), 22.

20. "Senate Group Questions Supreme Court Vacancy," *Rocky Mountain News,* June 28, 1968: 3; Ruth Starr to Lyndon Johnson, June 20, 1968, John Macy Files, Homer Thornberry folder, LBJ Presidential Library Oral Histories, LBJ Presidential Library, Austin, TX; George M. Heit to Lyndon Johnson, June 26, 1968, John Macy Files, Homer Thornberry folder, LBJ Presidential Library Oral Histories, LBJ Presidential Library, Austin, TX.

21. Henry Julian Abraham, *Justices, Presidents, and Senators: A History of Supreme Court Appointments from Washington to Bush II*, rev. 3rd ed. (Lanham, MD: Rowman & Littlefield

Publishers, Inc., 1999), 36; Recording of Telephone Conversation between Lyndon B. Johnson and Leon Jaworski, June 25, 1968, 5:56 p.m., Citation #13143, Recordings and Transcripts of Conversations and Meetings, LBJ Presidential Library, Austin, TX; Larry Temple, interview by Joe B. Frantz, June 11, 12, 26, August 7, 11, 13, 1970, transcript, LBJ Presidential Library Oral Histories, LBJ Presidential Library, Austin, TX; Mike Manatos, interview by Joe B. Frantz, August 25, 1969, transcript, LBJ Presidential Library Oral Histories, LBJ Presidential Library, Austin, TX.

22. Marvin Jones, letter to Lyndon Johnson, June 25, 1968, Homer Thornberry Personal Papers, LBJ Presidential Library, Austin, TX; Albert E. Jenner, letter to Ramsey Clark, June 26, 1968, Homer Thornberry Personal Papers, LBJ Presidential Library, Austin, TX; Charles Alan Wright, letter to the editor, *New York Times*, July 4, 1968: 18; editorial, "Thornberry for Fortas," 42; Leslie Carpenter, "Papers Back Thornberry," *Austin American-Statesman*, June 29, 1968: 9.

23. Martin Weil, "Homer Thornberry Dies at 86; Nominated to Supreme Court," *Washington Post*, December 13, 1995, final ed.: sec. D, 4; Charles "Tippie" Newton, interview by author, March 19, 2004; Hill, interview by author, August 30, 2000; Thornberry, interview by Joe B. Frantz.

24. John P. MacKenzie, "Thornberry Record Shows He's Not 'Soft' on Crime," *Washington Post*, June 30, 1968: A7; Thornberry, interview by Brian Davis; Weil, "Homer Thornberry Dies at 86; Nominated to Supreme Court," sec. D, 4; "Tower Joins Efforts To Block Court Posts," *Austin American-Statesman,* June 29, 1968: 6.

25. Hal Walker, CBS News, July 22, 1968; Roger Mudd, *Late Report*, WCBS TV News, June 26, 1968; Tom Dunn, *Late Report*, WCBS TV News, June 26, 1968; NBC News, July 23, 1968.

26. Temple, interview by Joe B. Frantz; Joseph A. Califano Jr., *The Triumph and Tragedy of Lyndon Johnson* (New York, NY: Simon and Schuster, 1991), 311-312.

27. Temple, interview by Joe B. Frantz; Robert Dallek, *Flawed Giant: Lyndon Johnson and His Times, 1961-1973* (Oxford, UK: Oxford University Press, 1998), 558, 563-564.

28. Temple, interview by Joe B. Frantz; George E. Christian, interview by Joe B. Frantz, June 30, 1970, transcript, LBJ Presidential Library Oral Histories, LBJ Presidential Library, Austin, TX.

29. "Thornberry Attends Ceremonies," *El Paso Times*, May 15, 1969; Tom C. Clark, interview by Joe B. Frantz, October 7, 1969, LBJ Presidential Library Oral Histories, LBJ Presidential Library, Austin, TX.

30. Lyndon Johnson, letter to Homer Thornberry, June 28, 1971, Homer Thornberry Personal Papers, LBJ Presidential Library, Austin, TX.

CHAPTER 12

1. Bass, "The 'Fifth Circuit Four,'" 32; Brown. *Race, Law, and Education in the Post-Desegregation Era*, 205-206; Grantham, *The South in Modern America*, 251; Bass, *Unlikely Heroes*, 325-326.

2. Erica Frankenberg, Chungmei Lee, and Gary Orfield, *A Multiracial Society with Segregated Schools: Are We Losing the Dream* (Boston, MA: Harvard University, January 2003),

67; Dara N. Byrne, ed., *Brown v. Board of Education: It's Impact on Public Education, 1954-2004* (Brooklyn, NY: Thurgood Marshall Scholarship Fund, 2005), 77; Bass, "The 'Fifth Circuit Four,'" 30; Bass, *Unlikely Heroes*, 332.

3. Couch, *A History of the Fifth Circuit 1891-1981*, 163; *US v. Georgia Power Company King*, 474 F.2d 906 (5th Cir. 1973); *Bing v. Roadway Express, Inc.*, 485 F.2d 441 (5th Cir. 1973).

4. Couch, *A History of the Fifth Circuit 1891-1981*, 161; Thornberry, interview by Brian Davis; Barrow and Walker, *A Court Divided*, 115.

5. Barrow and Walker, *A Court Divided*, 2, 5.

6. Ibid., 5-9, 11.

7. Ibid., 5, 6, 191-193.

8. Ibid., 191-193, 217; Bass, *Unlikely Heroes*, 303, 330; Thornberry, interview by Brian Davis.

9. Barrow and Walker, *A Court Divided*, 243-247.

10. Thornberry, interview by Joe B. Frantz.

11. Ronald Radosh, *Divided They Fell: The Demise of the Democratic Party, 1964-1996* (New York, NY: Free Press, 1996), 49; Weil, "Homer Thornberry Dies at 86; Nominated to Supreme Court," sec. D, 4.

12. Goodwin, *Lyndon Johnson and the American Dream*, xv, xviii; Lyndon Johnson, letter to Homer Thornberry, April 13, 1972, Homer Thornberry Personal Papers, LBJ Presidential Library, Austin, TX.

13. Dallek, *Flawed Giant: Lyndon Johnson and His Times 1961-1973*, ix; Caro, *The Years of Lyndon Johnson*, 760; Robert A. Divine, "The Johnson Revival," Robert A. Divine, ed., *The Johnson Years, Vol. 2: Vietnam, the Environment, and Science* (Lawrence, KS: University Press of Kansas, 1987), 5, 7.

14. Bass, *Taming the Storm*, 470; Mann, *The Walls of Jericho*, 503.

15. Mann, *The Walls of Jericho*, 503; Sitkoff, *The Struggle for Black Equality*, 221; "Voting Rights Act of 1965," *Encyclopaedia Britannica*, http://www.britannica.com/EBchecked/topic/633044/Voting-Rights-Act, accessed on July 7, 2014; Bernard Grofman and Lisa Handley, "The Impact of the Voting Rights Act on Black Representation in Southern State Legislatures," *Legislative Studies Quarterly* 16, no. 1 (February 1991), 112.

16. Homer Thornberry, speech, joint session of 63rd Texas Legislature, January 25, 1973, Austin, TX, Homer Thornberry Personal Papers, Box 3, LBJ Presidential Library, Austin, TX.

CHAPTER 13

1. Thornberry, interview by Brian Davis.

2. Bass, *Unlikely Heroes*, 264, 329-330.

3. Horrigan, interview by author, July 18, 2012; Carolyn King, interview by author, December 5, 2001.

4. Charles "Tippie" Newton, interview by author, March 18, 2004; Tommy Barton, interview by author, March 10, 2004.

5. *The Almanac of the Federal Judiciary,* vol. 2 (Englewood Cliffs, NJ: Prentice Hall Law & Business, 1991), 21.

6. Biographical Directory of Federal Judges, U.S. Federal Judicial Center, http://www.fjc.gov/history/home.nsf/page/judges.html (accessed June 24, 2014); Congressional Biographical Directory, U.S Congress, http://bioguide.congress.gov/biosearch/biosearch.asp (accessed June 24, 2014).

7. Thomas Reavley, interview by author, December 4, 2001; Bass, "The 'Fifth Circuit Four,'" 32; *Waltman v. International Paper Company*, 875 F.2d 468 (5th Cir. 1989); Jim Zook, "Emotions run high over low-profile judge," *Houston Chronicle,* July 28, 1991: 1A; King, interview by author; Brian Davis, interview by author, March 22, 2004.

8. Charles S. Bullock III and Mark J. Rozell, eds., *The New Politics of the Old South: An Introduction to Southern Politics* (Lanham, MD: Rowman & Littlefield Publishers, Inc., 1998), 255, 257.

9. "Austin's Growth Tops in Texas," *Austin American-Statesman*, October 6, 1963: 1; Douglass, *Austin Natural and Historic*, 231-236.

10. Thornberry, interview by Anthony Orum.

11. Lee Kelly, "'Horatio Alger' Thornberry Celebrates Career as Judge," *Austin American-Statesman*, July 11, 1985: J3; Lee Kelly, "Law Scholarship Established as Judge's Birthday Surprise," *Austin American-Statesman,* January 24, 1989: C3.

12. Hill, interview by author, August 30, 2000.

13. Marian Thornberry, interview by author, May 17, 2013; Thornberry, interview by Brian Davis.

14. Thornberry, interview by author.

15. Mike Burgess, "Robber Attacks Thornberrys, Maid in West Austin Home," *Austin American-Statesman,* June 30, 1994: B1+.

16. Pamela Ward, "300 Gather at Service for Federal Jurist Thornberry," *Austin American-Statesman,* December 15, 1995: B1; Memorial service for Homer Thornberry, University United Methodist Church, Austin, TX, audio recording, December 14, 1995, Audiovisual Materials, LBJ Presidential Library, Austin, TX.

SOURCES

MANUSCRIPT COLLECTIONS

LBJ Presidential Library, Austin, Texas
LBJA Congressional File
Office Files of John Macy
Senate Masters
Senate Political Files
Special Files Pertaining to Abe Fortas and Homer Thornberry
Vice Presidential Masters
White House Central Files Name File

ORAL HISTORIES

Austin History Center, Austin Public Library, Austin, TX
    Thornberry, Homer. Interview by Anthony Orum. February 24, 1984.
LBJ Presidential Library Oral Histories, LBJ Presidential Library, Austin, TX
    Christian, George E. Interview by Joe B. Frantz. June 30, 1970.
    Christopher, Warren. Interview by T. Harri Baker. October 31, 1968.
    Clark, Tom C. Interview by Joe B. Frantz. October 7, 1969.
    Elstad, Leonard M. Interview by David G. McComb. February 14, 1969.
    Johnson, Sam Houston. Interview by Michael L. Gillette. June 9, 1976.
    Johnson, Sam Houston. Interview by Michael L. Gillette. March 31, 1978.
    Manatos, Mike. Interview by Joe B. Frantz. August 25, 1969.
    Patman, Wright. Interview by Joe. B. Frantz. August 11, 1972.
    Pickle, J. J. "Jake." Interview by Joe B. Frantz. May 31, 1970.
    Temple, Larry. Interview by Joe B. Frantz. June 11, 12, 26 and August 7, 11, 13, 1970.
    Thornberry, Homer. Interview by Joe B. Frantz. December 21, 1970. AC 78-94, Interview 1, LBJ Presidential Library Oral Histories, LBJ Presidential Library, Austin, TX, http://transition.lbjlibrary.org/items/show/70971 (accessed June 28, 2014).
    Waldron, Bob. Interview by Michael L. Gillette. January 28, 1976.
Sam Rayburn Library and Museum, Bonham, Texas

Thornberry, Homer. Interview by Anthony Champagne. January 4, 1980.
United States Court of Appeals Library – Fifth Judicial Court, New Orleans, LA
Thornberry, Homer. Interview by Brian Davis. August 20-21, 1992.

INTERVIEWS

Barton, Tom

Bentsen, B.A.

Brooks, Jack

Brown, Vera

Carpenter, Elizabeth "Liz"

Crump, David

Davis, Brian

Fondren, Gene

Gideon, Olga

Hill, Kate Thornberry

Hobby, William, Jr.

Horrigan, Joseph

Jones, Bess

King, Carolyn

Newton, Charles "Tippie"

Pickle, J.J. "Jake"

Reavley, Thomas

Schwartz, A.R. "Babe"

Schwartz, Charles

Sparks, Sam

Spires, Brian

Thornberry, David

Thornberry, Marian Harris

Thornberry, Molly

Trabulsi, Richard

BOOKS

The Almanac of the Federal Judiciary. Vol. 2. Englewood Cliffs, NJ: Prentice Hall Law & Business, 1991.

Abraham, Henry Julian. *Justices, Presidents, and Senators: A History of Supreme Court Appointments from Washington to Bush II*, rev. 3rd ed., Lanham, MD: Rowman & Littlefield Publishers, Inc., 1999.

Alinsky, Saul. *Rules for Radicals*. New York City, NY: Vintage Books, 1989 (c. 1971).

Allen, Edward. *Sam Rayburn: Leading the Lawmakers*. Chicago, IL: Encyclopedia Britannica Press, 1963.

Barnes, Colin, Geof Mercer, and Tom Shakespeare. *Exploring Disability: A Sociological Introduction*. Cambridge, UK: Polity Press, 1999.

Barr, Amelia E. *All the Days of My Life: An Autobiography, the Red Leaves of a Human Heart*. New York City, NY: D. Appleton and Company, 1913.

Barrow, Deborah J. and Thomas G. Walker. *A Court Divided: The Fifth Circuit Court of Appeals and the Politics of Judicial Reform*. New Haven, CT: Yale University Press, 1988.

Bass, Jack. *Taming the Storm: The Life and Times of Judge Frank M. Johnson, Jr. and the South's Fight over Civil Rights*. New York City, NY: Doubleday, 1993.

Bass, Jack. *Unlikely Heroes*. Tuscaloosa, AL: University of Alabama Press, 1981.

Berry, Margaret Catherine. *UT History 101: Highlights in the History of the University of Texas at Austin*. Austin, TX: Eakin Press, 1997.

Brown, Kevin. *Race, Law, and Education in the Post-Desegregation Era*. Durham, NC: Carolina Academic Press, 2005.

Bullock III, Charles S. and Mark J. Rozell, eds. *The New Politics of the Old South: An Introduction to Southern Politics*. Lanham, MD: Rowman & Littlefield Publishers, Inc., 1998.

Byrne, Dara N., ed. *Brown v. Board of Education: Its Impact on Public Education, 1954-2004*. Brooklyn, NY: Thurgood Marshall Scholarship Fund, 2005.

Califano, Joseph A., Jr. *The Triumph and Tragedy of Lyndon Johnson*. New York City, NY: Simon and Schuster, 1991.

Campbell, Randolph B. *Gone to Texas: A History of the Lone Star State*. New York City, NY: Oxford University Press, 2003.

Carmical, J.H. "New regime faces farm prices riddle." *New York Times*. January 25, 1953: F1.

Caro, Robert. *The Years of Lyndon Johnson: Master of the Senate*. New York City, NY: Alfred A. Knopf, 2002.

— — —. *The Years of Lyndon Johnson: Means of Ascent*. New York City, NY: Alfred A. Knopf, 1990.

Champagne, Anthony. *Congressman Sam Rayburn*. New Brunswick, NJ: Rutgers University Press, 1984.

Champagne, Anthony and Edward J. Harpham, eds. *Texas Politics: A Reader*. New York City, NY: W. W. Norton & Company, 1998.

Couch, Harvey C. *A History of the Fifth Circuit 1891-1981*. Bicentennial Committee of the Judicial Conference of the United States, 1984.

Cox, Patrick. *Ralph W. Yarborough, the People's Senator*. Austin, TX: University of Texas Press, 2001.

Dallek, Robert. *Flawed Giant: Lyndon Johnson and His Times, 1961-1973*. Oxford, UK: Oxford University Press, 1998.

— — —. *Lone Star Rising: Lyndon Johnson and His Times, 1908-1960*. Oxford, UK: Oxford University Press, 1991.

Davidson, Chandler. *Race and Class in Texas Politics*. Princeton, NJ: Princeton University Press, 1990.

Divine, Robert, ed. *The Johnson Years, Vol. 1: Foreign Policy, The Great Society, and the White House*. Lawrence, KS: University Press of Kansas, 1987.

— — —. *The Johnson Years, Vol. 2: Vietnam, the Environment, and Science*. Lawrence, KS: University Press of Kansas, 1987.

Douglass, Curran. *Austin Natural and Historic: An Introductory Guide to Austin History, Natural History, Points of Interest, and More*. Austin, TX: Nortex Press, 2000.

Frankenberg, Erica, Chungmei, Lee, and Gary Orfield. *A Multiracial Society with Segregated Schools: Are We Losing the Dream*. Boston, MA: Harvard University, January 2003.

Frantz , Joe B. *The Forty Acre Follies*. Austin, TX: Texas Monthly Press, 1983.

Gardner, John W. *On Leadership*. New York City, NY: The Free Press, 1993, (c. 1990).

Gibson, L. Tucker, Jr. and Clay Robison. *Government and Politics in the Lone Star State: Theory and Practice*. 2nd ed. Englewood Cliffs, NJ: Prentice-Hall, Inc., 1995.

Gillon, Steven M. *The Kennedy Assassination: 24 Hours After*. New York City, NY: Basic Books, 2009.

Goodwin, Doris Kearns. *Lyndon Johnson and the American Dream*. New York City, NY: St. Martin's Press, 1976.

Grantham, Dewey W. *The South in Modern America*. New York City, NY: HarperCollins Publishers, 1994.

Green, George Norris. *The Establishment in Texas Politics: The Primitive Years, 1938-1957.* Norman, OK: University of Oklahoma Press, 1984.

Hardeman, D.B. and Donald C. Bacon. *Rayburn: A Biography.* Austin, TX: Texas Monthly Press, 1987.

Hendrickson, Kenneth E., Jr. and Michael L. Collins, eds. *Profiles in Power: Twentieth-Century Texans in Washington.* Arlington Heights, IL: Harlan Davidson, Inc., 1993.

Jankowski, Katharine A. *Deaf Empowerment: Emergence, Struggle, and Rhetoric.* Washington, D.C.: Gallaudet University Press, 1997.

Johnson, Lady Bird. *A White House Diary.* New York City, NY: Holt, Rinehart and Winston, 1970.

Johnson, Lyndon Baines. *The Vantage Point: Perspectives of the Presidency 1963-1969.* New York City, NY: Holt, Rinehart and Winston, 1971.

Keith, Gary A. *Eckhardt: There Once Was a Congressman from Texas.* Austin, TX: University of Texas Press, 2007.

Key, V.O., Jr. *Southern Politics in State and Nation.* Knoxville, TN: University of Tennessee Press, 1949.

Lezzoni, Lynette. *Influenza 1918: The Worst Epidemic in American History.* New York City, NY: TV Books, 1999.

Mann, Robert. *The Walls of Jericho: Lyndon Johnson, Hubert Humphrey, Richard Russell, and the Struggle for Civil Rights.* New York City, NY: Harcourt Brace & Company, 1996.

McCullough, David. *Truman.* New York City, NY: Simon & Schuster, 1992.

Morehead, Richard. *50 Years in Texas Politics: from Roosevelt to Reagan, from the Fergusons to Clements.* Burnet, TX: Eakin Press, 1982.

Murph, Dan. *Texas Giant: The Life of Price Daniel.* Austin, Texas: Eakin Press, 2002.

Ogden, Frederic D. *The Poll Tax in the South.* Birmingham, AL: The University of Alabama Press, 1958.

Orum, Anthony M. *The Making of Modern Austin, TX: Power, Money, and the People.* Austin, TX: Texas Monthly Press, 1987.

Orfield, Gary and Susan E. Eaton. *Dismantling Desegregation: The Quiet Reversal of Brown v. Board of Education.* New York City, NY: The New Press, 1996.

Patterson, Thomas. *The American Democracy*, 10th ed. College Station, TX: Texas A&M University Press, 2011.

Pickle, Jake and Peggy Pickle. *Jake.* Austin, TX: University of Texas Press, 1997.

Radosh, Ronald. *Divided They Fell: The Demise of the Democratic Party, 1964-1996.* New York City, NY: Free Press, 1996.

Richards, David. *Once Upon a Time in Texas: A Liberal in the Lone Star State.* Austin, Texas: University of Texas Press, 2002.

Rossell, Christine H., David J. Armor, and Herbert J. Walberg, eds. *School Desegregation in the 21st Century.* Westport, CT: Praeger Publishers, 2002.

Rutland, Robert Allen. *The Democrats: From Jefferson to Clinton.* Columbia, MO: University of Missouri Press, 1995.

Schlesinger, Arthur M., Jr. *A Thousand Days: John F. Kennedy in the White House.* New York City, NY: Fawcett Premier Books, 1992 (c. 1965)

Shelton, Emmett, Sr. *My Austin.* Boston, MA: American Press, 1994.

Silverstein, Mark. *Judicious Choices: The New Politics of Supreme Court Confirmations*. New York City, NY: W.W. Norton & Company, 1994.

Sitkoff, Harvard. *The Struggle for Black Equality, 1954-1992*, rev. ed. New York City, NY: Hill and Wang, 1993 (c. 1981).

Smith, Douglas L. *The New Deal in the Urban South*. Baton Rouge, LA: Louisiana State University Press, 1988.

Uhlberg, Myron. *Hands of My Father: A Hearing Boy, His Deaf Parents, and the Language of Love*. New York: Bantam Books, 2009 (c. 2008).

Unger, Irwin and Debi Unger. *LBJ: A Life*. New York City, NY: John Wiley & Sons, Inc., 1999.

Valenti, Jack. *This Time, This Place: My Life in War, the White House, and Hollywood*. New York: Harmony Books, 2007.

Woods, Randall B. *LBJ: Architect of American Ambition*. New York City, NY: Free Press, 2007 (c. 2006).

Woodward, Bob. *The Brethren: Inside the Supreme Court*. New York City, NY: Simon & Schuster, 1979.

Wormser, Richard. *The Rise & Fall of Jim Crow: The African-American Struggle Against Discrimination, 1865-1954*. New York City, NY: Franklin Watts, 1999.

ARTICLES

"A Curious Congress." *Austin Statesman*. September 6, 1962: A6.

"Another Party For The Thornberrys." *Williamson County Sun*. October 11, 1962: 2.

"Austin's Growth Tops in Texas." *Austin American-Statesman*. October 6, 1963: 1.

"Bastrop Chicken Fry To Honor Thornberry." *American-Statesman*. October 7, 1962: A4.

"Canonizing the Civil Rights Revolution." *Northwestern University Law Review* 103, no. 1 (2009).

"Centex Solons Support Dams on San Gabriel." *Austin American*. February 1, 1962: A29.

"City Candidates List Views on Bonds." *Austin American*. May 22, 1946: 9.

"Civil Rights Bill Ready for House." *New York Times*. April 20, 1960: 24.

"Committee Decides Next Week on Vote Recount." *Austin Statesman*. August 8, 1940: 13.

"Commodity Letter: A Special Staff Report on Price and Production Trends Affecting Industry." *Wall Street Journal*. January 6, 1953: 1.

"Complete Equality, Nothing Less." Special issue, "The Negro in America." *Newsweek*, July 29, 1963: 19-21.

"Congressman To Be Feted On October 4." *Williamson County Sun*. September 20, 1962: 2.

"Connally Says GOP Not Needed in Texas." *Austin Statesman*. June 27, 1962: 3.

"Council Hears Plea on Vet Beer Permit; Miller, Thornberry Clash on Zoning." *Austin American*. October 18, 1946: 17.

"County Vote Follows Trend Set In Texas." *Williamson County Sun*. November 8, 1962: 1.

"Dam at Laneport is Recommended." *Williamson County Sun*. February 1, 1962: 1.

"Dams! A Flood of Dams!" *Williamson County Sun*. October 11, 1962: 2.

"Definitions of Discrimination." Special issue, "The Negro in America." *Newsweek*, July 29, 1963: 18.

"'Democrats for Dobbs' Formed by Centexan." *Austin Statesman.* October 6, 1962: 5.

"Dobbs Says He's Gaining Staunch Demo Votes." *Austin Statesman.* October 2, 1962: 12.

"Ex-Teacher Dies in Washington; Funeral Here." *Lone Star* 80, no. 1. September 15, 1958: 1+.

"Farm Employment Hits Lowest Seasonal Level Since 1925, U.S. Reports." *Wall Street Journal.* January 14, 1953: 18.

"Friend Meets Girl's Uncle On Phone—It Was THE Lyndon." *El Paso Herald.* November 27(?),1963: sec. B, 5.

"From the Hornet's Nest." Unknown source. 1948(?). "AF-Biography Homer Thornberry" file. Austin History Center. Austin Public Library. Austin, Texas.

"Gallaudet's board ousts president." *Washington Times.* October 30, 2006. http://www.washingtontimes.com/news/2006/oct/30/20061030-122608-4001r/?page=all. Accessed on July 3, 2014.

"Gillis Post To Be Filled At Election." *The Austin Statesman.* April 4, 1946: 1.

"GOP in Hays County Fires Salvo at Court." *Austin American.* May 15, 1962: 19.

"Giveaways Draw Fire Of Dobbs." *Austin American.* March 28, 1962: 5.

"Hendrix Lashes At Democrats." *Austin American.* February 8, 1962: 38.

"'Hi, Homer.'" *Austin American.* October 5, 1962: 21.

"Homer Thornberry For Legislature." *Austin American.* February 9, 1936: 5.

"Homer's Party Huge Success." *Williamson County Sun.* Octoober 23, 1958: 1+.

"JFK Appoints Thornberry Judge, Keeps Promise to Sam Rayburn." *Austin American.* July 10, 1963: 13.

"J.F.K. Signs Bill For Dams." *Williamson County Sun.* October 25, 1962: 1.

"Jim Dobbs Repub. nominee." *American-Statesman.* May 6, 1962: A1+.

"Johnson Names 2 To Appeals Court." *New York Times.* June 18, 1965: 18L.

"Johnson Rolls In As Demos Sweep State." *Austin American,* November 3, 1948: 1.

"LBJ Cited for Service to the Deaf." *Austin Statesman.* March 24, 1967: 9.

"Laneport Project Is Blasted At Austin Hearing Monday." *Williamson County Sun.* May 3, 1962: 1.

"Lawmaker Tells Of Misery Found On Tour of Area." *Austin American.* January 24, 1938: 1+.

"Life and Labors of Thomas H. Gallaudet." *The North American Review* 87, no. 181 (October 1858): 517.

"Life on the Ranch: A Day at Home with LBJ." *U.S. News & World Report.* April 13, 1964: 67-68.

"None Dissent As Eilers Asks for Public Approval." *Austin American.* January 25, 1938: 1+.

"Odyssey of Homer." *Time.* July 5, 1968: 15.

"Patterson Undecided on Meeting Date." *Austin Statesman.* August 9, 1940: 1.

"Petitions Ask Thornberry on City Council," *Austin American,* March 10, 1946: 10.

"Poll: A Leadership Deficit." *U.S. News & World Report,* October 31, 2005: 80.

"Random Notes in Washington: Travel Likely for G.I. Families." *New York Times.* January 29, 1962, late city ed.: 12.

"Rayburn Is Dead; Served 17 Years As House Speaker." *New York Times.* November 17, 1961: 1+.

"Reception for Thornberry Turns Into 'Dam Party.'" *Williamson County Sun.* October 18, 1962: 1+.

"Rep. Thornberry Resigns House Effective Dec. 20." *El Paso Times.* September 27, 1963: 1A.

"Rep. Thornberry Secures Funds for Placement Officer." *The Modern Silents.* July 1937: 23.

"Rep. Young Will Be Named to Rules Panel; Texas Democrat Expected to Back Kennedy." *Wall Street Journal.* July 10, 1963: 7.

"Republicans Believe '62 To Be THE Year." *Austin Statesman.* February 15, 1962: A13.

"San Gabriel Dams Hurdle One Hump." *Williamson County Sun.* October 4, 1962: 1.

"Senate Group Questions Supreme Court Vacancy." *Rocky Mountain News,* June 28, 1968: 3.

"Texas Demos Could Lose Labor Support." *Austin Statesman.* September 19, 1962: 3.

"Texas Voters have Their Say In Vote Today." *Austin American,* November 2, 1948: 1.

"The SUN Endorses . . ." *Williamson County Sun.* November 1, 1962: 2.

"Thornberry Attends Ceremonies." *El Paso Times.* May 15, 1969.

"Thornberry Boosters To Honor Congressman Thursday." *Williamson County Sun.* October 25, 1962: 6.

"Thornberry Defeats Dobbs For 8th Term in Congress." *Austin American.* November 7, 1962: 17.

"Thornberry Flies to Washington To Push Public Works Measure." *Austin Statesman.* October 8, 1962: 7.

"Thornberry Has Operation." *New York Times.* July 3, 1957: 25.

"Thornberry May Push Ordinance." *Austin American.* June 6, 1946: 1.

"Thornberry Scores Complete Victory; Lee Allen Sheriff." *American-Statesman.* July 26, 1936: 1+.

"Thornberry Sworn In." *Austin Statesman.* June 6, 1946: 1+.

"Thornberry Tells Interest in City." *Austin American.* June 7, 1946: 1.

"Thornberry to Return to Texas as U.S. Judge." *Bastrop Advertiser.* July 11, 1963: 1.

"Thornberry To Take Oath On Dec. 21." *San Antonio Express.* December 4, 1963: final ed., 8B.

"Thornberry Voting Record That Of Moderate Liberal." *The Commercial Appeal.* June 29, 1968: 8.

"Thornberry Wins City Council Post." *Austin American,* June 4, 1946: 1.

"Thornberry's Name Filed." *Austin Statesman.* May 21, 1946: 1+.

"Those who write the news honor those who make it." *Austin American.* December 17, 1957: 17.

"Three-Dam Program Now Issue in Politics." *Austin American.* February 8, 1962: 19.

"Tower Joins Efforts To Block Court Posts." *Austin American-Statesman.* June 29, 1968: 6.

"Uninvited Guest Named Johnson is Graduation Speaker for Deaf." *New York Times,* June 14, 1966: 44.

"Will Homer Skip Court?" *Austin Statesman.* November 25, 1963: A1+.

"Young Republicans Rap Rayburn as 'Traitor.'" *Dallas Morning News.* February 26, 1961, early city ed.: sec. 1: 9.

"Youngest Deputy Sheriff in Texas Represents New Type of Law Enforcement." *Austin Statesman.* August 8, 1930: 5.

Albright, Robert C. "Mansfield Asks No Politicking Over Fortas." *Washington Post,* June 29, 1968: A6.

Arlow, J.A. "Communication and character: A clinical study of a man raised by deaf-mute parents." *Psychoanalytic Study of the Child* 31 (1976): 139-63.

Baskin, Robert E. "Rep. Thornberry Tested in Service, Found Strong." *Dallas Morning News.* July 10, 1963, early city ed.: sec. 1, 14.

Bass, Jack. "The 'Fifth Circuit Four.'" *The Nation.* May 3, 2004: 30-32.

Belair, Felix. "President on Way to Mexico Talks." *New York Times.* February 19, 1959: 10.

Brewer, Anita. "Distinguished Alumnus Homer Thornberry." *Alcalde, The University of Texas Alumni Magazine.* January 1966: 10-12.

Burgess, Mike. "Robber attacks Thornberrys, maid in West Austin Home." *Austin American-Statesman.* June 30, 1994: B1+.

Caro, Robert. "My Search for Coke Stevenson." *New York Times.* February 3, 1991: section 7, 1+.

Carpenter, Elizabeth. "Her Actions Are Her Words." *American-Statesman.* May 31, 1953: B-1.

— — —. "Mrs. Thornberry Marks 80th Milestone Today." *Washington Post.* May 24, 1953: 115.

Carpenter, Leslie. "Federal District Court Bench Is Logical Step for Homer Thornberry." *Corpus Christi Caller-Times.* August 4, 1963.

— — —. "Papers Back Thornberry." *Austin American-Statesman.* June 29, 1968: 9.

— — —. "Those Juicy Plums On the Federal Bench." *Austin American.* June 22, 1965: 4.

Casey, Phil. "$475,000 Gallaudet Center Opens." *Washington Post.* October 20, 1959: A14.

Castlebury, Glen. "Foreman Warns GOP To Solidify." *Austin American-Statesman.* October 6, 1963: F1.

— — —. "Housing Law Is Approved." *Austin-American Statesman.* May 18, 1968: 1.

Collins, Sara. "A Time Capsule Found at a Demolished Mary Thornberry Building." *SIGNews* 7, no. 6. June 2009: 17+.

Editorial. "'Full Mobilization,' Thornberry plea." The Editor's Notebook. *Austin American* (December 15, 1950), 4.

Editorial. "Voter IDs on Trial." *New York Times,* July 13, 2012, http://www.nytimes.com/2012/07/14/opinion/voter-ids-on-trial-in-texas.html?_r=2&hp (accessed June 28, 2014).

Editorial. "Thornberry for Fortas." *The New York Times.* June 27, 1968, late city ed.: 42.

Fisher, Kevin W. "A profile of the life and career of Judge William Homer Thornberry." *Fifth Circuit Reporter* 13.3 (1996).

Ford, Jon. "Congressman Visits All Spots in District." *San Antonio Express.* September 25, 1955: 3B.

Ford, Robert E. "Republicans Stage Run at Democrats." *Austin American.* February 7, 1962: 5.

Goldenberg, Suzanne. "'Not deaf enough' university head is forced out." *The Guardian.* October 30, 2006. http://www.theguardian.com/world/2006/oct/31/usa.highereducation. Accessed on July 3, 2014.

Graham, Fred P. "Coleman Picked For Court Post." *New York Times.* May 13, 1965: 24.

Grofman, Bernard and Lisa Handley. "The Impact of the Voting Rights Act on Black Representation in Southern State Legislatures." *Legislative Studies Quarterly* 16, no. 1 (February 1991).

Hamilton, Bill. "New Job's No Snap." *Austin American.* January 19, 1964: 1+.

Harbriech, U. "Influence of deaf-mute parents on the character of their offspring." *Acta Psychiatra Scandinavica* 59, no. 2 (1979): 129-38.

Hiott, Debbie. "Retired jurist Herman Jones, 'the gentleman of the courts,' dies at 83." *Austin American-Statesman.* October 28, 1994: B1.

Holland, William. "2 Buildings Honor Artist, Teacher." *Evening Star.* May 16, 1969.

Holley, Joe. "Holder calls Texas voter ID law a 'poll tax.'" *Houston Chronicle.* July 10, 2012. http://www.chron.com/news/houston-texas/article/Holder-calls-Texas-voter-ID-law-a-poll-tax-3697707.php. Accessed on June 28, 2014.

Hornady, Walter. "A Texan in Washington—Thornberry Wields Power as Rules Member." *Dallas Morning News.* December 28, 1959: 8.

Jones, Garth. "Texas GOP Pins Hope in Primary." *Austin American.* February 15, 1962: 3.

Kantor, Seth. "When Homer Finally Takes a Steady Job, It Is to Be a Dilly." *Houston Press.* July 3, 1963: 4.

Kelly, Lee. "'Horatio Alger' Thornberry celebrates career as judge." *Austin American-Statesman.* July 11, 1985: J3.

Kelly, Lee. "Law scholarship established as judge's birthday surprise." *Austin American-Statesman.* January 24, 1989: C3.

Krebs, Albin. "War Shattered Johnson's Dream." *Dallas Morning News.* January 23, 1973, 10A.

Lawrence, David. "Thornberry's nomination called reward from J.F.K." *Houston Chronicle.* July 13, 1963: sec. 6, 2.

Lawrence, W.H. "Democratic 'Advisers' Avoid a Party Split." *New York Times.* January 13, 1957: E7.

Lindell, Chuck. "The people's politician." *Austin American-Statesman.* June 19, 2005: A1+.

MacKenzie, John P. "Thornberry Record Shows He's Not 'Soft' on Crime." *Washington Post.* June 30, 1968: A7.

Mathis, Nancy. "Six decades of politics, Pickle-style." *Houston Chronicle.* April 9, 1994: 1A.

McClendon, Sarah. "Mrs. Thornberry In 'Perfect' Role." *Austin American.* May 6, 1957: 1+.

– – –. "Report by Towers Alters GOP Guess." *Austin American.* July 21, 1962: 1+.

Morehead, Richard. "Texas Racial Bars Tumbling Down." *The Dallas Morning News.* May 10, 1964, sec. 1: 16.

Murphree, Alex. "Texas Re-Discovers Its University." *Texas Weekly* 10, no. 15. April 14, 1934: 8.

Pearson, Drew. "Will LBJ Bow to Sen. Eastland?" *Washington Post.* December 16, 1964: B21.

Pickle, J.J. "Homer Thornberry, My Congressional Role Model." *Texas Law Review* 74, no. 5 (1996): 943-946.

Reavley, Thomas M. "Homer Thornberry." *Texas Law Review* 74, no .5 (1996): 947-948.

Scarbrough, Don. Editorial. "A Texan in Washington—Thornberry Wields Power as Rules Member." *Williamson County Sun*. January 7, 1960: 3.

Sevareid, Eric. "Sam Rayburn Believed Implicitly In America's Strength, Rectitude." *The Sunday Bulletin*. October 15, 1961: 2 VB.

Shanks, Dave. "Lawmaker At Home." *Austin American*. November 1, 1955: 17.

Simmons, Dale M. "Downtown post office renovations planned." *Austin American-Statesman*. September 15, 1989, final ed.: B3.

Trussell, C.P. "Civil Rights to go to Floor of House." *New York Times*. May 22, 1957: 22.

Ward, Pamela. "300 Gather at Service forFederal Jurist Thornberry." *Austin American Statesman*. December 15, 1995: B1.

— — —. "Judge recalled as quiet leader." *Austin American-Statesman*. December 15, 1995: B1+.

— — —. "Repackaged post office is renamed." *Austin American-Statesman*. January 19, 1993: B1.

Wagenheim, H.S. "Aspects of the analysis of an adult son of deaf-mute parents." *Journal of the American Psychoanalytic Association* 33, no. 2 (1985): 413-435.

Weil, Martin. "Homer Thornberry Dies at 86; Nominated to Supreme Court." *Washington Post*. December 13, 1995, final ed.: sec. D, 4.

Wheelock, Ernestine. "Austinite Receives Prestigious Appointments." *Austin American-Statesman*. January 26, 1969: C2.

White, William S. "Civil Rights Compromise Set to Pass House Today." *New York Times*. August 27, 1957: 1.

White, William S. "Democrats Spur Civil Rights Vote." *New York Times*. August 20, 1957: 1+.

Whiteman, Marj. "Thornberry Given Okay." *Austin American*. July 16, 1963: 1+.

Wright, Scott. "Austinite with gift for justice dead at 86." *Austin American-Statesman*. December 13, 1995: A1+.

Zook, Jim. "Emotions run high over low-profile judge." *Houston Chronicle*. July 28, 1991: 1A.

INDEX